St. Joseph's Hospice Association
Jospice International

Impossible dreams ... some fulfilled

IN THEM WE TRUST

Francis O'Leary M.H.M.

ISBN 0 903348 54 3

Printed and Published in Great Britain in 2004 by

Print Origination

Ince Blundell, Formby, Merseyside

Father Francis O'Leary M.H.M.

Acknowledgments

My thanks are due to Mr. Ian MacNicol, a friend from my student days at Glasgow University, who has spent many hours reading the proofs of this book. His patience has been remarkable.

My thanks also go to my secretary Miss Cathie Moran for the long hours she spent in typing out my meanderings.

The initial preparation for the printing and publication of this book was carried out by Mr. Philip Daley of C & D Printers, Liverpool. To him my grateful thanks.

Note

Mill Hill Fathers usually have M.H.M. (Mill Hill Missionary) after their names. As there are so many fathers' names mentioned, I have omitted these initials after the name.

F. O'L. March 2000.

Prologue

FRANCIS ALOYSIUS O'LEARY was born on June 18th, 1931 in Crosby, Liverpool. He went to SS. Peter and Paul's School in Crosby and then, at the age of 11, entered the junior seminary of the Mill Hill Fathers at Freshfield, to the north of Liverpool.

After progressing through the seminaries at Burn Hall, Co. Durham, St. Joseph's College in Roosendaal, the Netherlands, and St. Joseph's College, Mill Hill, he was ordained on July 8th, 1956. He was sent to Glasgow University, graduating in 1960 with an M.A. Degree and received his first posting as a missionary priest to Rawalpindi, then the capital city of Pakistan. He was moved by all the poverty and deprivation he saw and resolved to do something about it. The opportunity arose two years later when he was asked to help a Pakistani woman, Mrs. Jacob, who was seriously ill. He found an outhouse in the church compound—it was really a mud hut—and into this Mrs. Jacob was carried. She was the first patient of Jospice International, as St. Joseph's Hospice Association came to be known. The date was November 19th, 1962, the Feast of St. Elizabeth, Patroness of Nurses. Two years later the first Hospice, at Westridge, Rawalpindi, was opened.

Being inspired by Mother Teresa and her work, he asked her for advice. Her reply was not to worry about money and to place one's trust in God and He would look after everything. Fr. O'Leary took that bit of advice and keeps thinking of her words day by day.

In the 38 years since then Jospice has grown. There are now two Hospices in Pakistan and centres in India. Other Hospices have been established in Colombia, Peru, Ecuador, Honduras and Guatemala. In England there are two Hospice buildings at the Headquarters of Jospice in Liverpool and another in Ormskirk, nine miles away. In 1997 a Hospice was opened in Mexico, at Nezahualcoyotl, in the suburbs of Mexico City, and it is hoped to start another Hospice in Bogota, the capital of Colombia. The work of Jospice has helped millions of people at home and abroad and Fr. O'Leary is widely regarded as one of the founders of the hospice movement.

His work has received recognition from many sources. On television in 1973 he was the subject of This Is Your Life, hosted by the late Eamonn Andrews. The following year in Peru he received the Daniel Carrion Medal, an award for medical services to the people of that country. In the 1996 Queen's Birthday Honours List he was awarded the M.B.E. for his services to the hospice movement.

The pages which follow not only record the history of Jospice, they demonstrate the personality of Fr. O'Leary. There is the concern for the patients, and his working through the night. There is the sense of awe at a most unusual happening, when a dying patient left the Imprint of his body on a mattress cover, an Imprint which has defied all attempts to remove it and which has left forensic experts baffled. There is the urge for innovation, like the Live Crib every Christmas involving friends and Jospice staff, as well as live animals to lend an air of reality.

Throughout it all, there is someone who manages to keep his sense of humour, no matter the circumstances, and who manifests his great love of music to the extent of organising Gala Concerts with the Royal Liverpool Philharmonic Orchestra. These and other entertainments have been warmly appreciated.

I. MacN P. C. D.

Foreword

"Come, consider the wonders of God, the astounding deeds he has done on the earth."(Psalm 46,8). Those words of the psalmist seem to me to be a fitting introduction to these Memoirs.

Sixty years ago, a Mill Hill Missionary visited SS. Peter and Paul's Elementary School (as Primary Schools were then called) to talk to the children about the missions. That priest could not have imagined what would happen as a result of his talk. One of the children, Francis O'Leary, decided there and then that he wanted to be a Mill Hill Missionary. Although he was only nine years old, he never wavered from that decision and soon afterwards entered the Junior Seminary to study for the priesthood. Thus, although he could have had no inkling of it at the time, that visiting priest was in a real sense laying the first brick of what was to become St. Joseph's Hospice Association.

These Memoirs are inevitably bound up with the story of St. Joseph's Hospice Association. One is tempted to describe them as the history of the Association, but the word 'history' might well conjure up the idea of something dull from the dead past. On the other hand, as W. H. Auden wisely suggests, "There is no such thing as history. . . only biographies." History is produced by the lives, the actions and the decisions of people.

The pages of these Memoirs surely illustrate that statement. They are filled with references to real people. For the most part, you will notice, the people involved are not the rich and the famous. Rather they are just 'ordinary' people who, pulling together and inspired by Fr. O'Leary's vision, have brought about the miracle of St. Joseph's Hospice Association. Whether they be nurses or patients, donors or doctors, working together in faith they have created–and keep in existence–an organisation which has already touched the lives of literally millions of sick and destitute people in so many parts of the world.

As a lifelong friend of Fr. O'Leary I have witnessed the burgeoning of the seed which was sown so long ago in that elementary school. I have also had the privilege of being associated, albeit in a small way, with the work of St. Joseph's Hospice Association both here and abroad. It has always been for me a source of wonder and not a little awe.

My prayer is that these Memoirs not only prove interesting reading, but also an encouragement to the members of the Association and an inspiration to those who are not members to join in the work.

"We give thanks to you, O God, we give thanks to you, as we call upon your name, as we recount your wonders." (Psalm 75,1)

Mgr. Vincent Hughes

Our Lady of Lourdes, Birkdale, Southport, Merseyside.

Mgr. Hughes wrote these words when Fr. O'Leary had completed the bulk of his Memoirs. Sadly, Mgr. Hughes died on March 14th, 2000 as the final touches were being made to the book. There are many references to Mgr. Hughes in the Memoirs, written when he was still alive. For the most part Fr. O'Leary has left them unchanged, because although Mgr. Hughes is dead to this world he is still alive in heaven, enjoying his eternal reward.

Preface

When Father O'Leary was finally prevailed upon to write his Memoirs, the question of a title naturally arose. Various suggestions were made and discussed but none seemed to appeal to him. I don't know how he arrived at "IN THEM WE TRUST" but it is apt enough to be inspired; for these Memoirs, selected from so many memories, tell of a journey of trust.

Throughout his life, Our Lady and St. Joseph have been, and are still, his travelling companions. (There have been times when those of us on his Management Committee have been worried when there was little or no money in the bank to see us through, but Father would say, "Pray to Our Lady and St. Joseph.")

The character of the man becomes apparent as the chapters of the Memoirs unfold; his humour, love of music, single-mindedness, his refusal to see problems . . . only solutions, his enthusiasm and ability to make people go where they would rather not and do what they would rather not do!

He is stubborn, persistent, infuriating, incredibly generous and hospitable, impish, untiring and totally human. He is beloved, warts and all, and loyally served by many dedicated people.

To lesser men, the obstacle and lack of resources would be too daunting to make the dream reality, but through his trust in Our Lady, St. Joseph and all the patients who have died and are in Heaven, Father O'Leary has accomplished the impossible dream and St. Joseph's Hospice Association continues to grow. It has been a privilege to be Chairman of its Management Committee for the past 20-plus years and part of that growth . . . life has been enriched.

Perhaps these Memoirs will sow a seed in some unselfish heart and bring forth a willingness to give of oneself in the service of others through St. Joseph's Hospice Association.

May those who follow be blessed with the same spirit of the love and generosity of its Founder.

John C. Carson   *Chairman*

Prior to this book being published John Carson sadly died. He was a tireless and dedicated worker for Jospice for many years and was deeply involved in the final preparation of this book.

Contents

This gentleman, together with Mrs Jacob, our very first patient in Rawalpindi, Pakistan, are the founders of Jospice International.

They provided the inspiration on which Jospice became established.

Our Inspiration

THE photograph appearing on the previous page I took more than 38 years ago. This poor man epitomises the state of the world at present, a microcosm of the world's greediness and lack of compassion. He is just one of those people who starve to death every year. It was taken in India, but it could easily have been someone from Central or South America, Vietnam, Cambodia, or any shanty town dweller. There are millions of people suffering in this fashion. His was an extreme case, because his body had begun to rot even before his soul had gone to God. He would have been an excellent model in an anatomy class and a wonderful specimen for any laboratory technician wishing to do research in skin decay or the life cycles of the body-eating louse. It was no use giving him a rupee for he had not the strength to hold it; besides, some passer-by would have stolen it. At least 500 people passed him by in the 20 minutes I was observing the situation.

Human degradation is a terrible thing and yet that poor man, even though he never knew it, had the power within himself to beget compassion and love in thousands of individuals over these past years, for he has been a constant reminder to all Jospice people, since he has been portrayed so often in our magazines and this photograph peers at us from every angle at Jospice Headquarters. He is one of the people talked about by representatives of the world's governments, and they are still talking . . . Of course, some groups have tried to take up his case, but what has really happened while they have all been talking ? . . . Admittedly, the task is not an easy one because the words "Third World" are not understood by the majority of pundits who use those words. Believe it or not, it is an extremely delicate operation, in these days of individual political structures and nationalism, to feed a hungry person or to give an injection to a Third World sufferer. The operation is confused, not only by political, geopolitical and economic difficulties, but by the gross misunderstanding of the nature of a Third World exercise. Thank God Jospice has tried to help him over the past 38 years. Although he has been a pawn in the rich man's game, he became, and still is, the source of our inspiration. Christ still speaks to us through him.   F. O'L.

Mrs Jacob

The first patient of Jospice International
She died in Rawalpindi Pakistan in 1962

How it all began in Pakistan -

It all started in a little mud hut in Westridge, Rawalpindi, on November 19th, 1962, the Feast of St. Elizabeth, Patroness of Nurses. An old lady, Mrs. Jacob by name, lay dying from multiple strokes. She died in this very humble dwelling–a mud hut, and together with the poor man she provided the inspiration to start the work of Jospice in Pakistan and in other parts of the world. This is how Mrs. Mahmood, an observer at the time, told the story of the first St. Joseph's Hospice in Rawalpindi, Pakistan.

A few years ago, an old woman hobbling along the outskirts of a park in Rawalpindi, Pakistan, caught the eye of an American woman driving by in a small car crowded with young children. Glancing in the rearview mirror, she marvelled that one so bent could manage to move at all and wondered where she could be going so far out of town.

At that moment, the old woman fell by the wayside. Instinctively the driver lifted her foot from the accelerator and then, guiltily, sped on. After all, she argued with herself, what could she do with her if she stopped? There was no room in her car and there was no ambulance she knew of which would come to carry the woman away. If there were, where could she be carried? The few hospitals scattered throughout 'Pindi were unable to care for all the sick and so had to stick closely to rules–military patients in the military hospital, railway employees in the railway hospital, government employees in the government hospital, and so on.

Although tremendous changes had taken place during the past ten years in Rawalpindi, schools, hospitals, industries, food–all such basics to a good life– were still inadequate for the needs of the great population of this new Muslim nation. For many suffering souls there was just no place to turn. A penniless villager, the American realised, would be turned away from every door for there was just no bed which could be given.

Unable to accept her own rationalising, the woman dropped her children at home and drove back to the park to take the stricken woman to her own house. The road was empty. Somehow the ancient crone had moved on. The image of her, however, returned again and again to haunt the American for it seemed so imperative that some place should be found for such desperately needy people.

Fr. Francis O'Leary, a young priest from near Liverpool, was thinking the same thing at the same time. He had arrived in 'Pindi in 1960 to teach in a Pakistani boys' school and to be parish priest of the Sacred Heart Church in Westridge, a small community on the outskirts of 'Pindi. It was his first assignment as a priest and as a foreign missionary. The overwhelming poverty, illness and urgent need of mankind in Asia gave him no peace. Although old timers in the East usually learn to live with this ache and some, in self defence, even blind themselves to it, for him, newly arrived, it was a daily sorrow which had to have some answer somewhere.

What could he advise his poorest parishioners who lived crowded in a one-room mud hut with an incurably sick grandfather? They could not care for him and the overcrowded hospitals needed their beds for younger people who had some hope of being cured. What could he do with children so badly undernourished that they could not walk because their four-year-old legs were mere sticks? With money medical care could be had, but for the poor, which made up the major part of his parish, there seemed to be no answer

Then, one day in 1962 he found himself with the responsibility of a paralysed old lady whom no hospital would take. He realised that the work which he must do in Pakistan was not just teaching children and performing his parish duties but that somehow he must start a hospital for people suffering from incurable diseases, and for the poverty-stricken sick who fell outside of the scope of the medical help which the Government of Pakistan was able to give.

That November night as he finally found an empty room in Westridge for his dying patient, the seed, which was to become St. Joseph's Hospice for the terminally ill, was planted. One year later to the day, a ceremony of turning the first soil took place next to the church of the Sacred Heart. Two years later, the sight of the low, cream-coloured building, gaily decorated with rows of potted plants, is a warm image in the hearts of most of the people of Rawalpindi. For the old and suffering they know there is a final place to go if their need is great enough. For people grateful for their own blessings it is an ideal place to give donations as thanksgiving. For everybody, it is a triumph of hard work, great optimism and unrelenting faith.

Obviously, the Hospice didn't just bloom overnight. Every brick and curtain and medicine bottle had to be begged one way or another by Fr. O'Leary and his dedicated Committee members. The Bishop of Rawalpindi gave him his blessing and the go-ahead sign. The first donation was 10 rupees–about 75p– and that started the young priest on his initial venture in fund-raising. His first debt for the Hospice came at the same time as he printed leaflets to be sent all over the world for donations. It was hit and miss at first. Getting the addresses from magazines of any organisation which looked solvent, he bombarded dude ranches, hospitals, hotels, medical companies, and any other likely, or unlikely, organisations for help. But Rawalpindi, tucked in the foothills of the Himalayas, must have seemed too far away, for the answers only cleared the printing debt. Advertisements in English newspapers began to produce a slow dribble of funds and Fr. O'Leary's Mother collected the first donations amounting to £86.

The summer of 1963 Fr. O'Leary spent in Karachi going from medical firm to medical firm collecting medicines and funds. With support and help from Mr. and Mrs. Pitman, two valued friends living in Karachi, he went from business house to business house selling industrialists on the idea of helping in this philanthropy. By October, 1963, he had gathered the equivalent of $5,000 and this was security enough to start. The foundation was laid for a one-storied, long, low building with a large ward on either side, one or two offices and treatment rooms, a tiny nursery, a kitchen, several bathrooms and a long shaded verandah for patients to lounge on and to serve as a temporary dispensary for local out-patients. The hope was to expand some day, but for the moment, if just this much could be completed it would seem a miracle. As the funds dwindled to less than a hundred dollars it was apparent that nothing short of a miracle could carry it on. Then this miracle happened. Misereor, a German foundation started by Catholic clergy in Germany to help atone for war atrocities, donated one and a half lakhs of rupees (about $30,000) for the use of the Hospice. From that moment the future of St. Joseph's was certain and the completion of the building was just a matter of time.

Once the building was secure the next problem was a nursing staff. As luck would have it the Mother General of the Franciscan Missionaries of Mary, a nursing order, was in Lahore. She was approached with the request for nurses and readily saw the value in such a plan. Six nuns were sent to Westridge and were later joined by a seventh. Fr. O'Leary hastily prepared a small convent for them adjacent to his parish church and next to the Hospice. Led by Sister Dolores from Spain, this small group of Indian, Argentinian, Irish and Pakistani nuns, have taken over the complete management of the hospital. Four of the nuns are nursing sisters and the others manage the kitchen, the convent and the teaching in the parish school.

Because of the obvious impossibility of caring for the in-patients and the out-patients who come to the Hospice each day for medical care, the nuns are training aides to help them. This has been a blessing in the parish because the daughters of the poorest people, who would normally have no chance for education, can be trained in a paying and useful career and earn money, food and lodging as they are being trained. Since the opportunity is such a good one the nuns have had no trouble in selecting intelligent and capable girls.

The first glimpse inside the Hospice is something of a shock–a very pleasant shock! One could expect gloom in a building devoted to patients who cannot be cured. Of the many words which could be found to describe St. Joseph's, "gloom" is just not on the list. When Fr. O'Leary came to his choice of colours he had none of the housewife's prejudice about right combinations and wrong combinations. Not knowing that yellow and pink are not normally put together and that orange and turquoise can be quite startling side by side, he chose his colour scheme with careless abandon and unbelieving joy that he had gone far enough along in his plans to need a colour scheme. The results are delightfully gay and cheery with the charm of a summer garden. Ruffled white curtains frame the many large windows, multi-coloured lampshades cast rainbow tints in the roomy wards, and brightly designed quilts on each of the 20 beds in a ward make it into a homely atmosphere. For many of the patients it is their first time ever to live in a room with electricity or to use a bathroom with plumbing and it seems to them as though heaven has arrived on earth. For most of them their death had been accepted. The unbelievable thing is to have the last days or months or years in such a surrounding of comfort and love. This seems to set the keynote of the Hospice and though it is a place for the dying the emphasis is on living.

The beginnings of Jospice..... the mud hut, Westridge, Rawalpindi

The patients, who come from all castes and creeds, from all over Pakistan, and from widely scattered backgrounds, offer the widest possible range of human suffering and a moving sight of human drama as well. On the verandah of the Hospice sits a man with no legs and partially deformed hands winding bandages with a lot of enthusiasm. He is suffering from Buerger's disease and has just had his fifth operation. Sitting in a wheelchair in the sun a 90-year-old lady with no known relatives to care for her, quietly dozes the morning away. A non-infectious leper happily paints some furniture in the garden. A mental patient of massive proportions proudly sits guard near the hanging laundry so that the possible rogues passing by cannot steal it across the low wall. A young girl, discarded by her husband because of an injury to her spine, crouches near an ancient Singer sewing machine on the verandah ripping up second hand clothes to make baby clothes, table napkins and anything else the nuns show her how to do. At mealtime an old and crippled deaf man who was found dying of malnutrition by the roadside, contentedly feels his worth in the Hospice as he feeds a helpless patient suffering from Parkinson's disease. Three spastic children endeavour to learn greater control of their bodies as the nuns give them lessons. An old gentleman dying of cancer in the men's ward is visited by his arthritic wife who lives nearby in the women's ward. At the far end is the nursery where wasting children begin to show a rosy glow of health from the regular meals and loving care of the nurses. There is an intangible sense of happiness in the air despite the gravity of the illness all around. The illness was there anyway but to be ill in St. Joseph's is a blessing which none of the patients really takes for granted. The love and careful nursing, the regular meals and helpful medicine make all the difference to each of these helpless people approaching the end of their lives.

Mrs. Mahmood

Rawalpindi, Pakistan 1965

My Father Arthur Joseph

My Mother Anne Josephine

The Beginnings . . .

1

MY Father Arthur was in the Royal Marines during the war about 1916. He and his company had been detailed to sail for the Dardanelles on H.M.S. New Zealand. He was friendly with my Mother, Anne Russell, at the time. She lived in Little Crosby, near Liverpool. He was down in Portsmouth ready to set sail for the area of fighting.

My Grandfather took my Mother down to Portsmouth to say their goodbyes to my Dad. They went down by train and my Grandfather squared the attendant of the dock to allow him access to the ship. At this very time my Father received an order from the deck sergeant to take three steps forward and he was marched off the ship and told to go and play at a concert which was being given by the Royal Marines in Portsmouth that evening.

The pianist for the concert had fallen ill. They knew my Father was an accomplished pianist and so an order was given that he play at the concert. Once off the ship he was whisked away to where the concert was being held. While my Dad was playing the ship sailed and when he came came back to rejoin the ship he was told that it was impossible because the company had left without him and he was given a posting elsewhere. H.M.S. New Zealand sailed away but it was blown to pieces by enemy fire and every man of the ship's company was killed.

This tale about my Dad is a neat little story but if it had not taken place I would not have been here to write my Memoirs. It is very difficult to imagine how one is completely in the hands of God and how He ordains things to take place as He wills. My Grandfather and my Mother were obviously sad about the loss of the ship's company but relieved that my Father was not among them. However, they could hardly judge the consequences of this at that time. The whole of one's life is determined by God. It is easier to see it now in retrospect in the events I am about to unfold, all of which were God-orientated in as far as He seemed to be able to fix everything as He willed it.

My mothers family Fr Willie Russell,
Auntie Bet,   Uncle Frank,
Mum, Uncle Charlie, Auntie Mary

Mum and Rita with our cousins, Dot, Joan,
Sister Thomas More & Fr Willie MHM.

My Great Grandfather (Wall)

My Great Grandmother (Wall)

It was on September 2nd, 1942, that I started my missionary career, if you like, by joining the Junior Seminary of the Mill Hill Fathers at St. Peter's College, Freshfield, near Liverpool. I was then 11 years of age and found myself among a group of 32 students of similar age, who were joining the Mill Hill Fathers, in preparation for the priesthood. I was 25 years of age when I was ordained a priest at St. Joseph's College in Mill Hill, London. I studied six years at St. Peter's College, Freshfield, two years at St. Joseph's College, Burn Hall, Co. Durham, two years at St. Joseph's College in Roosendaal, the Netherlands, and a further four years at St. Joseph's College in Mill Hill.

When I was eleven and went to Freshfield I felt quite lost, but a young Franciscan Sister of St. Joseph, Sister St. Anne, came to my rescue and helped me sort my things out. She took us for lessons in table manners and brainwashed us into the niceties of behaving like young gentlemen. Sister St. Anne subsequently served many years in Africa. Like the Mill Hill Fathers, these Sisters were founded by Cardinal Vaughan and they cared for our community with great devotion and pride.

I remember her buying a big statue of The Little Child of Prague for the Junior Dormitory and she introduced us to the delights of having splosh for supper !!

These seminary years were on the whole happy ones. The regime was a strict one; a mixture of study and prayer, but there was time for recreation and I remember the sport with great feeling. In the junior seminary football was the highlight of the week. There were four football pitches. Sadly those fields today have been handed over for housing and the college itself has been knocked down and replaced by a Cheshire Home.

I also enjoyed the singing in my student days. I remember one concert when Archbishop Downey came as the guest of honour. The announcement was made that the "Junior Choir will now sing Ave Maria, Sweet and Low, All Through the Night" which received quite a guffaw !! Bishop Campling, the great missionary bishop, was present on that occasion. The priests on the staff were extremely good. Fr. J. P. Kennelly was a strict Rector but there were among the staff devoted men like Fr. Tubby Preston, Fr. John Larkin, Fr. Jim Heery, Fr. Tom Sheridan and Fr. John McMahon who was a fine organist. He arranged for the choir to sing the Ave Maria my Dad had composed. I have forgotten the feast day on which we sang this motet, but it was enjoyed by all the students.

Under Fr. Kennelly the regime was very disciplined but despite this I enjoyed my sojourn in college. I was happy enough to get through my examinations.

The concerts and football kept us on our toes and the singing in the junior choir I found most enjoyable.

In the senior seminary at Mill Hill the harmonised choir had great ambitions and I recall us singing Beethoven's Die Vesper, a beautiful piece with magnificent harmonies. No feast day would go by without the descant version of Te Joseph Celebrent sung with great enthusiasm. It is amazing how small things affected one's life. The more adventurous of us would go and sneak into the refectory to see if dessert spoons and forks were placed on the table for lunch and we would look forward and sometimes guess correctly what the dessert would be !

The Sisters did all the cooking and we used to look forward to our meals—being the hungry lads that we were. During meals there was silence apart from the odd 'et reliqua' when we were allowed to speak.

It was the custom, for example, after breakfast to say one's grace facing the Crucifix and I remember the voluminous big pockets we had in our cassocks surreptitiously being stuffed with knives and forks, butter and bread and anything else that was available on the table. All manner of edibles were slipped into the cassocks of those who were saying their grace. One fellow, I remember, had a knife placed down his sash ! As he walked out of the refectory, the Rector, Fr. Martin, was following him and made some remark about being stabbed to the unsuspecting student.

We had some great smoking concerts in Mill Hill. When a missionary came back from abroad, he was always given a great reception and at the last minute we would put together some witty sketch or some form of concert which always ended with a version of words put to the tune of the popular radio show Much Binding in the Marsh. They were usually very funny. I remember they were composed by Brian Conneller and Jim McKinnon would accompany on the piano.

We were studying the Pentateuch in Scripture at the time and our discussions were centred round the fact of Moses' authorship of these books. Fr. Heuthorst was our scripture professor and went on for weeks lecturing about Moses. Brian Conneller, to celebrate these discussions, made up a verse as follows:-

> At St. Joseph's at Mill Hill,
>> Fr. Heuthorst got a letter about the book
> At St. Joseph's at Mill Hill,
>> which we know by the name of Pentateuch
> Dear Sir, it ran upon my word
>> it's time discussion closes
> For writing Pentateuchs I swear
>> is not a bed of roses,

and I should know, I wrote it
   Yours sincerely
Mr. Moses !
   At St. Joseph's at Mill Hill

Brian Conneller was very smart at writing these versions. I regret now I did not collect more of them as they were often brilliant.

Memoirs are for memories and an abiding one in my mind from my footballing days at Mill Hill, was a brilliant goal I scored against St. Edmund's, Ware. The team had travelled from Mill Hill to play what was hoped would be an annual fixture.

Mill Hill First XI
Back Row: O'Reilly, Akker, Fox, myself, Melis, Van Leeuwen
Front Row: McKinnon, Kiggen, Brentjes, Ahern, Hogenkamp.

We prided ourselves at being the best seminary team in the London area. I was playing inside left and was able to stream out magnificent passes to a Dutch student called Hogenkamp. Hogey had a tremendous left foot and he could send the ball across at a searing pace if he caught it correctly. I anticipated this. The ball came hurtling across the goal area about four foot high at a tremendous speed. I remember running into position for it, diving headlong and catching the ball beautifully with my head. It sailed into the goal. It was a quarter of an hour before the game restarted because the pitch was on the top of a hill and it took that time to go and find the ball !! There were no nets, of course, and the ball went right down the hill. It was a muddy pitch and I recall how elated I felt at having made contact with such a fierce drive.

I often relate this incident with a certain amount of pride and it is a story you can exaggerate as much as you like because the people you are telling the story to were not there. Normally you leave them with a feeling of disbelief !!

There were incidents like that which made the seminary life exciting and enjoyable. I think it was the attitude of the Fathers who were training us like Fr. Paddy Morris, Fr. Duijvenstein our Theology Professor, Fr. Maserai who took us for Canon Law and Fr. Knuwer our Ascetic Theology Professor. They were very prayerful men and acted as good guides with our first steps, if you like, into our Mill Hill sphere of spirituality.

I suppose each college has its moments of hilarity. The one that stands out most for me concerned St. Joseph's College, Mill Hill. The winter had been very severe and the pond had frozen over. After lunch it was the custom to 'do a round', that meant walking round the grounds and most of the students, when the pond had frozen over, congregated round it. I remember one particular day when we were daring one another to walk across the ice.

Piet Kok accepted the challenge and I think also Johnny Fraughan with Fokko Ros. They got on to the ice to try and venture to cross to the other side of the pond. Half way across the ice began to crack under Piet and we egged him on further to complete his crossing. The more earnestly he tried the more the ice cracked and he went into the water a few times. We enjoyed the situation hugely. Piet Kok came out of the pond filthy dirty and shivering. I remember asking him later why he hadn't turned up for lectures that afternoon. He told me that he had an appointment to see the doctor as he suffered from rheumatism. I thought that was a classic answer !

We didn't seem to take many photographs in those days, but some bright spark, Gerry Lebbink I think, caught some snapshots which I reproduce here. Piet, Johnny and Fokko went on to ordination and did great work on the missions. These great men were part of that tradition passed on to us by Cardinal Vaughan, our Founder, and which is the hallmark of all Mill Hill men.

The so-called rigours of the seminary I didn't find very harsh or arduous and it was with a sense of pride that we became Mill Hillers.

Those seminary years were on the whole happy ones. When I got the idea of entering the seminary and told my Father, my Dad said immediately, 'I'll give Fr. Winstanley a ring and arrange a meeting with the Mill Hill Fathers.' My Dad phoned Fr. Jim and he fixed an appointment with Fr. Kennelly, the Rector of Freshfield, who came out to see me.

The Winstanleys had been friendly with my family for some years and Fr. Jim seemed to be the best contact. I remember going round to Fr. Jim's house many times and in the course of one of my visits I recall his sister-in-law, Mrs. Winstanley, telling me that she was worried about another of Fr. Jim's brothers, who lived in North Lancashire and had fallen away from the Church for a number of reasons, one of which was that his wife would not allow the priest over the doorstep.

My class at Mill Hill July 1956. (not in order) J Akker, T Beemster, J Dijkman, J Gasser, A Geerts, J Groessens, B Keaney, J vd Kligt, F Kwik, H Melis, R McGorty, J McKinnon, W Naylor, F O'Leary, L Purcell, E Roebroeck, F Ros, J vd Salm, J Stampfer, J Thompson, W Tuerlings, F Vester, F Wessels, L Wiedemayr, D Wolbers, J Zonneveld.

Anyway, I had occasion to ring the Winstanley family and it was in the days before S.T.D. came into play and the Crosby numbers had GRE before the number. So I phoned GRE 1234. The telephone rang and when answered I spoke to the lady and asked could I speak to Jim please. She said there was no Jim there. I apologised and said I was sorry that I must have had the wrong number but that it was a family called Winstanley that I was trying to contact. She said their name was Winstanley, then added, "I'm sorry, I can't spend more time speaking to you as my husband is extremely ill and is dying." She put the telephone down.

In my mind I related this to the statement of Mrs. Winstanley, that she was very worried about this particular relation, so I rang the number again GRE 1234 and who should answer it but the other Mrs. Winstanley, I told her that I thought I had been talking to a relation of hers in North Lancashire and that a Mrs. Winstanley had said that her husband was very ill and was dying.

Mrs. Winstanley thanked me for the information and had time to ring the parish priest in that area to let him know of the circumstances. In those days to call North Lancashire one would have to go through an operator and the possibility of ringing a Crosby number and getting the other family of Winstanley in North Lancashire was so very strange. An angel must have been very busy re-routing my call to the required branch of the family !!

With Rita and 'young' Jim Winstanley at Mill Hill

My first High Mass at St Peter's College, Freshfield,
assisted by Fr. Anthony Stark and Fr Jim McKinnon

On July 8th, 1956, I was ordained a priest by Bishop Craven and after the Ordination ceremony, the Rector Fr. Martin read out our appointments. To my surprise, I didn't get a mission appointment but was told to go for higher studies at Glasgow University. It was with fear and trepidation that I entered on my university course and I graduated in 1960. Of course, I was awaiting my appointment to a mission territory and my Mother, who had come up to Glasgow for my graduation, was as anxious as I was at the prospect of my receiving such an appointment.

With my brother Arthur and Mum at graduation

I was sent to Rawalpindi, Pakistan. I didn't know anything about Pakistan and I just wondered what it would be like. Bishop Nicholas Hettinga was in charge of the Diocese of Rawalpindi. His diocese must have been one of the biggest in the world, stretching from near Lahore on the Indian border to the peaks of the Himalayas in the North and to the West it bordered on Afghanistan. I departed on November 5th, 1960 from Liverpool, on the M.V. Cilicia and arrived three weeks later in Karachi. Dad had died in 1958 but my Mother, Brother Arthur and Sister Rita bade me farewell at Liverpool Landing Stage. A rather sad farewell it was. My Mother's parting words to me, which I will never forget, were "Francis, always be a good priest." These words have always stood me in good stead. Excitement, mixed with a certain amount of fear, are always present when one is undertaking a serious commitment but I felt reassured by the love and commitment of my family, as I set out on my journey. Mr. Menezes, a travel agent who acted on Bishop Hettinga's behalf, met me in Karachi and promptly ordered a camel tonga to take all my luggage to the railway station. It was an overnight train to Rawalpindi. The only thing I can remember about it was a very fervent passenger kneeling down in the train at three o'clock in the morning facing Mecca. He was saying his prayers. I do not know whether or not I was included in his prayers but it was a good start to my stay in Pakistan because prayer was to play a great part in my life. The journey took a full 24 hours. Although I was feeling quite tired, I was heartened by the great welcome given to me by Bishop Hettinga, Fr. Fred Moss, Fr. Bill White and Fr. Paddy Byrne.

Graduation at Glasgow University

Bishop Hettinga had asked me to take out some material to form a backdrop to the High Altar in the Cathedral of Christ the King. The Bishop also had requested a couple of guns for shooting wild boar. And another priest, Fr. Nobby Turner, had asked for some fishing tackle and golf balls. I was quite relieved to hand over all these goods safely.

My first morning in Rawalpindi was a strange one. I went out to say Mass in the Cathedral and as I approached I saw the Bishop's dog, Jack, on the Cathedral steps. He looked quite vicious and I was taken aback with fear. So I hunted round the house for a back door but could not find one. There was only one way into the Cathedral and that was through the front door to face Jack. I met one of the priests who killed himself laughing that I was afraid of Jack !!

Jack was a huge alsatian and made friends with everyone, much to my relief. He used to go in and out of Bishop's house as if he owned the place. There was a big bowl of water for him in the vestibule and he was always looking for scraps. I remember one day the Bishop saying, "Dogs not allowed" and immediately Jack went out. The Bishop used to take Jack out for a stroll every evening into the Cantonment. When the weather got very hot and people were thinking of taking to the hills, Jack was the first to go. He was the first one to feel the heat and let everyone know that it was time for holidays when he kept slumping down in the vestibule of Bishop's house.

The priests who were free used to go up to a town called Murree for their summer holiday. I was amazed when it came to my turn to find that all the dogs in Murree looked like Jack and there was a crowd of them. Murree was a delightful spot. In the British days it was a holiday camp for the troops. The troops, though, had to march, and various areas of the route were marked where they were allowed to rest.

My first appointment which the Bishop gave me was to a place called Dalwal in the Thar Desert. I remember being sent with the cook as a companion and we arrived at Chellagang. The cook said we had missed the last bus to Dalwal and I suggested that we get a taxi of some kind which he agreed to. The alternative was just to kip down somewhere. I was anxious to get to Dalwal because I still had a deep feeling of being lost.

Fortunately a driver agreed to take his car through the hillside. There was no lock on the steering wheel and we had quite a hazardous journey. Then out in the distance I saw a lamp being shone towards me. It was Fr. Tobias, a Franciscan from Lahore.

He was the parish priest at Dalwal. There were only three Catholics in the area, I recall, and I joined up with three American priests to learn Urdu. That was my task there. There was no electricity and very little in the way of conveniences like running water. Fr. Tobias was a great man. He spoke Urdu perfectly and knew the script of the language, so much so that he was asked by the Pakistan authorities in Karachi to go down and organise an Urdu library for them there.

The salt mines in Khewra wanted a priest for Christmas. Fr. Tobias thought my Urdu was at a level at which I could deliver a sermon. My Urdu was not brilliant in any way but I was able to get through a sermon which Fr. Tobias had typed for me in Roman Urdu. The congregation consisted mostly of Goans who worked in the salt mines.

The head of the industry was an Englishman who had a beautiful bungalow, nicely manicured lawns and servants. I remember him shouting to me "Happy Christmas, Father" with an accent–a most peculiar one as if he had a hot potato in his throat. I said Holy Mass in a type of shed and then went to the bungalow for Christmas dinner which I enjoyed. I said that I had to get back to Dalwal that evening. He volunteered to give me a lift. Unfortunately, he wouldn't turn off the main road but dropped me off at the track which led me to the Mission Station. He informed me that he had a new car and the road was too bumpy to take me back to the school.

It was a beautiful night, not too cold and the moon shone very brightly. I looked at my watch. It was six o'clock in the evening and I thought of home and the time it was there which would have been just on one o'clock in the afternoon. I thought of Christmas at home and how cosy and affable it would be. There I was trudging on my own along this lonely path, quite scared and not really knowing my way.

Soon after this the Bishop requested the three American priests and myself to go to Rawalpindi. It was great fun going into the city and meeting ordinary folk again and, above all, speaking English.

I got friendly with Danny O'Dowd and his wife Felicity. He represented American Express in Rawalpindi and he invited me round to his house a few times. I was in Rawalpindi for a week or so and then had to get back to Dalwal to carry on with my studies. What amazed me was that the little children could speak Urdu fluently and I had a grammar book trying to learn postpositions and things of that nature.

But I was very happy and getting to know Pakistanis. The countryside was beautiful but there was little one could do except study Urdu. The time went very quickly and I used to look forward to the Crosby Herald arriving which old school friend Hughie Sankey sent out to me every week. I had read the Crosby Herald on occasions before I left for Pakistan but now I used to devour every page and every advertisement the day it arrived.

I was very impressed with Fr. Tobias and the way in which he would converse with people and had become one of the community even though there were only three Catholics to minister to.

In my third month in Dalwal I was called back to Rawalpindi and appointed to teach in St. Mary's School, Murree Road, with one of my classmates, Fr. Bill Naylor.

An old soldier of the Indian Army, by the name of Mr. Hudson, used to be a frequent visitor to SS. Peter and Paul's Church, in Crosby. On one of my visits, he sidled up to me, having heard that I had been appointed to Pakistan, and said, "When you get to Rawalpindi, go to Westridge. I used to be in the barracks there." I mentioned this to Bishop Hettinga who confirmed that I had the right place, commenting, "Westridge, the arsenal of India." Westridge was to feature very much in my work in Pakistan because it was there that I founded the first Hospice of St. Joseph's Hospice Association.

When I was on board the Cilicia, I met a couple who had recently been married, Margaret and Peter Seymour-Eyles. They were a very nice couple and interested in what I was hoping to do in Pakistan. One day Margaret said to me, "What are you thinking about, Father? Why don't you come over to India and visit us?" I accepted the invitation readily. So, in 1962, I got permission from Bishop Hettinga to travel to India during my summer holidays. I had never been on a plane before but the only way to get to their place was to travel from Rawalpindi to Lahore by plane, Lahore to Dhaka in East Pakistan (now Dhaka in Bangladesh), Dhaca to Calcutta and from Calcutta up to Tezpur, quite a distance for a first time traveller by air. It was a great experience to be able to see a different country, though India, basically, is the same as Pakistan. I stayed at Bishop's house in Dhaka and the Fathers there made me very welcome and put me on a plane to Calcutta, to catch my connection to Tezpur. However, in Calcutta, I had to stay overnight and I went to the Irish Christian Brothers in Chowringhee. They knew of their Congregation's house at St. Mary's College in Crosby and made me feel at home. The next day I caught the plane to Tezpur, situated in India's eastern state of Assam. When I arrived, there was no-one at the airport to meet me. It was my fault really, as I had not informed Margaret or Peter of my exact date, because of communication difficulties.

There was only one other person at the airport, which was not much bigger than a landing strip, and that person asked me why I had come to Tezpur. I said, "For a holiday." "What, you've come to Tezpur for a holiday?" he said in amazement. I gazed on the jungle which surrounded me. There had to be a Catholic Mission nearby. I was put into a tonga and was taken to the nearest Catholic Church, which was about half an hour away. The Mission consisted of a huge school, which accommodated hundreds of students from the surrounding area. The priests were Indian Salesians. The only trouble was that they all went to bed at half past nine and I was left on my own. There was no electricity, just a small tilly-lamp and I asked one of the priests if he had anything for me to read. He passed me an American Catholic paper and I read a few pages. To my surprise, I found the obituary notice of my great uncle, who had recently died in the U.S.A. – Austin J. Wall. Having read the obituary, I made tentative efforts to get to bed but from a little hole in the bathroom door, I saw a huge centipede crawling through. I switched my torch on it and it disappeared back into the bathroom. These creatures are extremely ugly, huge fat things, and I wasn't in any way anxious to make contact with it. It happened on about four or five occasions, that the centipede tried to get out of the bathroom and went back again when I shone my torch. I got on to the bed but was afraid to take off my clothes for fear of this enormous creature. I battened down the hatches, as they say, as I tucked in my mosquito net and gradually fell asleep. I could hear the Brahmaputra River flowing by and it was a great experience to hear the sound of the jungle. I fell asleep under my mosquito net but was wakened by the fact that something large and cumbersome was settling on my nose. I don't know if it was the centipede, but whatever it was the weight of its body bore down on the net. I jumped up excitedly but could find nothing. I waited until day broke and scoured the area for this unwanted creature. There was no trace of it, thank God, but I felt very ill at ease, having seen it. I said Holy Mass and attended the Assembly of the school, very dutifully done and great order existed among the pupils of the school. At lunch time I said to the parish priest, Fr. Joseph, who was incidentally later to become Bishop of Tezpur, "I had better be on my way, Father, I've got to go on to Dering." He replied, "I can't see how you are going to get there, as you will have to cross the river and the rivers are all swollen. You won't be able to cross." But I insisted that he had mentioned the fact that a train crossed the river, even though he had said there was absolutely nothing on the other side. I thought that there had to be some transport and that I could get a lift somewhere when I got to the other side. He tried to dissuade me by saying, "It's not safe to travel that way. I feel responsible for you," but I persisted so much, that he said, "Right, I'll give you a few sandwiches and some tea, which you can take on the train." He kindly made them and took me to the railway station. I didn't quite believe him when he said there would be no motor vehicles at the end of the line, but it was true. There was nothing there at all. The line petered out at the other side. It was dark and by this time, quite late at night. I turned for help to a young Bengali lad and told him I wanted some transport to get to Dering, which was still about 25 miles away. He said, "You'll have to walk back over the railway line, into the jungle area. I know that some people are there." We duly retraced our steps down the railway line. "Mind the snakes," he kept saying to me. He needn't have reminded me of that fact, as I felt reassured because he was walking in front of me. After three quarters of an hour, he took me into the jungle, to a clearing where there was a huge tent. I went inside it. I was in my cassock and sash and a gentleman shouted to me.

"Come in, Father, you are welcome." It was a Mr. Lucas, who was in charge of the men who were building the railway.

I told him of my need for transport. He was surrounded by all his lady friends but he got up and said, "Follow me." He put his big gumboots on and got hold of a mighty stick, saying "Come on, Father, follow me" which I did and saw to my surprise that we were standing at the backside of a wild elephant. I shouted, "Mr. Lucas, Mr. Lucas, there's an elephant here," and with the greatest understatement of the year he said, "Don't bother him, Father, and he won't bother you." He took me to a makeshift dormitory, where all the men were asleep and procured a lorry for me. He hammered on the door. Everyone, but everyone, was fast asleep. Eventually the whole group of men who were there awakened, came out and got on to the lorry. He gave directions to the driver on how to get to the nearest inhabited dwelling.

After travelling for half an hour, we arrived outside a huge bungalow with beautiful lawns and flowers everywhere. A bearer came out and took my case and went inside. I hadn't even seen or spoken to the Sahib yet. "You'll be all right, Father. I'll fix you a room; the Sahib is out. He has gone to a party." I went in and was offered bacon, egg and toast–a lovely repast really. I was very hungry after such a long journey.

After my meal, I sat down and fell asleep and awakened at the sound of a car. I thought that I had better get to the door and introduce myself to the Sahib.

32

He took one look at me, dressed as I was, in my white cassock and sash. He had had quite a bit to drink and he seemed stunned as I stood there. "It's all right, Father, it's all right," he kept saying. "You can have what you want." We chatted for a while and I told him of my ambition to get to Dering. Fortunately, his driver had not gone home. It was five o'clock now, in the morning, so he told his driver to return at seven o'clock, to pick me up and take me to the Catholic Mission. When I arrived there, the priest, Fr. Cherian Moolamattan knew of my existence because Peter and Margaret had left a note that when I arrived, a message should be sent to them.

I went down to meet Margaret and Peter Seymour-Eyles who were at the very beginning of our work in Assam, India, they now live in the south of England.

They lived five miles away in the middle of nowhere ! The priests were very welcoming, as usual, and they sent a runner, literally, to tell Peter and Margaret that I had arrived. Within a couple of hours, I was chatting to Peter and Margaret and they took me back to their bungalow. I then discovered that I had run out of cigarettes and told them that I was going to the local shops. Astonished, Peter asked where I was going. I told him of my need and he replied that I wouldn't find any shops around there, that there was just nothing outside the bungalow. How right he was. Outside the bungalow, there was a huge jungle, in which roamed tigers, leopards, snakes of every description and I was ordered not to venture out on my own. The following morning, I thought I would take a stroll, to have a look at the area, and followed a path which went right into the jungle. After half an hour, I heard a big sound, like a roar, to my right. The thought crossed my mind–Bengal tigers !!! I was petrified. Although the temperature was up in the 90's, I came out in a cold sweat and shook with fear. I thought, "How could I defend myself ?" Although there were bamboo shoots to my left, I was stiff with fright and could not put my hand out to get one. My only defence was my small camera. I thought of my head being mashed to pieces in the jaws of this tiger and whether or not I should make an Act of Contrition. I did, as I thought death was so close to me. The thought, too, of my Mother receiving a telegram, as to how I had died, came into my mind. I don't know how long I was in this state, but when I regained my senses, I turned round and found myself on tip-toe, making my way back. Eventually, I came across Peter, who was in such a rage, because he feared I had been mauled to death. I have never had such a telling off in my life before and felt quite humiliated that I had acted so rashly. Peter and Margaret were very kind to me. They provided me with everything. Peter apologised later but explained the dangers to me again and after the telling off, I had no temptation of disobeying him a second time.

On one particularly fine morning, I was looking for my dressing gown, because Margaret had told me that my breakfast was on the loggia. I could not find my dressing gown but as I passed Margaret and Peter's room, I thought I had spotted it. Margaret, I imagined, had collected it for the dhobi by mistake, so I promptly retrieved it and took it to my room. Later, that morning, Margaret said to me that I had Peter's dressing gown on. I denied it, of course, and said it was mine.

Ten minutes or so later she came into my room and said that she had found Peter's dressing gown. It turned out to be exactly the same as mine. "Where did you buy it?" I said. She explained that they had caught the boat train from London and when they arrived in Liverpool, she remembered that Peter needed a dressing gown. So when they got off the train, they went into a large store next to the station (which had to be Blacklers) and bought it. I said that my Mother had taken me into Liverpool to the same shop and we had bought an identical dressing gown, exactly the same size, colour and design. The chances of this happening six thousand miles away, in the foothills of the Himalayas, seemed to me to be particularly small.

Margaret and Peter were great hosts and took me all over the surrounding area. Peter demonstrated for me how the tea was plucked and processed. The next time you are enjoying a cup of 'Brooke Bond' tea, think of me and a place called Dering in the foothills of the Himalayas.

I was there two weeks and took off from Tezpur once more to Calcutta and stayed a couple of nights with the Irish Christian Brothers. It would be a great opportunity to meet Mother Teresa, I thought, and made for her headquarters on South Circular Road and asked to join the Sisters in their work. They willingly agreed and gave me the opportunity to travel with them round their points of call. On their journeyings they said prayers and dispensed medical treatment for their leper patients, who arranged themselves in queues at determined stops. I was so edified by their work and their devotion to duty and above all, by their simplicity. What attracted me was the way in which God was so evidently with them.

Mother Teresa whose work inspired me.

Having left the Sisters and seen where Mother Teresa had been a young nun, I went to their Hospice, at the Kalighat Temple in Calcutta. I took a photograph of a poor man lying on the street, with a cow next to him. Soon afterwards, the Sisters called me into the Temple to tell me that the same poor man had been brought in to them and was dying. I took another photograph of him (reproduced on Page 10). He inspired me and thousands of other people who have since seen his photograph and have similarly been affected. This old man has been our greatest fund raiser. I then thought how nice it would be if I could do the same kind of work as these Sisters and when the opportunity came along with Mrs. Jacob, I readily grasped the chance of doing this type of work in Rawalpindi.

Mrs. Jacob, an old lady, was our first patient in a makeshift Hospice, which was virtually a mud hut. This all happened in 1962. Mrs. Jacob lay dying in a rat infested dwelling and one Sunday evening, after Mass, I was walking across the compound and a Pakistani lady came up and explained to me that she had in her care an old lady whom she no longer could look after. She, apparently, had been abandoned in her house and could I do something to help her.

I went round to see this lady. She lay motionless on a bed in this rather tumble-down house. My ministrations towards her seemed to be meaningless. She obviously had had a stroke and I felt totally useless. Whilst I was with this lady there happened to be a meeting of the Catholic Young Men's Society of Rawalpindi, which I had started the previous year. I sent a message for a few men to come round to help me to carry this lady down to a taxi which I

35

had summoned. I didn't know at that time where I was going to put her. However, I knew some nuns in Rawalpindi who would willingly look after her. I went to the Convent and received a great welcome from Sister Margaret and Sister Cervera, both Franciscan Missionaries of Mary. They readily volunteered to give this lady a bed for the night. Unfortunately, they stated they were unable to care for her longer, as the bed she occupied was needed on the following day. I recall Sister Cervera pouring some liquid into Mrs. Jacob's mouth and one of her eyes opened. She poured some more liquid in and the other eye opened. The lady was very much alive and I then rang every hospital to see if she could be admitted but all refused. "There is nothing we can do for her," they said. But so much could be done for her with proper care and attention. Later that evening, when I was lying on my bed, wondering what to do with this patient, I thought of the little outhouse in Westridge. It was a former servant's quarters, attached to the Church of St. Mary. There was nobody inhabiting this small house, which was virtually a mud hut, so a few of us got together and were able to obtain an ambulance to transport Mrs. Jacob there, through the good offices of Dr. Mumtaz Husain, the chief medical officer of the combined military hospital in Rawalpindi.

St Joseph's Hospice – our first -1964

In November it was cold and the old lady would require some heat. Thank God, the family in the adjoining mud hut were very friendly and extremely helpful. I knew them well, because I had been saying Mass every Sunday morning in this Church of St. Mary and had become quite friendly with Mr. Sadiq Masih and his wife, Alice, and their young daughter, Rita. In fact, the whole family cleared up and made habitable this mud hut, into which we placed a warmed charpoy, in time to receive Mrs. Jacob when the ambulance arrived.

There was a water tap in the compound which had running water and we fixed up a line from the Church, to provide electricity. The Sisters and a few friends gave Mrs. Jacob a big welcome. They washed her and made her comfortable and every day we organised some transport to bring them from their convent, three miles away. Every evening the Sisters and their helpers cared for Mrs. Jacob and saw to her needs.

One evening, I received a message from the catechist to say that Mrs. Jacob had had another stroke and was close to death. I went round in the car of Captain Alun Williams, an American Army officer who was stationed in Rawalpindi, and I was mesmerised by the fact that the only thing she recognised was the Crucifix. My Dad had given me this Crucifix some years earlier and I placed this in front of her. This was the very first time she gave a sign of recognition. I had presumed she was a Muslim, as ninety-nine per cent of the population were Muslim. I placed it in front of her, thinking that if she were a Christian, it would give her some consolation and this is what happened. She raised her head and kissed the Crucifix and kissed it continuously for the next four or five hours, until she died.

We were all struck by this happening and astonished. On the day Mrs. Jacob arrived, I remember going into the little sacristy of St. Mary's and saying to Mr. John Pinto (who was to become a member of our Committee), "We will have to remember this day, November 19th, the Feast of St. Elizabeth, Patroness of Nurses, because it might be important one day." So, on that day, St. Joseph's Hospice was founded and from then onwards, great things happened. Bishop Hettinga was going to the Vatican Council and he had promised to contact the German Bishops to raise some money for the new Hospice we were planning in Westridge.

Very kindly, the German Bishops gave us a donation and we were on our way to building the first Hospice of St. Joseph's Hospice Association. Mr. Mir, a local building contractor, worked to the plans drawn up by Mr. Vizzosi, an Italian architect working in Rawalpindi, and in 1964 our Hospice was ready for opening. Cardinal Alfrink, of Utrecht, who happened to be visiting Rawalpindi at that time, was invited to perform the opening ceremony on November 26th. We were all so excited that such an event could take place and soon the Hospice was filling up with patients. Today, that Hospice has been extended a couple of times, to provide the first child clinic in Pakistan and it now has physiotherapy and nurses' quarters.

..and, typically Spanish. She would be nice to you one day and if you hadn't behaved yourself, she wouldn't talk to you the following day ! She was, however, a great and prayerful soul and under her leadership, the Hospice made great strides.

Turning the first soil for the Hospice with Mr Faizi and Mr Sylvester Gulfam

When it was time for me to come home, I realised that Mr. Hudson, who had advised me to go to Westridge, advised me well, because our little Hospice in Westridge has been the inspiration for all our work in England and in Central and South America.

Our reports from abroad keep us in good heart. For example, I received recently a letter from Sister Lucille Viau about her work in Rawalpindi. She writes . . . .

Dear Father,
S... was returning after a hard day's work when a gang of robbers came upon him and his companions, demanding at gunpoint their meagre earnings. Upon their resistance, two were killed on the spot whilst S... received a bullet in the spine, leaving him paralysed. For him this might have been the end of his dream (to raise and educate his children). The shadow of death passed over him. Sorrows, desperation, almost despair took hold of him until the day he crossed the threshold of St. Joseph's Hospice.

Like so many others, he underwent several weeks of physiotherapy, was fitted with orthopaedic shoes and calipers and given a special type of wheelchair so as to enable him to go daily to work and continue to provide for his four children.

Once again, we have seen signs of death and the seeds of life.

I could elaborate on many, many similar cases, which we witness daily, experiencing God's continual blessings.

Sister Lucille Viau F.M.M.

St. Joseph's Hospice, Rawalpindi

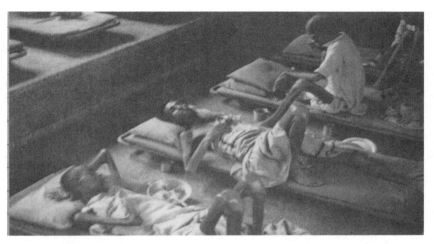

Some of Mother Teresa's patients in the Kalighat Temple in Calcutta

Bishop Nicholas Hettinga, first Bishop of Rawalpindi.
I had great admiration for him.

La Casa de San Jose, Thornton,Liverpool

First Faltering Steps

2

ONE might think it would be very difficult to collect funds for a Christian institution in Pakistan. It would have been if I had not obtained the help of two people, Edna and Peter Pitman. They were passengers on board the Cilicia when we left Liverpool on November 5th, 1960. They kept in contact with me when Bishop Hettinga sent me to Dalwal to the mission school in the Thar Desert to learn Urdu.

Each week they sent me the International copy of The Times. I had no funds and decided in 1963 to use my summer holidays collecting money in Karachi. I had not thought that Edna and Peter were still living in Karachi and it was only when I was travelling down to Karachi that I had the idea of contacting them. I got into conversation with an Anglo-Indian gentleman on the plane and I remember telling him of my hopes and that really I needed a driver and a car to take me around Karachi, because it was a city with which I was not familiar.

When we got off the plane, I remember saying to him, "Give me ten minutes to look through the telephone directory" in the unlikely event of my being able to contact the Pitmans, otherwise I would have had nowhere to stay. Fortunately, the name of "Pitman" loomed through all the names in the directory. I was quite surprised ! Peter answered the phone and I asked him if he remembered a Fr. O'Leary on board the Cilicia. He said that he did and gave directions on how to get to his house to my Anglo-Indian friend. Within twenty minutes or so, I was at Peter's house. Peter met me and said, "Go inside; Edna will be delighted to see you again." I was therefore able to go in and say, "Hello, Edna" and greet her warmly.

We sat well into the night, discussing my plans for a new Hospice in Pakistan. A Dr. Simcox had been invited round for dinner and he told me he had established a hospital in Karachi. Eventually the bearer came in with a glass of whisky and said, "Father, your bath is ready." I was then shown the bedroom where I was to sleep. Nicely coloured sheets dressed the bed and a two-ton air conditioner was in the room. Karachi was terribly hot and I was thankful for a cool bedroom.

I planned to say Mass early next morning in St. Patrick's Cathedral and the chokidar wakened me at six o'clock. I took a taxi to the Cathedral, said Mass there and arrived back at the house at eight o'clock. Peter was getting ready to go out to work but before I had seen him, the bearer walked in with my breakfast and the morning paper on a trolley. Peter then came in and said that he was going to work but that I could have his car and Abdul, the driver. "He will take you wherever you want to go," he said. I was delighted, of course, that I had the services of a driver, but more particularly, that Peter had set up for me a meeting with the British Chamber of Commerce in Karachi. I went there first and received the addresses of all the British companies in that city.

Dressed in my white cassock and sash, I went from company to company and did that for a whole month. My only cost was the price of a supper for Abdul each evening. Peter and Edna could not have been more hospitable. They became, as it were, part of the project. My first collection in Karachi amounted to over twelve thousand rupees–about £1,000.

Before I left for Karachi I had received a strange telegram. I remember it was Good Friday. It read simply – "Do not do anything until I come to see you" signed Dr. John Bunyan. Further correspondence with this gentleman gave me the details of his arrival in Pakistan from Salisbury (Harare) in Southern Rhodesia (Zimbabwe). This coincided with my visit to Karachi so I went down to the airport to meet this doctor. I contacted a Dr. Pinto to get some moral support and backup, because this was a highly placed Harley Street specialist coming to see me. I prepared the staff in Rawalpindi to receive him in a true Pakistani way.

Rather excitedly I waited for the East African Airways flight to arrive. Dr. Pinto, who was very influential and knew many people in Karachi, got permission for me to stand on the tarmac so that I would be the first person to meet Dr. Bunyan.

He was first off the plane and with a great wave of the hand said, "Fr. O'Leary, very pleased to meet you." I replied as courteously as I could and introduced Dr. Pinto to him. Dr. Pinto assured him that there were only a few niceties to go through customs-wise and we were prepared for a speedy departure to the Beach Hotel in Karachi where I had booked a room and put on a nice meal for him. The cook had made a special cake and everything seemed to be in order.

A speedy departure seemed to be on the cards for Dr. Bunyan and I remained outside the immigration area waiting with Dr. Pinto. We had been chatting for about half an hour but Dr. Bunyan was still in immigration. I looked through the glass partition and was quite disturbed when I saw him taking his tie off and loosening his shirt.

It was quite a humid and an extremely hot evening. The perspiration was rolling off him. He got up and came to the door and said, "Father, they are not going to allow me to enter the country." Both Dr. Pinto and myself were disappointed because it meant that we would have to cancel all our preparations. On enquiring why from the immigration officer, he told me that Dr. Bunyan's papers were not in order in as far as he hadn't had the required vaccinations.

Dr. Pinto said that he knew Mr. Bhutto, the then Foreign Secretary of Pakistan, and would get the required permission. The immigration officer was adamant and said that even the President of Pakistan couldn't allow this gentleman to come into the country. It was against all the legal rules and medical regulations. Dr. Bunyan protested that he had had all the necessary injections but the health authorities insisted that the East African Airways plane had landed in a country which was an endemic area for yellow fever. Poor old Dr. Bunyan. The alternative to being dispatched immediately home on a B.O.A.C. plane waiting in Karachi airport was to be taken to a house in isolation in a desert area beyond Karachi.

I was given permission to visit him the following day. I bought a bottle of whisky for him so he could drown his sorrows that night and the following day accompanied by a Pakistani doctor and Dr. Pinto I visited him at his house in the desert.

There were huge padlocks on the door inside and outside and there were soldiers on duty outside. There was no fear of Dr. Bunyan escaping from that lot. We were fumigated on arrival and sat down to listen to what he had to tell us. He explained that he had invented a new bed called the Bunyan Bed and he advised us to use it in our Hospice work. We went through all the blueprints. I knew myself that we probably wouldn't take them because of the expense and so we put the matter on hold and arranged to see Dr. Bunyan at the airport before he took off for England.

We waited for the special car to arrive. It resembled a tank rather than an ordinary medical vehicle. The weather was blisteringly hot and once again we had pity for the poor old doctor. We said our goodbyes and Dr. Bunyan left on the evening flight to London. He had explained that he was a direct descendant of the Bunyan of Pilgrim's Progress so we wished him the best of luck on his journey. A week later I received a letter from him telling me of his disappointment at not being able to speak to me properly. He described the terrible heat and the food and went on to say that he must have caught some sort of a bug on the flight home and had been extremely ill.

Dr. Bunyan, who died in 1983, was an international expert on medical inventions, especially the Bunyan bag which was widely used during the 1939-45 war to treat burns. He was President of the Royal Microscopical Society and in 1968 he invented a sterile recovery unit to keep transplantation in a germ-free atmosphere. Hence, it was for me a great privilege to have met him. I am sure he is saying a prayer for our 'Pindi Hospice in heaven now and that we 'pilgrims' here on earth will make good progress !

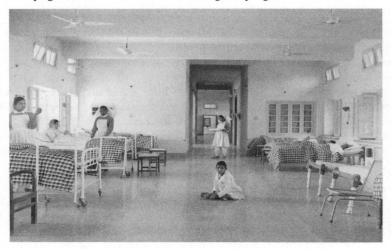

St Joseph's Hospice: The women's ward. Little Annie in the centre.

I returned to Rawalpindi after that delightful month in Karachi and told Bishop Hettinga of my experiences. He seemed overjoyed and excited and, lo and behold, the Hospice would soon become a reality. The establishment of a good nursing team came about through the kindness of the Franciscan Missionaries of Mary. Their Mother General was arriving in Lahore and the Sisters, when I went to visit them, expressed the fear that they were going to miss Holy Mass the morning she arrived. The train was leaving 'Pindi at 3 o'clock in the morning. To allay their fears, I volunteered to say Mass for them at 1 o'clock and, of course, the nuns were delighted. Naturally, that was the first thing they told Mother General when they arrived in Lahore. Through these Sisters, I made a special appeal to the Mother General to supply nursing sisters for our new Hospice. She immediately approved of her Sisters working with me. It all seemed so easy in those days. Many prayers were offered up to God to grant all our wishes.

It was a wonderful feeling to drive on my little motor scooter out to Westridge, to see the great work the Sisters were doing. They attracted other people to help them, notably the Quadros family, with whom I am friendly to this day.

A Committee was formed to see to the day-to-day running of the Hospice. The Hospice then became part of my parish, as I was put in charge of the Sacred Heart Church, in Rawalpindi, in the grounds of which the Hospice was situated. I also had my duties in St. Mary's Church, further along the road. All this parochial work had to be linked up with my job as Vice-Principal of St. Mary's Academy, a huge new school, built by Bishop Hettinga.

If one has sufficient anxiety and verve about solving a problem the impossible can become possible. Let me give you an example. My first appointment after I had completed my studies in Urdu was to St. Mary's School in Murree Road, Rawalpindi. Fr. de Jong was the headmaster and I remember being very nervous when I was introduced to the Junior Cambridge Class which I was to teach. They were all very clever lads and I enjoyed the programme that was set for me. But I had obligations also as a curate at the Church of Our Lady of Lourdes in Dhok Elahi Basksh. The Catholic population of the parish amounted to a few hundred souls.

Sister Patrica F.M.M. with Anwar Jan, one of our first patients.

One afternoon the catechist asked me to go round to see a lady who was very sick. She was a young person of about 26 years of age and had three or four children. She lived in great poverty and it was obviously a great struggle for the family to keep together. This poor lady had a growth in her stomach and was very poorly. She said to me, "Father, if they could only keep me alive for a few more months because I am anxious about my children." I consulted with the doctor in the Holy Family Hospital, Dr. Anne Dolan who was also a missionary nun. She told me that the only way she could help this lady was by giving her an injection of Nitrogen Mustard.

I made enquiries around the various hospitals in 'Pindi but they didn't have this particular drug. I thought then of obtaining the drug from England and with this idea in view I sent a telegram to my friend Fr. Vincent Hughes. He was in a parish in the Liverpool Archdiocese. I asked him in that telegram to request the drug from my Sister Rita who was a nursing sister in the Northern Hospital in Liverpool. She in turn asked the almoner in the hospital, Pauline Farrell, if she could acquire the drug. Pauline rang Boots in Nottingham who were the manufacturers and she obtained about 20 vials of this Nitrogen Mustard

The difficulty, of course, was getting them sent out and I knew that this could be awkward to arrange. I sent telegrams to the Red Cross in Geneva for help and as I was passing the PIA airline office there was a chap working on a teleprinter. I asked him could he send a message to the airline in London to see if they could bring the necessary medicine out to me on one of their flights. I also contacted the head of the Pakistan Airlines, Colonel Mohd Nur, and asked him for assistance. Eventually, the medicines arrived in Lahore but were impounded in customs.

Meanwhile the lady was waiting desperately and hoping that something would happen. I managed to get the authorities in Lahore to release the medicines and fly them up to Rawalpindi. I couldn't contain my excitement when I went to celebrate Mass the following day in the Holy Family Hospital and told Dr. Dolan that I had the required medicine. After Mass I popped in to see the lady and told her not to worry that I had the medicine which would be injected into her that day. She gave me a beautiful smile of relief and I went off to the school for the Assembly. Later that day the catechist came to see me in the school to tell me that all hell had been let loose in Holy Family Hospital. The lady in question had started to shout out "I want to become a Christian, I want to become a Christian" much to the disquiet of the Sisters. I wasn't very popular at that time because the Sisters thought that the hospital might be closed down because of the rumpus that this lady had kicked up. So I sent the catechist back with the information that I would be visiting later that evening.

Fortunately, when I arrived I met Dr. Dolan and she assured me that she would protect me against the other nuns !! I remember going through the door feeling very uneasy and walked with Dr. Dolan to the ward where this lady was. If a nun gives you a dirty look you necessarily start feeling afraid.

Anyway we got round it all right. I was able to pop in to see this lady and was able to anoint her. I was delighted, of course, with all the various forces that had been galvanised into action for this lady to take the decision she had so bravely made. I went away that night having left the ward feeling like a million dollars.

At this time I lived in the priests' house which was attached to the school. One day in my first week there I went along the corridor and found one of my colleagues studying very hard. I walked in and greeted him, and asking what the problem was as he looked so studious. He explained that he was taking a Degree at Lahore University and part of his course was studying Latin.

Initially I was surprised that one could take a subject like Latin at a Pakistani University. Apparently the papers were set and marked by the Franciscan Fathers in Lahore. On making further enquiries as to why he had a problem he replied to me that he had a particular passage in Virgil's Georgics to translate and could not make head nor tail of it. Simon Almeida was the priest's name. He was a product of the seminary in Colombo in Sri Lanka.

When I saw the passage which was causing such a problem I recognised it immediately as I had done my Degree in Latin at Glasgow University a few months previously. The Latin professor in Glasgow had earmarked this particular passage as being very difficult construction-wise. I had taken it that this could have been a spot question in the Degree exam and I had studied it thoroughly. I even remembered it by heart so I started off by saying, "Where is the verb, Simon? No, not that one, the main verb, Simon" and so we went on to find the subject and all the causal clauses. Anyway I put down the translation as I remembered it and poor old Simon thought I was brilliant and he went off and told the other priests how clever I was. I just tossed it off as another event and walked out of the room and said, "If you have any more difficulties, Simon, just let me know."

Fr. Simon was an extremely good man and a very arduous worker. He went on to get his Degree and is now teaching, I think, somewhere in the subcontinent.

Simon had been going on about my translation abilities so when a letter came in from Sri Lanka I pretended that I could read it and I said, "I will read the letter out for you, Simon." Previously, he had told me about his friend having to undergo a kidney operation and half way down the letter it had the word 'kidney' written in English. So I started off as one would start off any letter 'Dear Simon, thank you very much for your last letter. How are you keeping? My operation was very successful and my kidney is now functioning' – or words to that effect. It turned out that my translation was correct. If you saw the Sri Lankan script it just looks like a series of O's with little tangents on them, so I was able to pull Simon's leg a second time. Then I said to him, "Any more translations, Simon, just give me a call !!" When I said goodbye to Simon, he had a very bewildered look on his face.

The Story unfolds . . .

3

FATHER Paddy Byrne was the instigator of St. Mary's Academy, a new school built mainly for the influential people of Rawalpindi. At this time, Rawalpindi was the interim capital, whilst Islamabad was being built. So I found myself teaching the sons of army people from the President down to the lowest subaltern. Similarly, the daughters of these families went to the Presentation Convent, run by the Irish Presentation Sisters. The former Prime Minister of Pakistan, Benazir Bhutto, was a student there before she took off for higher studies at Oxford. The President's sons and the son of the Commander-in-Chief of the Army, Hassan Musa, went to St. Mary's Academy.

The establishment of our Hospice was all part of a personal Christian witness in our apostolate as missionary priests in Pakistan. Dr. Mumtaz Husain sent his sons to our school and his wife, Mary, was a very good and devout Catholic and both gave tremendous support to Bishop Hettinga in those days. The Bishop and all the priests were always welcome in their home. All these factors seemed to be part of a divine plan to get the Hospice going. God was bringing us all together, to show that His plan for the Hospice was born in a beautiful way. Those first friendships, thank God, still continue. Although Mary Husain died in the 1980s, I am still in contact with Mumtaz and his family. Periodically, Mumtaz comes over from Pakistan to visit our Hospices in England.

As I reminisce in St. Joseph's Academy, here in Thornton, the Secular Franciscan Order are holding their Divine Mercy Sunday today. This is indicative to me all these years later, of the need we have for our closeness to Christ and how necessary for us to have Christ's mercy and His grace to keep us going. About 130 people are attending today to pray here in this Academy. They pray for us at home, of course, but also for our other projects in Pakistan and in Central and South America. The prayers of these people are highly valued by me, because it seems that without a spiritual intervention, our work would falter. People often ask me, "How do you manage, Father ?" Invariably the answer is prayer and the intercession of Our Lady and St. Joseph and all our patrons. So particular emphasis is placed on their patronage, because we need them at every step we take. Our reliance on their intercession is total. They are part of us and we in prayer ask for their help all the time.

In April, 1966, I came home in time for my Mother's 70th birthday, on April 23rd. I am grateful that I was still able to rejoice in my family. My Mother had suffered a stroke while I was in Pakistan and she became totally dependent on Rita, my Sister, my Brother Arthur and myself. Fortunately, Rita was a nursing sister in the Northern Hospital in Liverpool and a small room on Ward 10 was made available for my Mother. Every night, the three of us would go in to visit her.

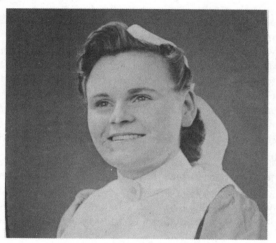

My sister Rita in her nursing days

It was a great privilege to be able to take Mum Holy Communion every day and to have that unification with Christ through her. During the four years Mum was a hospital patient I was busy trying to establish our Association in South America and forming what would become a Management Committee in England. My friend Margaret O'Donovan held the first official meeting at her home in Everest Road, Crosby on August 19th, 1966 and our first Minute Secretary was Helen Downie.

We have moved on a bit from there, of course, but the people who attended those first meetings became part and parcel of our organisation. The Committee, I suppose, became more established when it met in Seafield Convent, a large convent school in Crosby.

At that time, Bishop Gerry Mahon was the Superior General of the Mill Hill Fathers. It was he who gave me permission to establish our Association and it was with his blessing that our work could be established in South America and here in England.

The Management Committee of St Joseph's Hospice Association who carried the cares and worries of our work in the '70s and '80s

Back row : Terry O'Leary, Jack Keating, Filomena O'Leary, myself, John Carson

Front row; Jim Allen (RIP), Rita Allen, Colette Keating, Mary Carson, Dr Marie Cleary (RIP), Peter Carter

Our Beginnings in
South America and England

4

OUR first efforts in South America were concentrated on a small town in Colombia called San Bernardo del Viento. Idyllically situated on the Caribbean, it stands on its own. The nearest town, Lorica, is about ten miles away and there is nothing between it and the Panama Canal–just jungle and beautiful sandy shores. We were advised to go there because I had met Mother Peter, the Superior General of the Franciscan Missionaries of Mary, on a visit to Rome. She had just returned from South America and said that San Bernardo del Viento was a town which, in her opinion, needed our help most. One morning Eily Cropper, one of my Committee, came to me as I was going into SS. Peter and Paul's Church and showed me an advertisement for Coseley Buildings, a comparatively small firm manufacturing ready-made buildings. That day I went by train to Wolverhampton to see Coseley Buildings and gave them a rough idea of what was required. Within a couple of months they produced drawings and appointed a clerk of works named Chris O'Reilly. Chris came up to see me and we had lunch at the Blundellsands Hotel in Crosby before he left for South America.

He set out quite bravely, I thought, to this area in Colombia, to meet the building which had left by ship some weeks beforehand. Catholic Relief Services supplied lorries to take the prefabricated parts from Barranquilla to San Bernardo. Chris had the uphill task of recruiting local people, whom he had to instruct in foundation work, electricity and all the other things that go into erecting a building. He had the Hospice structure up within six months and it was a wonderful moment when I went out in 1967 to turn the corner in the jeep and see our first building in South America.

A nursing team was recruited here in England and in the States. The Hospice opened for its first patients in the spring of 1968 under Sister Redencion and other Franciscan Missionaries of Mary. It was fun starting out in this fashion. We did pub crawls and flag days and all the other things that go into fund raising, to pay off the £25,000, which was the cost of the new Hospice.

Our Hospice in San Bernardo del Viento, Colombia

When I visited South America for the first time, I didn't realise that the Colombian Consul in Liverpool had arranged for people to meet me at Bogota Airport. As the plane headed for Eldorado Airport, I had been thinking where I could say Mass when I got to Bogota. However, before I could make any plans, a gentleman met me at the airport before I went through customs and said to me in English, "Is your name Fr. O'Leary?" I told him it was and he said, "Well, I have the great granddaughters of General Danielo Florencio O'Leary here to meet you" and there, in front of me, were Carolina Blanca and her four sisters, descendants of General Danielo O'Leary. In the middle of Bogota there is a big statue commemorating his memory, because he was a great friend of Simon Bolivar and considered one of Colombia's liberators. Apparently, he was a great man–well, he must have been, if his name was O'Leary. We got into a couple of cars and I was whisked round to the Pombo-O'Leary household.

I mentioned that I wanted to say Mass and immediately Cardinal Concha was told of my arrival. The Cardinal very kindly allowed me to say Mass in his private chapel. We went back to the house and had a very enjoyable meal. I did mention that I was flying that evening to Cartagena. Arturo telephoned his sister in Cartagena who met me at the airport and took me to the Franciscans, who arranged for me to say Mass the following morning before I departed for San Bernardo.

I was quite anxious about this new venture. I landed in a town called Corozal, to be met by Sister Redencion, the Franciscan Missionary of Mary who was in charge of our new project. We then went by jeep to San Bernardo and received a great welcome from the Sisters there. One of the prominent citizens of that small town was Senor Negrete and to this day, he is one of our best supporters. His son, Raul, came to visit our Hospice in Thornton and is now a well-qualified doctor back in his own country.

After my journeying in Colombia, I took off to visit my friend, Fr. Vincent Hughes, who was stationed in Peru. We had been altar boys together in SS. Peter and Paul's Church, Crosby, and I thought that this was a golden opportunity to pay him a visit in his new surroundings. Vincent had volunteered the previous year to work for the Archdiocese of Liverpool in Peru and he was stationed in a small town in the north of Peru, called Negritos. However, before visiting him, I popped in to see the Auxiliary Bishop of Lima, Bishop Santoni, and he requested a Hospice for Callao, just north of Lima. I accepted his request, not knowing, of course, how anything could be worked out to put up another Hospice. However, we have never refused anyone.

Our Patron St Joseph

From Lima, I took a plane to Talara and was met by Vincent and Fr. Martin O'Grady. I told them about my journeyings and the fact that I had promised Bishop Santoni a Hospice in Callao. Immediately, Vincent said, "You have to start one here too." That is how our Hospice in Negritos originated.

My travelling was not over yet, because I crossed into Ecuador and then took a plane to Guayaquil and from there to Mexico City, because I wanted to visit the shrine of Our Lady of Guadalupe. Our Lady of Guadalupe appeared in Mexico as the pregnant mother of God to Blessed Juan Diego, an Aztec Indian, on December 9th, 10th and 12th, 1531. She left a Miraculous Image of her appearance on his cactus fibre cloak, or tilma, which still exists today for all to see in the Basilica of Our Lady of Guadalupe in Mexico City.

Our Lady came to offer faith, hope and consolation to the oppressed natives of Mexico and to reconcile them with their Spanish rulers. She put an end to the bloody human sacrifice of the Aztecs and converted ten million natives in the next ten years !

That was a wonderful experience and thank God I was able to re-live those first moments, when I had the opportunity, in early 1995, of returning to Guadalupe. I had the great privilege of going back to Our Lady of Guadalupe's shrine again, in the latter part of 1995, to experience a renewal of faith and trust in Our Lady. The apparition of Our Lady to Juan Diego is something very special and again, the urge came within me, to build a Hospice in Mexico City, which is the biggest city in the world. At that time they did not have a Hospice, or a similar institution, to care for the dying. Happily they do have one now, since our new Hospice opened there on September 28th, 1997.

By 1970, the San Bernardo Hospice was in full swing and our first Hospice in Peru, Negritos, had left Liverpool in crates. It opened the same year. The prefabricated parts for our Hospice in Callao were still stored in a warehouse on the docks and one evening I went down with Filomena O'Leary, our Nursing Superintendent and Honorary Secretary, to show her how it was to be assembled. She had joined our Committee three years earlier. After visiting my Mother who was a patient in the Northern Hospital, we saw the loading on the M.V. Vallegos a couple of days later and made a point of going down to Crosby shore, to see the ship on its way to Lima, Peru. Then, three weeks later, we flew to Lima and saw the crates on the dockside in Callao, the port of Lima. Believe it or not, it took nine months to get clearance from customs. Why it took so long, I can't really remember. All sorts of technicalities had to be completed before the crates were allowed to leave for the site of the Hospice, a mere two miles away. We had so many negotiations to work out with Sinamos, which was an organisation representing workers in Lima, but eventually the crates were deposited on land which had been made available to us by the Peruvian Government, since we were giving the Hospice to the poor people of Lima. At that time Lima was surrounded by thousands of families living in shacks on the mountainsides. So sad it was to see them all huddled together in dire poverty with so many of them in poor health.

Sister Triona F.M.M. was our first representative in Callao. She was a fluent Spanish speaker, having trained as a nurse in Spain. She was from Ireland and had difficulty in restraining her temper when dealing with officials !!

We found that negotiations in Peru were extremely difficult, despite Sister having fluent Spanish. She was joined by a group of nurses who had volunteered to work for us in South America. The priest in charge of Callao, Fr. Bernard Toal, was a great help to all our girls. Within nine months the Callao Hospice had then been erected and in 1973 it was opened in the presence of the Bishop of Callao and the British Ambassador to Peru. Another Hospice had arrived from Liverpool for an area south of Lima, Villa el Salvador. There were in Villa el Salvador 500,000 people who had come down from the mountains of Peru at the time of the terrible earthquake in 1970. There was no accommodation for them in Lima, so they settled on this huge sandbank which was Villa el Salvador. They built shacks for themselves and it was amazing how so many thousands of people survived in these surroundings. There was no water or electricity–absolutely nothing–yet they did survive. Our little Hospice was put into Sector 1 and it too opened in 1973. A lot of tramites or negotiations had to be gone through to get an electric line to the Hospice. When that happened, people in the surrounding area took their electricity from that line. We rejoiced that so many people benefited.

Today, Villa el Salvador has changed completely. Irrigation has made it possible for trees to grow. Schools have been built and when I went on a recent trip to Peru, a brand new church had been built, ultra modern and very artistically designed. What a change it was to find that one priest, Fr. Joe the Pole, with 500,000 parishioners was a thing of the past and that there are now many parishes, each with its own identity. The Society of St. James the Apostle made this possible, as many priests from Europe and America had volunteered their services to that Society in Boston, U.S.A.

The early '70s were very busy and we saw the implementation of a lot of our plans.

In 1973, for example, as well as the two Hospices near Lima we opened one in Tambo, in the High Sierra of Peru, and a fourth in San Francisco, the other San Francisco in the Peruvian rain forests. There was also a big surprise in store for me that same year, but more on that matter later on.

I'm inclined to ask myself what would have happened if Sister Bernadette Horvath, a Hungarian nun I met in Rawalpindi, hadn't thrust into my hand the famous picture of St. Joseph and Child.

The clinic in the Holy Family Hospital where she worked was crowded and her hand shot over the heads of what seemed to be hundreds of people to give me this holy picture. Into my wallet it went and there it stayed for all of nine years.

In 1972, when the time arrived to bid for the property at Thornton, Liverpool– property now known as San Jose–I had no idea from where I was going to get the money to reach the reserve price of £120,000. Then I thought of the wonderful spiritual trick Cardinal Vaughan played when he had his eyes on the property which was to become part of St. Joseph's College in Mill Hill. He had visited the owner of the house so many times without getting a positive answer.

So Cardinal Vaughan, being the man of faith he was, went to Burns and Oates in London and bought a small statue of St. Joseph. He wrapped this up in brown paper and decided to visit once more the owner of the house. He told him that he hadn't got much time and was forced to go on further and would he mind keeping the parcel he was carrying until his return.

The owner consented not knowing what was in the parcel. In Cardinal Vaughan's own mind St. Joseph had already taken over the property. Subsequently the owner consented to sell the house to the Cardinal. St. Joseph had operated in his usual wondrous way.

When I was standing in the grounds of Thornton Wood, the building which is now our Hospice in Thornton, and not knowing what to do I wondered whether it was worthwhile playing the same trick in order to get the building. I then realised I had in my wallet a holy picture of St. Joseph which Sister Bernadette had given to me in Rawalpindi. I promptly took it out and went towards the building and placed the holy picture just inside the door and prayed and prayed.

After the auction the auctioneer came out and, although I was not bidding in the auction, I couldn't because I did not have the necessary ten per cent deposit, he agreed to let me have the property by private treaty over a period of three months. So I assembled six or seven telephones in my office and asked my helpers to ring round convents in the British Isles requesting each convent for a loan of £500 with a promise of returning that loan within two years. I also placed an advertisement in the Universe and within that period of three months I had raised £56,000.

I promptly went into the Nat West Bank and presented them with this money. The manager agreed to loan me the rest of the money which was required to clinch the purchase. We all went to Bremner Sons and Corlett in Liverpool and signed the contract. The only trouble came a year later when we had to submit our annual accounts. The bank manager was very concerned about the overdraft but more troubled about the unsecured loan which was registered at £56,000.

Official opening of the Thornton Hospice by Colonel Raul Montero, Vice-Minister of Health, Peru, and his wife Gladys

I assured him that we would do our best to pay those loans back, secretly hoping that the good Sisters would not come down too heavily on me to repay the loans. They didn't, of course, and within a relatively short time (about ten years) we were clear of debt on the building. So St. Joseph worked in the same way for me as he had done for Cardinal Vaughan and we were very thankful to him for this great act of kindness.

Despite our feelings of wellbeing at securing the property our thoughts were directed to the sad news of the tragic death of my friend, Fr. Gerry Weston. I had been speaking to Gerry a couple of weeks beforehand and he was telling me of his plans and what he hoped to achieve. He had some wonderful tales to tell of his life as an Army chaplain and the stories he related about his free fall parachuting made me feel that I was out of the action.

He had gone for a simple lunch appointment with some officers in Aldershot. The I.R.A. had planted a bomb inside a car and parked it beside the officers mess. When it blew up Gerry and six other people were killed.

He lived in Enfield Avenue where I live and I knew his mother very well. I went to see her that evening to offer my condolences. It was sad news and all the parish of SS. Peter and Paul's, Crosby, were affected.

This Is Your Life . . . .

5

IN April 1973 Filomena and I visited our Hospices in Peru and on May 1st I flew home from Lima on an Air France flight at eleven o'clock in the morning. Before boarding the aircraft I said goodbye to a team of nurses, including Filomena, and gave her instructions to pass on to various people. That morning I had hoped to say goodbye to Fr. Vincent Hughes but he wasn't at the airport. "Ogger" (as he was known at school) usually made a point of coming to say goodbye but he wasn't there, so I departed. The first stop was Paris. I didn't realise it at the time but someone was there, observing that I did get my flight and there was also someone in Paris who saw me getting off the flight and that I had got the London connection.

I arrived in London early the following afternoon and was met by Paul Frayne who had done some photographic work for us earlier that year in our Hospices abroad. I was due to meet various producers of programmes to make a TV programme of our work and I had thought that a meeting had been set up through Tom Brennand, an old school friend. He held an important position at Thames Television in those days and I thought he would be a good contact for our Association. I didn't realise it, but Tom Brennand had got in touch with Tony Cooney, one of our helpers who in turn telephoned family and friends. A room had been set aside at the Clive Hotel for our meeting and I was so tired that I just wanted to go to sleep and in fact dozed off as I was having a cup of coffee. No producer had turned up yet and it was after five o'clock.

I said to Paul that I had to go and say Mass although I didn't know where I was going to say it, but I thought that there must be a Catholic Church in the vicinity. So off I went. Paul said that he wouldn't come along. Little did I realise that he had to be the main contact with the studio.

As I walked out of the hotel, I saw a priest on the other side of the road, so I went over to him and asked his permission to say Mass in his church, which was just around the corner. This I did and finished Mass at 6.15 p.m. The parish priest invited me in to the presbytery for a cup of tea, which I enjoyed, but was conscious of the fact that I had to be back for a producers meeting at seven o'clock. I left the priest's house and arrived at the hotel at ten minutes to seven. I am being very precise about the timing because, unknown to myself, I had to be on stage at seven o'clock. Tom had what seemed to me a triple gin waiting for me and as I tackled it, he leaned over and said "Finish that off as I have a chaser waiting for you." I said that I couldn't drink any more because I would be under the table, as I was so tired.

At six minutes to seven he said, "Come on now, let's go. We have to see the producers after this programme so come along with me." I did and went along with him. The Clive Hotel was only two minutes walk away from the studio.We went straight into the studio. A comic was warming up the audience and there were a couple of seats vacant. Tom told me to just go and sit in them, which I did with Tom. I was rather bemused at the whole paraphernalia of a television studio, but still I didn't know that I was to be the subject of the programme, the victim if you like, because it was quite a harrowing experience, apart from being an enjoyable one.

At seven o'clock precisely, Eamonn Andrews walked on to the stage and the programme began. Many of you may have seen the programme 'This Is Your Life'. As I have said, it took me completely by surprise. Within the next half hour I was surrounded by family and friends, some of whom I hadn't seen for years. First on stage was Rita, my Sister, followed by Arthur, my Brother. I had in fact a return rail ticket, thinking I was going to meet Rita on the midnight train to Liverpool. She had told me she was at a nursing conference on that day in London. Then came Jim McKinnon and Brian Conneller, both of whom had been my classmates at Mill Hill. They had their stories to tell, which created a few laughs and then Millie Quadros was called on to the stage. She gave the background to the establishment of the Hospice she was involved in and my work in Pakistan. The stage became more crowded with the coming on of Terry and Filomena and their whole family, Anne-Marie, Paul, John, Ruth, Catherine, Bernadette, Claire, Elizabeth and Patricia. Little did I know that Filomena had taken a plane from Lima just an hour after my plane had left. It was also a surprise to see Fr. Vincent Hughes on the programme. He had left Lima at half past six in the morning by an Air Panama flight, so no wonder he wasn't at the airport to say goodbye to me. To wind up the programme, Edna Pitman came on with her story of my visit to her in Karachi. It must have cost the programme makers a great deal of money to fly all these people to London and to get my friends from the Liverpool area to come down.

During the programme a film made in Pakistan was shown. It involved Rita, who is the daughter of Sadiq and Alice. Rita had a young brother, Francis O'Leary ! I mentioned this in the programme–how Francis was called after me and took my surname. It was all great fun and after the programme there was a meal awaiting us all.

It is strange how these events happen and watching the video is interesting now because you are viewing people as they were so many years ago. The programme had the highest rating for the number of people viewing that week–something like eight and a half million. One wonders what good it has been for us. I suppose it captures for us all, events which happened so long ago and it is nice to see everyone looking so much younger. People who were not Catholics learnt something about the Church in a roundabout way. As I have said previously, it was good fun and many people who belonged to our Association were brought together and a certain type of happiness was created, which to this day is maintained. It also showed that the Church takes under its wing all those thousands of people who are destitute and abandoned.

Mentioning 'This Is Your Life' makes me think of our first movie film showing the beginnings of our work in San Bernardo, Colombia. This was taken by Terry O'Leary in his own inimitable way. Writing about Terry prompts me with the thought that he is the envy of every Management Committee Member, since he is the only one whose face, over the years, hasn't changed. He has kept his youthfulness and ebullience and is the envy of us all. A teacher of Spanish, now retired, he is wonderful in the way he has given lessons to every girl who has gone abroad for us and drilled the language into each one. We are very grateful to him and so are the girls, of course. Some of them have developed their language quite well and can speak Spanish without any trouble.

Quite often, on my visits to Central and South America, one of the girls translates my talks into Spanish with ease and I think of them sitting behind a desk in Thornton earlier, and I marvel at their progress.

Likewise, we are all thankful that we have had Filomena, Terry's wife, as our Honorary Secretary. She is a past master at writing Committee notes and minutes. She too is fluent in Spanish and there have been so many occasions when I have had papers for translation, and difficult letters to unravel, which she has always done very competently.

With Some of Our Patients at Home

6

OUR Hospice in Thornton was opened on the Feast of St. Joseph March 19th, 1974. Our first patients, Eileen Gibson and Bob Kinder, were admitted that day and stayed with us for many years. Then there was Dan Howard and Eileen McGonagle, the first patient who died with us.

Other patients Lydia Howell, Stan Kennedy and Bob Shaw spring readily to mind. Lydia's strong point was singing "Hail Queen of Heaven" after Mass and ringing the bells at the Consecration. As Lydia got older and more frail, it was not unusual for her to start singing "Hail Queen of Heaven" at the Our Father and her request to me was to see that it was sung at her funeral. It was a terrible morning and the rain was pouring down on the few of us who gathered together for her funeral and we bravely sang the first verse.

Stan Kennedy, a former fireman, was excellent at telling jokes–the cornier the better ! I remember one he told me about the man who had two wooden legs, who enjoyed a pipe every morning after breakfast whilst reading the morning paper. The only trouble was that he wouldn't throw anything away and after a few months, the room in which he lived was stacked with paper. One morning, when he was lighting his pipe, he didn't blow the flame out but carelessly threw it aside and within minutes, the whole house was ablaze. He managed to ring the Fire Brigade. The firemen came out, put the blaze out, but he was burnt to the ground !! He really did enjoy corny jokes !

Patient Bob Shaw did his typewriting at two o'clock in the morning, to the great surprise of everyone. He was, in fact, fundraising for us and every now and again would present us with a large cheque.

In particular, I recall Eileen Gibson, sitting in the corner, bravely enduring her illness without one word of complaint. She was a real saint. These patients

63

created the spirit of Jospice, the spirit we are always trying to emulate but never succeed. They provided that spirituality which is at the root of whatever success we have made for our Association and, of course, their work still goes on as they pray for us. Whenever I want a special intention to be answered, with my invocation to Our Lady and St. Joseph, I always call in the troops and ask them to work on it. They always seem to oblige ! They are still with us, praying for us in heaven. It is absolutely amazing how we keep going, but with these prayers we have been able to manage.

It was with the same type of joy that we admitted a patient called Norman who used to live in San Diego in California. He was terminally ill and wanted to come back to Liverpool to die. Norman had a brother who was dying in Walton Hospital at the same time. It was a great happiness for us to be able to grant his dying wish and to give him a bed. The same type of happiness we experienced when little Yusuf, whom I will refer to later, could walk again and was able to go back to Pakistan accompanied by Jean Dodd and Anne Kirkpatrick.

Bereavement can have its lighter side and very often the sayings and the doings of a loved one who has just died can have a saving effect on those they leave behind. There was Denis Ryan for example–tough guy by any standards, who was dying of a nasty illness. He asked our Nursing Superintendent, as he tossed and turned in the bed, if he were going to die soon. After all, what was the use of just lying there he grumbled, when nothing could be done for him !!

"Look, Denis, my dear", said our Nursing Superintendent, Filomena, "You've been lying there for three whole months without doing a tap. You've only had to press a button and await a bevy of beautiful nurses to attend on you. It's now your turn to do something for us ! We've been praying to Our Lord, Our Lady and St. Joseph to look after you, but at the moment, Denis, think of us. We need several thousand pounds in the bank, a new washing machine, and all the items I've got listed here are sorely needed. When you see Our Lord, Our Lady and St. Joseph, the first thing you must do is to say– and this is before the particular judgement – 'Before you say anything, Lord,– St. Joseph's Hospice needs the following . . .' " Immediately Denis replied with thumbs up, "Right, Filomena, you're on !!" Denis died 20 minutes after this conversation and before the 24 hours were up we had everything provided–washing machine and all !!

Denis realised the meaningfulness of this part of his life, battered though it was. He had discovered a reason for dying ! It was necessary for him to help us who had been caring for him. This was a type of spiritual blackmail, but it worked with Denis and with so many hundreds of patients who have followed him. How could one grieve for Denis when he was so obviously working for us in heaven !!

It only goes to show the intercessory power of a patient. How can we estimate the power of all our patients when you add up those that have gone through our care in Pakistan, Peru, Colombia, Ecuador, Honduras, Guatemala, Mexico and here in England. When somebody says to you "Count your blessings," we can quite literally count thousands of them. Just add up all the saints who have been cared for by St. Joseph's Hospice Association. Everyone of us would become a saint, if we were to take the example of the patients with whom we have come into contact. Why should we worry, when we have such a power of prayer going before God all day and every day ?

I recall when Mrs. Jenny Ryan contacted me about her husband, Bill. He was in great distress and the local nursing staff had done their best to make him comfortable. Eventually he came to our Hospice in Thornton and enjoyed being in St. Elizabeth's room. Jenny was a nurse herself and so she was able to lend some support but his condition had worsened and she needed more help. Bill was a very staunch Catholic and it was a great privilege to give him the consolation of our Holy Church. Jenny was grateful for this and that marriage bond which existed between them seemed to be enriched by our ministrations.

One night I was quite astonished when I had taken Holy Communion to Bill. He woke up (it was about midnight or the early hours of the morning) and told me about the dream he was having. "It was more than a dream because it was so realistic," he said.

He related to me that he had been in the Holy Land with a friend and he was walking along the road feeling the heat and experiencing the dust and the grime, when who should accompany him but Christ Himself. They kept on walking for some time and then he said that Christ leaned over and said to him, "Would you like to receive Holy Communion, Bill?" At this point he woke up and there I was with the Blessed Sacrament. He couldn't get over the coincidence, if you like, of the two events.

The walk he described in the minutest details, and it was so very real to him that the perspiration was rolling down his neck. He received Holy Communion very devoutly and soon after this event Bill died.

Bill's wife Jenny and the family have kept in contact this long while and I've been promising to have lunch with her for many a long day but haven't got round to it yet.

I readily recall a patient, Patricia Butler. She was a very prim and proper person and made sure that everything about her was neat and tidy. She had suffered for some years with a terrible pain from a distressing condition. When people enquired about her religion, she would reply, "I am a D.I.Y. R.C."

She was very fond of reading and had read a lot of Catholic literature. For many years she and her husband had lived in East Africa which they had enjoyed and were the last two, you might say, of the old British Colonial group. Her husband Jack tried to do everything to relieve the pain from which she was suffering but without much success. She had heard about us through her contacts at St. Joseph's Hospice in Mare Street, London, and they recommended that she should contact us.

We brought her to our Hospice in San Jose where she stayed for a short time and thank God we were able to treat her illness with some success. She then prepared to go home and Jack arranged for nurses to call in to see her in Southport. She was a great lady and a very brave person. I recall going to visit her in Southport and was with her shortly before she died. I anointed her, for which she was very grateful, and our consultant Dr. Marie Cleary and Filomena accompanied me. We did our best and prayed very hard for her. Jack, her husband, was so brave and we were very pleased that her final days were peaceful and free from pain.

Work with Fr. Frank Smith . . . .

7

HOW difficult it is to get the right type of person to serve on a Committee. It is hard to find that sort of person but still we have to persevere until the right one comes along. We have 14 people on the Management Committee at the present time and we have always had a similar number from the year we began. Committees are made in Heaven. The Members of my Committee will laugh when they read this, but there is no doubt about it. God sends the right people along at the appropriate time. In other words, vocation ! God calls the person to do a particular job for our Association. I don't think he chooses us as Committee Members for our brain power. Some of us speak Spanish and that is a great help. Others may be more proficient in organising but whatever we can do, all our efforts must gel together, otherwise nothing would be achieved.

It becomes apparent, as new projects present themselves, the way in which we think collectively. Out of 14 people, there can be objections to this or that. Sometimes the Committee Meetings work out in an unpredictable way and we don't seem to have accomplished anything. What we have to do is to look back and find out what has happened and then we are amazed. When we examine particular projects, we feel we have contributed very little but usually, in some wonderful way, Our Lady and St. Joseph make their Will known. We have to pray to them, always, because they are the final arbiters of what takes place.

As we make our way through the story of St. Joseph's Hospice Association, there are a few highlights that have to be mentioned. 1973 was a busy year for us. We opened four Hospices in Peru, at Callao and Villa el Salvador, near Lima, at Tambo in the High Sierra, and at San Francisco in the tropical rain forests of the department of Ayacucho. I don't know where we found the time to carry out all theses activities, because in the same year we were busy preparing and refurbishing Thornton Wood, as it was then called, the house in Thornton, near Liverpool, which was to become the Headquarters of St. Joseph's Hospice Association.

At this time Fr. Frank Smith was looking after the Hospice in San Francisco. Frank had done his nursing degree at Sheffield University. It was very unusual at that time to find a priest who was also a nurse and I recall how Frank came into my office, bemoaning the fact that Mill Hill had not given him permission to do nursing. I took Frank to the Shaftesbury Hotel and gave him a meal and three gins and brought him back to my office. I had on my desk the private number of the then Superior General, Fr. Noel Hanrahan, and I dialled it while Frank was carrying on about getting permission or not. I handed the telephone to Frank and he found himself talking to Noel Hanrahan and I remember hearing him say, "That will be great, Noel, that will be really great." Frank got his permission to study and he graduated from Sheffield University in 1973 and we, of course, willingly agreed to his secondment to us as it were. Frank is a great battler and he gets things done where many another person would fail. He did wonderful things in San Francisco, and managed the small Hospice there very well.

On one of my visits to Fr. Frank Smith in San Francisco, I met up with one of his fellow missionaries who was a Benedictine in that area. I had taken the plane from Heathrow to Lima and as was my custom I picked up a copy of that week's Punch magazine. When I arrived in Lima I was fortunate enough to be able to catch a flight the same morning to Ayacucho. I counted myself lucky to catch this flight because there is only one per day.

I arrived in Ayacucho after an hour's flight and managed to get some transport from the local hospital to take me over the Andes right down into the rain forests where San Francisco is situated. This is a very long journey but the view of the Andes and the jungle covering the mountains is absolutely superb. It was very hot and I stopped at a wayside cafe (if that is the right terminology). A gentleman walked in, obviously European, sat down and ordered a cup of tea. In this particular area it would be very unusual to see a fellow European apart from our own workers in that area. After a few minutes we started to chat and he told me his name was Fr. Michael, a Benedictine from the Mission farther up from our clinics on the River Apurimac.

When it came time to make our goodbyes I noticed that he had no transport so I asked him which way was he going. He replied to my astonishment that he was walking to the next village, then farther on to three or four more villages in that area and as he said that, he pointed to a huge area of jungle. He had sent notices out to the people of the area to say that he was on his way. Fr.

Michael said that he just bedded down in a hut and carried very little with him in the way of change of clothes and things of that nature.

He told the story of one night sleeping under a table and that he felt restless and couldn't get to sleep. So he thought he would say some of his breviary. He put his hand out into his bag and got bitten by a viper. "Dear me," he thought, "that was careless" and put his hand in a second time to reach his breviary and got bitten a second time. As there was no electricity in the hut he could not see anything and thought the snake had crawled away somewhere. I thought to myself what a marvellous man he was doing this type of work–real missionary work. Before we departed, I asked him if he had any reading matter for that night. "No," he said, "it is difficult to read by a tilly-lamp. That's all that I've got." I said, "Father, take this" and gave him that day's Punch magazine. He was so grateful, you would think you were giving him a bar of gold and he thanked me profusely. That day's date was printed on the cover of the magazine and he couldn't believe he had it in his hand. I haven't seen Fr. Michael since then but I am sure that he will be doing great work now as he was in those days.

On one such visit to Fr. Frank Smith, Frank decided to do a baptism among the Campa Indians. The baby was on the other side of the River Apurimac. He said, "There is no bridge across that river and no ferry to take us over," and then said to me, "We will stop this fellow" who was punting a small plank along the rough waters. Frank begged a lift to the other side. The boatman agreed and told Frank and myself to take our positions on the plank. We had to take a sort of crouch on our haunches. When I got on to the plank, with my weight, the plank went under the water.

Frank and I eyed one another with a rather scary look. It was necessary to keep perfectly still and put our trust in God. Why, I thought to myself, have I put myself in this situation, when the slightest movement could have resulted in both of us being swept away in a whirlpool. I was very scared and so was Frank. We asked one another for absolution in case it was necessary and the chap punted away up river in order to connect with the current to take us to the other side. My feet were soaking wet of course and so were Frank's. Was I relieved when we 'docked' at the other side. We got off and went up the bank and could see the Benedictine Monastery that we were heading for. Frank said to me that the field would be swarming with snakes and that we would have to give them good warning by making a noise with our feet. I can see Frank now jumping in the air as we went through the grass. Fortunately we got to the Monastery safely. It was nice to sit down and have a cup of tea with the monks. They were so surprised to see us.

When we got to the village there were only women there. The men were out getting the tea. They were firing into the trees to kill a few parrots in order to have a tasty morsel for their families to eat. Whilst they were away I saw a big bowl being passed around and everyone seemed to be spitting into it. The only difficulty was that everyone had to drink out of this bowl but my stomach got the better of me and I only pretended to take a gulp–it was very revolting stuff but gave me an insight into how life was lived among the Indians. Having taken a tangerine from a nearby tree I carried on to do the Baptism.

Frank also ran the river clinics which he set up on the River Apurimac in Pichari and several other places. However, that area became too tricky to work in, for the drug trade was starting even then and San Francisco was regarded as a rendezvous for drug traffickers. Because of this we eventually pulled out of San Francisco in 1975. Frank then crossed into Ecuador to find a suitable site for a new Hospice. He chose a place called Suburbio, on the outskirts of Guayaquil. It opened that same year. Later the Hospice moved to a new site a few miles away, at Isla Trinitaria.

One of Fr. Frank Smith's nurses at this time was a girl called Maria Luisa Plaza Vergara. Her whole family have for many years been associated with Frank's project in Ecuador and have given him support. Maria Luisa and her sisters Obemia, Carmen, Trinidad and Dora, have given maximum help to Frank in his efforts in caring for the sick and the poor in Guayaquil. Their mother too, whom I have met, is their inspiration. They all form a wonderful team. In all his exploits he received great help from Anne Klapper and Rosemary Monaghan–both very devoted girls.

Frank is full of innovative ideas and in consultation with ourselves, he decided to build an extension to his clinic in Ecuador and dedicate it to the memory of a previous Superior General of the Mill Hill Fathers, Bishop Gerry Mahon. This he completed without any fuss and a lot of hard work. It is interesting to note that it is the only building commemorating the memory of Bishop Mahon. I think it very fitting to call the extension after him because Bishop Mahon was the person to whom I went to get permission to do Hospice work. I recall seeing him at Freshfield and requesting his advice and permission to establish our first Hospice in South America. With great enthusiasm (Bishop Mahon was full of that sort of thing) he gave permission immediately.

I recall seeing an advertisement after I had arrived back from one of my trips to South America, that the Empress of Canada was selling off many of its goods and chattels at low prices. I went along to the dock in Liverpool and I recall that woollen blankets were £1 each. Cups, saucers and plates, some of which we use to this day, were going for a song, as well as some lovely damask serviettes. They were goods which we would have to buy for

Thornton and I think that the total bill for this equipment came to £4000. What a job it was collecting the stuff ! But it was all put to good use.

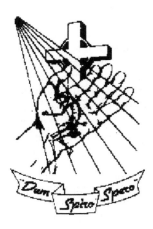

Further Steps Abroad
and Three White Horses

8

IN 1974, Dr. Marie Cleary joined our Committee and became our Medical Officer. How fortunate we were, how blessed we were really, by having such a person to take care of our patients. She was an outstanding doctor and I have never met any other like her, particularly with her bedside manner and her prayerfulness. Her spiritual input was something special and if you happened to ask for prayers for someone who was very sick, she would reply "Well, the Archdiocese is going to Lourdes next week and they will say some prayers for the patient"-an outstanding person, one of great faith.

Filomena and Terry, other Committee members, were already well acquainted with South America, through their own visits there. Management Committee members John and Mary Carson and Rosaleen Faulkner also visited our Hospices in South America. This journey was particularly tiring for them but it had its amusing moments. I remember John trying to wade through a hoard of frogs which had gathered outside the Hospice in San Bernardo and the horror Rosaleen expressed as she was finishing her fish soup in San Francisco and saw a big eye and the head of a fish staring at her. Mary seemed to take it all in her stride.

On our way back from San Francisco, we had to pass through the town of Ayacucho which boasts of being a town with the greatest number of churches in the world and I called Rosaleen, who was a very devout person. "Come and have a look at this church," I said and she replied, "Father, I couldn't care less !" which, coming from Rosaleen, made us all go into fits of laughter. Mary Carson often recalls that story with glee.

1974 also saw the arrival of our first Peruvian Nurses, the first of many to come over to England to see how we ran our Hospice. Their names were Natividad Espinoza and Hilda Palomino. It was in 1974 also that Willie Nieto was invited to join our Committee. He was the Peruvian Consul in Liverpool and introduced us to some acquaintances of his who were influential in various departments in Lima.

Very often some of us would pop round to Willie Nieto's house in Wallasey. We could be assured of a great welcome from Willie and his wife Bruna. Willie enjoyed classical music and he had in those days a very good record player. He would always offer us something to eat and drink. We felt very welcome in his home.

One particular night I recall visiting his house to discuss something or other about our Peruvian projects and we were quite a few hours in serious talk. It was about three o'clock in the morning when I departed with our two Peruvian nurses, Natividad and Hilda, Yves our French cook and Filomena. About five minutes after leaving Willie's house I saw someone lying on the roadside, so I stopped to find out what the trouble was. I found a poor motor cyclist who had come off his bike and lay injured.

I looked for a telephone kiosk and within a few minutes was on the telephone to the local police. I introduced myself by telling the policeman on duty who I was and where I was from. He replied, "You are up very late, Father, high time you were in bed, what can I do for you?" I told him about the poor man on the road and could he send along an ambulance and some assistance. "I'll do that, Father," he said and put the telephone down. We waited for about ten minutes until the arrival of an ambulance into which we placed the injured motor cyclist. We got back into the car and it was getting lighter by this time and I drove towards Liverpool. I turned down the appropriate by-pass and went on to the M53 heading for the dock entrance of the Mersey Tunnel.

To my surprise I saw three white horses galloping along the motorway in the opposite direction. I felt astonished and then enquired of the others had they seen three white horses passing by. Yes ! I was not dreaming as the others had seen them as well. So when I got to the next intersection I turned on to the other side of the motorway and followed the horses as quickly as possible.

I soon caught up with them and managed to steer them into a cul-de-sac and thought of telephoning the police again for assistance. I blocked the road as much as I could with my car and saw a light on in one of the houses nearby. I knocked on the door. It was about five o'clock in the morning by this time and a rather startled gentleman opened the door. He was in the middle of a shave and wondered what I wanted. I explained the circumstances and asked could I use the telephone.

I dialled 999 and to my astonishment heard the same voice which had replied to me the previous time I had phoned the police. "What is your name" said the policeman on duty, I said, "Fr. O'Leary", "By Jove !", he said, "you are having a busy night tonight, Father, what can I do for you?". I explained that I had three gleaming white horses in a cul-de-sac and gave him the name of the road. "My word, you are getting into a serious situation, Father, I'll send what help I can." Within 10 or 15 minutes our anxieties were lessened when we saw two or three policemen coming to our aid. They were carrying long ropes which they put round the necks of the horses. By this time the horses were very excited and were he-hawing all the time. The policemen took two of the horses and then for the third horse they handed me the rope and said, "Follow us, Father."

I felt such a mutt walking along the roads of Birkenhead pulling a horse. Dock workers on their way to work couldn't hide their surprise and as they passed said, "Good morning, Father" and then looked around again to see if they were seeing things. I found that I had run out of cigarettes and as I was passing a newsagents, I thought that I would call in. So I tied up the horse outside the shop and walked in and asked for a packet of cigarettes. The shopkeeper couldn't believe his eyes and asked, "Is that your horse, Father ?" I replied in a deadpan voice, "Yeah !" "Where are you taking it ?" he said. I replied, "The horses are lost and they haven't told me who the owner is yet but the police outside seem to have everything under control." (It's a pity you can't take photographs of the people who are genuinely astonished.) I collected my cigarettes and followed the other horses with their policemen. They had decided to place the horses in a school playground and told me to wait until the owner had arrived.

Apparently these horses had broken out of a field which was near the motorway and had gone for a trot themselves. It was about nine o'clock before the owner turned up and after quite a long night I made my way back home. Willie Nieto was very surprised when I rang him the following day and told him about my horsemanship. He roared with laughter at the situation comedy which had followed my visit to his house. Willie became a great friend of our Association and we were sad when he left Liverpool about a year later to take up a posting at the Peruvian Embassy in Belgrade, the capital of what was then Yugoslavia.

It was around this time too, that Fr. George Lynch, who was a curate at St. George's parish, Maghull, had got together a group of people. They adopted as their slogan, "Maghull cares" and apart from the many other smaller events which they initiated, they decided to buy an ambulance for Fr. Frank Smith's Hospice in San Francisco. The Sudbury Group (near Harrow) was in operation and the Dublin Group was in full swing. Both are doing wonderful work for us to this very day.

A young John and Mary Carson with their friends who formed the Maghull Group.

Their chaplain was Fr George Lynch

A Special Medal
and a Live Crib . . .

9

ON September 2nd, 1974 I had the great honour to receive on behalf of St. Joseph's Hospice Association, the Daniel Carrion Medal, which is a Peruvian award for Medical Services rendered to the people of Peru. It was presented by General Miro Quesada, who was, at that time, Commander-in-Chief of the Air Force. Willie Nieto, the Peruvian Consul in Liverpool, was delighted that his Government had thought fit to grace our presence in Peru in this way.

Wonderful reports were being received from Villa el Salvador: that 554 emergencies had been dealt with in one month and that there had been 627 consultations. We had also, it was reported at that time, an outreach of 600 families–marvellous going for a new Hospice. San Bernardo had been operating very well and their little group of nurses were very sad to say goodbye to our nurse, Dina Smith, who became the longest serving representative of the Association at that time. She had done six years in that very remote area of Colombia.

At Christmas time, I had thought it would be a good idea to have a live Crib. We had a wonderful setting in our grounds but of course a live Crib means a live Crib. David Mahon was closely associated with us at that time and Rita, his wife, was expecting their third child. Their baby was an obvious choice for the baby Jesus and his wife as Our Lady, with David in the role of St. Joseph. Peter Kaye came out from Liverpool and took some wonderful photographs. We had a real camel and when I was trying to hire it, I thought it would be a good idea to ring Chester Zoo. I asked them if they would put me in touch with the Camel Department. The telephone rang and to my surprise there was such a department. The fellow who answered the telephone wasn't too enthusiastic about hiring out a camel, especially on Christmas Eve. "Too late at night, Father," he said. "Camels can get quite stroppy and they are dangerous animals." I put the telephone down and rang Belle Vue Zoo in Manchester. They had better news for me and said that they would certainly send a camel to us on Christmas Eve. They delivered a huge camel-box and this gorgeous animal strolled out on to the middle of the lawn, looking down disdainfully on all those who were admiring him. The cows had to be returned to the farm because they began to sweat but the donkey from the adjoining farm came over on time to carry Our Lady. We had chosen some nicely-sung Christmas carols and played them over the loudspeaker. A very memorable night indeed and one which, thank God, we can repeat every year. Believe it, or believe it not, that same donkey, Jenny, is still playing her part in our Christmas Pageant, a quarter of a century later.

In 1976 I sent Anne-Marie O'Leary, the eldest of the O'Leary family, to reconnoitre Honduras for us just after her 21st birthday. It was a great adventure for her and the fact that she was able to speak Spanish fluently was extremely useful. She was also a girl I could trust and it was her wanderings which resulted in our choice of the town of Morazan as the first place for a Hospice in Honduras. She was driven there by a Brother Jaime O'Leary, who was a Jesuit. Anne-Marie was surprised when she introduced herself and he said, "My name is O'Leary too." A very good friend he became and helped us in many ways, along with Fr. Pat Wade S.J., Fr. Bob Sullivan S.J. and Fr. Francis Hogan S.J. This was our first effort in Central America. At this time, of course, there were very few lay people doing our type of work. The pioneering nature of this work appealed to us and became more exciting.

The later years of the 1970s, in one sense, were unremarkable, insofar as nothing spectacular happened. However, in another sense, that is not true, because the Committee and all our helpers were engaged in raising funds and keeping the Association going from day to day. At the end of each week, it was difficult to reconcile the income and expenditure, in order to give us that safe feeling; safe, in the sense that we had next week's salaries in the bank on the Friday evening. I often worried about the following week as to how we would keep in business so we had to pray harder and come to the realisation that everything depended on prayer.

Our Lady and St. Joseph, we knew, would stand by us in any difficulty as they have done so often. That we are here today is indicative of the fact that many of our friends and helpers stood by us so loyally. In my letters to our supporters and helpers, I always have mentioned the fact that ours was a hand-to-mouth existence. I suppose Our Lady and St. Joseph were proving to us that we were totally dependent on them for they took a very active part in keeping the Association together, but the work had to continue.

The nurses from abroad were coming back home for holidays, giving us excellent reports, whilst we were busy recruiting new members to take their places. Fortunately, we had some excellent nurses who stood by us through thick and thin and our Committee Meetings on a Sunday evening lasted for about four or five hours. These events we sometimes look upon as unimportant, and that the Committee Meetings are humdrum, dealing with the work of the past week or fortnight and making preparations for the future. We look back on events that have happened–the growth of our young Hospices and, of course, the numbers of patients who have been treated. We have constantly appealed for prayer and more prayer and, thank God, the happiness of our Hospices has been brought about, through each individual nurse's spirituality. It is hard to realise sometimes, but it is prayer that keeps us united, and that prayer has been put into practical effect with the people with whom we were associating.

I am thinking of Mr. Robin Downie, a great surgeon who operated on me for peritonitis in 1975. I had suffered with pain for quite some time and I had taken Fortral pain killers. The trouble was that I was travelling in the Andes at the time and I remember meeting a doctor in Ayacucho, to whom I mentioned my difficulty. He said, "You have obviously got an appendix problem. There is no problem–I'll operate on you this afternoon." I didn't feel like chancing myself to him so I carried on my journey to San Francisco. Whilst there, Fr. Frank Smith decided to do a visit to the out-stations along the banks of the River Apurimac. There was an awkward point to traverse and to the right of the boat there was a huge rock, to the left, a whirlpool. For the sake of ballast, Frank put me in the front of the boat, revved up the outboard motor and we rocketed, I don't know how many feet, into the air and crashed down on to the other side of these objects. Crash, bang–I got my pain back again !!

Consequently, soon after I returned home, I was carted off to Walton Hospital. Thank God, everything went well.

Archbishop Erasmo Hinojosa came to see us in the late '70s, and made a great impression on us all. Our Hospice in Negritos, Peru, is situated in his diocese and he came to give us a personal report on the activities of the priests, Fr. Hughes, Fr. O'Grady and the Sisters of St. Joseph of the Apparition. They were all doing wonderful work and it was a great pleasure to receive a visit from such a saintly man.

Charles Evans and John Lyons at this time were doing the first of their many marathons to Walsingham from Liverpool. I gave them a lift through the Mersey Tunnel to Birkenhead and dropped them off where you get the first sign for Tranmere. They did it well and I always think of them when I pass that sacred spot !

So the '70s ended on a high note and we thank God, Our Lady and St. Joseph for guiding our steps so surely and helping us to overcome our problems, of which there were many.

At the Hospice we opened our little Chapel, which used to be a greenhouse, and so the '80s began well. It was amazing how quickly the Chapel was erected. It took exactly five days and it is a little gem. Tony Claro and a friend of his did some foundation brickwork. Two carpenters came into my office and said that they were looking for a job. I said that I had one–to build a Chapel ! They worked from the Monday of Holy Week to Holy Saturday afternoon. I said that it had to be finished for the Vigil Mass on Holy Saturday night. They worked day and night and lo and behold, our Chapel was opened with the Easter Vigil Mass on Holy Saturday in 1981. That was not the only building to be erected, because at that time our hydrotherapy pool was opened and also our new Hospice in Ormskirk, Hettinga House, was being prepared. We had purchased this property in 1976 and it seemed to take an eternity, before operations began in 1981. Archbishop Worlock officially opened it for us on February 9th, 1982.

Hettinger House Ormskirk

Fr. McKenna and Marie Woods invited me to have lunch with them and during our talks, they offered me the services of "Tomorrow's People Today." The upshot of it was that they put into Hettinga House a marvellous team who got the refurbishment of the whole building completed within twelve months. We couldn't have opened Hettinga House if Fr. McKenna hadn't come forward to offer us the services of his organisation, because "Tomorrow's People Today" must have saved us thousands and thousands of pounds. At this period of 1980, we were in debt to the tune of £132,000, owing various banks and committed to our tasks here at home and overseas. However, Mr. Peter cheered us up by writing a very heartening letter from Rawalpindi. He occupied the chair of Secretary in the Hospice and said that everything was going well and the Sisters were doing excellent work.

Some of the staff at Hettinger House

The Clinic we had sent out to Bangladesh was stolen in Chittagong but there were various rays of sunshine which shone on us during what could have been termed a troubled time. John Fish was putting on some shows for us in Blackburn. We had a really good night at Fr. Hughes' celebration of 25 years in the priesthood in Thornton. In the diary we read "Thanks to Mary Carson, Rosaleen Faulkner, Maureen Schroeyens and the O'Leary family for their help." John Carson, our Chairman, read out a glowing report on the refurbishment taking place at Hettinga House and said that very heartening reports from overseas had been received.

Francis Xavier Newton had very inventively got together a film about our work and we had a private showing of this in Warrington. I myself gave a lecture in the Faraday Theatre at Lancaster University, which seemed to go down well and we had great celebrations for Mrs. Kinder's 90th birthday. Meanwhile, Nina Arpino and the Group in Sudbury were instilling into us great enthusiasm by the parties which they were putting on to raise funds for us. Nina was particularly keen to help us. The Allerton Group arranged a marvellous evening in the Church Hall of St. Anthony of Padua, in Mossley Hill and Ron Watt (R.I.P.) held a meeting in Birmingham for the flag day they were holding. It was one of the most successful flag days that we have ever had. Not to be outdone, Michael Everett's sister, Lynn, put on a pantomime for us over the Christmas period. Michael Everett was one of our longstay patients and was a great friend to us all. Berta Mejia Medina went back to Guatemala. Berta had been with us for nine months and became acquainted with our Hospice work here in Thornton. She was later able to project this type of work in Guatemala, for which we have to thank her.

Archbishop Worlock at the opening of Hettinger House on February 9ᵗʰ 1982

A Couple of Nuns . . .

10

NUNS   or Sisters have figured prominently in the work of St. Joseph's Hospice Association. Two of them, I would like to highlight here, because I doubt whether either of them realises the part she played in my life. The first is the Good Shepherd Nun, Sister of the Divine Shepherd. It was a tradition that the nuns in Finchley would adopt spiritually, one of the students of Mill Hill who was preparing for the priesthood, particularly in the final year before Ordination. Mine was Sister of the Divine Shepherd and we were given permission to go and visit the nuns shortly before ordination. I remember saying "Hello" to the young Sister and introducing myself as Francis O'Leary. We didn't exchange much conversation but I expressed my gratitude to her for her prayers.

The last year before Ordination can be a difficult one. Students can be afflicted by what they termed Deaconitis–often acting in strange ways and so I was extremely grateful for the prayers of this Sister. Well, I got through my last year all right, was ordained and sent to Glasgow University and then I received my appointment to Pakistan. I served my time there and came home in 1966. Since my ordination I had given a thought to Sister of the Divine Shepherd only now and again and it was 40 years later when I decided that I would make contact with her. Through the kindness of the Sisters at their Provincial House, I found that she had changed her name to Theresa and was working in Edinburgh. I telephoned her and said that this was a voice from the past–a distant past and I explained who I was. Her immediate reply to me was, "Father, I have prayed for you every single day since I was requested." I felt so thankful that God had brought her into my life, as you might say, this good nun who dutifully prayed for me daily. I said that I would try and visit her one day and I still intend to do that, so maybe later in my narrative, I will refer to my meeting with her.

The second nun I wish to mention is Sister Dominic of the Notre Dame Congregation. Sister Dominic was at the University with me and was in the same class. We both did, believe it or not, the subject, Scottish History and Literature–a brave subject to tackle for a Sassenach like myself, but I was in a bit of a fix. I could not understand the professor's accent so I decided to skip his lectures. However, the testing time came with the Degree exams getting near. I did not have any notes or books on Scottish Literature and began to panic and thought I would go to the convent where Sister was staying, which was just up the road from the priests' house, and request to see Sister Dominic. I asked Sister if she had any notes from the lectures and she provided me with a wad of paper, about two inches deep. This was on the Wednesday morning and the exam was on Friday. It was nine o'clock in the morning and I mention the time because time was of the essence. I went back to my room in the house in Prince Albert Road and got some paper the same size as the notes that Sister had given me. I spent all that day, taking down the operative words for each page and studied Sister's notes. This took all that day, from nine o'clock to half past five the following morning and then I said Mass and started studying again. After Mass I went through all day Thursday and didn't have a wink of sleep that night, until 5.30 the following morning and went to sleep until seven o'clock. I then went down and said Mass, followed by breakfast, after which I went to the University, sat a three-hour paper, from nine o'clock until noon, went to the Catholic Society, had a cup of coffee and a Blue Riband biscuit and studied again from half past twelve until five to two. Then at five to two, I went back to the University and sat another three-hour paper and came out exhausted at five o'clock. I passed and was eventually awarded my Degree at the University. I felt quite relieved that there was such a nun as Sister Dominic around to help me through my ordeal, and what an ordeal it was !

Sisters have played a prominent part in all our activities. Some have served us in Central and South America, like Sister Marie Julie S.N.D. and Sister Kathy Murphy, and our Hospice in Pakistan has, of course, been under the care of the Franciscan Missionaries of Mary. Sister Josephine Wall S.N.D., my cousin, has always given us great support and Sisters Annunciata, Bernadette, Catherine, Julia, Zita, Margaret, Shelagh and Maria Crehan have been so supportive and downright good. Their goodness is shown in their nursing care and the comfort and solace which they have rendered to our patients.

Our thanks are due also to so many priests who have supported our efforts like Fr. Jim Russell and Fr. Don Gorski from the States, Fr. Joe Cunningham, Fr. Godfrey Carney, Fr. Bert Shaw, Mgr. John Furneval, Fr. Roger McGorty, Fr. John Gough, and a host of others too numerous to mention.

Quite often people ask me, "How do you relax, Father, what really takes your mind away from the worries and cares of the day?" When one passes the 65 mark that answer is simple to give, because one's activities sport-wise are things of the past and are now confined to a game of snooker once a week. I used to enjoy my sport very much, particularly football and tennis. No relaxation in those pursuits nowadays, worse luck !!

So today I choose more leisurely pursuits like listening to a concert of nice music particularly by Rossini or I might opt for viewing the shenanigans of Sergeant Bilko. I am a fervent admirer of the Bilko stories and I have a collection of about 90 episodes of Bilko which I never tire of. He always makes me smile and helps me on my way.

I find relaxation in the company of folk who come to see me. For example, one evening when I was chatting to Dr. Marie Cleary, our consultant, a Mr. Brian Noon came to visit me. He was very worried about his wife who was suffering from a very serious complaint. I promised to go round to see her even though she felt unsure whether or not to take up my offer of a bed. As usual I felt very awkward when I went round to see her. In fact I telephoned Brian from the car.

When he asked me where I was I answered that I was directly outside his house. He ran down the stairs and opened the door to greet me and said his wife would be overjoyed for me to visit her. Eventually, I agreed with Brian and his wife to say Mass in their house next to her bedside. One of her visitors was so overjoyed that everything had happened so quickly and that arrangements had been made so immediately that when I was leaving she said, "Don't forget to bring a Bishop along with you."

In actual fact I had to go to Freshfield to see Bishop Bonaventure, a Bishop from Pakistan who had requested me to go along to chat with him. I explained to the Bishop that I could afford little time to be with him and explained the circumstances of Mrs. Noon's indisposition and that I was going to say Mass there. Immediately Bishop Bonaventure said that he would come with me and I was delighted and thought that the lady who had uttered those remarks would eat her words when I went into the house.

I arrived with all the requisites for Holy Mass and for good measure introduced the Bishop to everyone. They were all overjoyed and the Bishop's presence made Mrs. Noon seem very important. We said the Mass and then I took the Bishop back to Thornton because it was a Friday and I was due to celebrate Midnight Mass, as I do every Friday, for the sick of the world. After Mass, it was a beautiful evening so we sat chatting for a long time outside.

I gave the Bishop a drink and he seemed to enjoy being at our Hospice. I happened to mention that Sister Bernadette from Hungary (the same sister who had given me the holy picture of St. Joseph) had recently contacted me. I had her telephone number in her home town of Pecs and even though it was about 3.30 in the morning I phoned her to say that there was a long lost friend to greet her. Bishop Bonaventure had known Sister Bernadette from his visits to Rawalpindi and was so pleased to be able to greet her. It was nice putting them in touch with one another after so many years.

Some Meanderings
our Patients and our Dogs ...

11

ON July 8th 1981, I celebrated my Silver Jubilee to the priesthood, with Holy Mass on the lawn at Thornton and afterwards a nice meal at the Blundellsands Hotel. The de Brandt family from Belgium, whose daughters had worked at Thornton, came over from Brussels and provided us with some very beautiful motets, especially during the Mass. It was a great occasion. In the evening Fr. Bill Naylor, Fr. Louis Purcell and myself celebrated in grand style at the Mill Hill Fathers house in Freshfield hosted by Fr. Paddy Doyle.

I have a little note beside the next item 'Terry to go'. It was a function put on by Bell's Fishing Tackle at Seaforth Docks. This would have been unheard of ten years previously, but the Mersey had been cleared of debris and the fish had come back again. Joe Cotter, a seminarian from Mill Hill, arrived at this time and he joined Filomena and myself on a trip to Crosby shore. Filomena was playing one of my tapes at the time – 'A Medley by Charlie Kunz.' – whom, incidentally, my Sister had nursed at one time in Pinner. It happened to be three o'clock in the morning and he was playing a tune with that title. This was followed by an overture by Rossini. Joe, who seemed very knowledgeable on all subjects, I tested by saying, "I bet you don't know what that one is, Joe?" He was stuck for an answer, but was not going to be defeated and replied, "La Gazza di Seta." Now, Rossini wrote one opera called La Gazza Ladra and another called La Scala di Seta. Joe got the two mixed up ! Other musical items were included in my diary–Mozart's Twelfth Mass was performed at Holy Trinity Church, in Formby and there is a note on September 22nd, that I went to see to the Barber of Seville.

The topic of euthanasia was being discussed at this time and so we formed a small organisation, called 'Exist.' An article or two appeared in the Catholic Press. It was, of course, a play on the word, 'Exit' which the Euthanasia Society had adopted as its main title. A deacon, Douglas Denny, was anxious to become part of this organisation and he came on a visit to Thornton. It was he who then got the idea of starting a hospice in the Thames Valley area. He brought this idea to fruition some years ago and, in fact, Her Majesty the Queen accepted an invitation to open the hospice in the Thames Valley.

The Union of Catholic Mothers put on a function in St. Anne's, in Ormskirk and Dr. Don Heffernan had a very successful fundraising evening in Newport. He raised £200. Amy Deegan was carrying on with her charity stall in Kirkby Market.

Miss Cranney, who had been a great supporter of ours, had been raising money from the Harvest Festival which the ex-employees of Johnson's Dye Works held every year. She was well into her eighties but dutifully held a function each year on our behalf.

Frank Kearney put on a cheese and wine party in his house and Margery Corkhill took over the car raffle in Maghull. North of the border, Anne McManus had a ceilidh for us in Kirkintilloch and it is reported that we all enjoyed ourselves at the office Christmas party at the Blundellsands Hotel.

Entries appear for letters either received from or sent to Fr. Frank Smith, Fr. Jose, Fr. Paddy Doyle, Anne-Marie Rice and all the other nurses who were acting for us overseas. On February 9th 1982, 'Hettinga House opened its doors today' reads the diary. Ted Caddick, who had been a great helper, was one of our first patients and it was a great consolation that we could find him a bed at our new Hospice in Ormskirk.

On a lighter note, in March of this year, there is an entry about the 'Dog & Partridge' in Chipping. What wonderful memories that little hotel has for me. When I arrived back from Pakistan, Fr. Hughes suggested that Rita and myself and my Mum should go there for lunch one day. When I had been in Pakistan, my Mother and his Mother, looked forward to being taken out for lunch to the 'Dog & Partridge'. I have made one or two visits since then. It always seems to be associated with Fr. Hughes' Monday off. We used to go into the Church of St. William of York, not far from the 'Dog & Partridge,' a small church, going back centuries. It was nice to pop in there to say a prayer for all our work.

Mgr. Ireland, a retired Mill Hill Missionary, who had worked in the Falkland Islands, used to come in to see us and always expressed his admiration for our work.

Two wonderful patients we had in our Hospices here at this time: Alice Benson, in Thornton, and Fr. Kevin Kelly's mother, in Ormskirk. What an example these two people were to our nursing staff and visitors alike. Alice Benson, I remember, wanted to keep all her furniture with her. It was a job trying to fit wardrobes and a chest of drawers into her room. However, she insisted and so we emptied her house and she gave us all her prized possessions, which were very bulky. Fr. Kelly's mother, I always remember, when I enquired where she was going–it would be to the chapel–and as she was shuffling along she always answered, "I am going to see the Lord." A very comforting thought when one is bewildered or distracted by various happenings, to be given the realities of life by a very simple person. They are both in Heaven now, of course, praying for us and naturally are part and parcel of our achievements here at this present time.

During all the comings and goings, I had noted that Jim Culshaw had organised a rota of ladies to prepare and cook lunches at Hettinga House and that we had the joy of receiving the wedding guests, on our front lawn in Thornton, of Anne-Marie O'Leary and Ken Brzezecki. Our grounds, of course, provided the perfect setting for the wedding breakfast and everyone enjoyed themselves as the O'Learys always do when they gather in strength. We had visits from the Eliot family, who made it possible for us to have an extension to our building and to have lifts installed, both in Thornton and Hettinga House. I noted too, that Ruth O'Leary went on a reconnoitring trip for us to Brazil and whilst all this was going on, Eliza Lopez was holding one of her many functions with the Allerton Group and Ramon Remedios gave a concert at the St. George's Hall. It was noted, also, that Mrs. Sharples had organised a meeting to establish a hospice in the Preston area. I was requested to go along to speak to the Group. It was after such a meeting that the Lostock Hall hospice was organised and I had the great pleasure some years ago of going to view it. As usual Joe and Myra Lovelady were always there to be called upon with their marvellous group in Litherland as was Marie Porter and her friends in St. Helens who used to busy themselves with our newsletter.

There is a reference about an appointment for Sebastian with his veterinary surgeon. His photograph is in my office being a constant reminder of his fidelity and lovableness. He was an Old English Mastiff and always looked worried. He had a lot of extra flesh on his bones and he would often have that hang-dog look about him. He became great friends with my Sister Rita, and Marie Wills, who daily visited Hettinga House. He used to get upset when I went to visit the Hospices abroad and always made some sort of protest, like stealing my alb and putting it into a corner of the chapel and lying on it. Priests who came in to supply for me were often horrified at the sight of Sebastian. He weighed about twelve stone and stood very high, putting the fear of God into many people. He was, however, gentle and quite a coward. He had a way with him did Sebastian and there wasn't much happening that he didn't know about. Policemen, particularly, held him in great awe and they were noted for standing motionless when Sebastian was around. When the police were called out by the night staff, they always enquired whether Sebastian was outside the building, or safely inside, because I am sure they would have rather met an intruder than face Sebastian.

The life of a dog in Rawalpindi is hard and arduous. Pakistanis don't make friends easily with dogs and if they do possess one, it is hard for the dog to keep up with the lifestyle of its owner. Kim didn't know his good fortune when he was adopted by me and took up residence in the courtyard of the priests house in 'Pindi. He was an alsatian, very likeable and full of good fun.

Every evening he would go up to the room of one of the teachers, John Pinto (whom I have mentioned earlier) and John would give Kim a piece of bread and some water. One night when John was playing with him and teasing him, Kim accidently nipped the thumb of John and he came down to my room in a terrible state. "Your dog has just bitten me," he reported and there was a terrible look of fear in John's face. I asked him what he was worried about. He said, "Rabies, Father." The time was 11.30 at night. John was extremely worried in case he had picked up this dreaded disease. I asked John where the dog had bitten him and he pointed to his thumb. As there was only a slight mark on the underside of his thumb, I tried to assure him that I was sure it would be all right, but that he should report to the Holy Family Hospital. I said to John, "The only reason great precautions are taken is because it is such a horrible death" and then told him that there were one or two tests which would determine the onset of the illness.

"Let's test Kim with a bowl of water," I said. If the dog were suffering from hydrophobia, he would go away from the water, adding that this was a sure way of determining whether or not the dog had rabies.

I knew Kim always veered away from water, so I poured some out into a bowl and called Kim in. Obediently Kim came along, looked at the water and moved his face away from it. I said, "Oh dear, John, that's not a good sign, but you will be all right, I will keep Kim locked up in his kennel for the night and I will see how he is in the morning."

Every morning, as was his habit, Kim went up to John's room for his daily piece of toast. So dutifully the next morning Kim went to John's room but he had developed that night a terrible type of dog flu and I could see that Kim didn't feel well. John saw Kim swaying from side to side. He was convinced that the dog had rabies. He rushed down to me and said, "Father, Father, the dog is very sick." I looked at Kim and knew that he had caught a bug and was in fact not so ill, but I said to John that he had better hurry and get to the hospital. Poor John didn't know what to say to the nuns when he got there except to tell them that he had been bitten by a dog which was suspected of having rabies.

John had to re-arrange his teaching programme and got a taxi and went to the hospital. When he returned he reported how he had got on with the Sisters. There was no evidence of any bite on his thumb and there he was checking in for rabies !! He got a telling off from the Sisters when he told them it was my dog that had caused his fear. It was John who came home with his tail between his legs.

Another dog in my life was Snuff. I got Snuff when he was only a few weeks old. He was a yellow Labrador and went to live in the O'Leary household. He kept everyone awake on his first night by crying all the time, even though we had put an old sock under his jaw. Snuff was a great character. He became a frequent visitor to my office and would always welcome a person with a scarf or a pair of shoes or slippers or whatever he could get his mouth on.

He became friends with my Brother, Sister and myself and would always accompany us wherever we went. Snuff was a demolition expert par excellence and was liable to tear to pieces anything that he could get his teeth on. I recall one evening at a party at the O'Learys when I found the remains of what had been a delightful green hat. I gathered up the evidence and put the pieces in the bin. When the party was over a lady announced to all, "Has anyone seen my green hat ?" Snuff and I kept quiet. Well I didn't really. I said, "I'm sure I saw someone going off in a green hat just now," and there the matter ended. Only Snuff and I knew what had happened.

When we opened the Hospice in Thornton my Brother Arthur was accustomed to bring Snuff for a run every evening. He used to visit the patients and was a great favourite with them. I often recall the time when I was saying the eleven o'clock Mass in SS. Peter and Paul's Church in Crosby. I was at the lectern giving a sermon and to my horror I could see Snuff making his way up the central aisle to the sanctuary, having heard my voice.

I had to stop sermonising, of course, and Snuff didn't want to be caught. He ran all over the sanctuary evading my clutches. Eventually I caught him and took him outside through the sacristy. I was very embarrassed by this incident and went back on to the sanctuary to conclude my remarks to the congregation. Little did I realise that Snuff had found his way to the entrance of the church again and to my consternation was making another attempt to reach me on the sanctuary.

Fortunately someone collared him before he could make this second attempt and I breathed a sigh of relief. He was a good pal and gave happiness to many of our friends and acquaintances. He now lies alongside our other canine friends under the inscription "Semper Fidelis."

There are constant references about Frank Fox and his wife, Betty, who were wonderful supporters for us in the Wolverhampton area. A reference is also made regarding Ron and Mary Watt and the flag days in Birmingham and yet another entry about Rossini's Petite Messe Solennelle. We all seemed to be so busy.

August 1983 was a busy month for us. Joe and Rosemary Purcell were celebrating their Silver Wedding at St. George's Social Club and John Richardson was doing his Weekly Draw. Terry O'Leary, it was noted, had left for a visit to Honduras. We had hoped to have done something in Brazil, but the people we spoke to had little idea about terminal illness, or caring for the chronic sick. It is only now that their people are beginning to realise that there is a big problem. Nevertheless, our enthusiasm was kept alive by people like Rita Walker, who ran a shop for us in the town of St. Helens. She was a wonderful lady who worked for us effortlessly. She is enjoying a well-earned reward in Heaven this long while–a great lady and we were much indebted to her. We were grateful to Wyn and Dennis and their family and friends in Blackpool for their wonderful support, especially the fudge !!

I was trying, at this time, to find the whereabouts of a girl called Angela Maxwell. The only information I had about Angela was that she had attended a school in Rochdale. She designed our logo. It was in reply to a notice I had circularised to schools for an idea for our logo. Angela's entry was by far the best and she won first prize (I think it was £8). I photocopied the drawing and I have used it many times in my advertisements in the Catholic Press. I was anxious to meet her. As I said, the only information I had was that she had attended a school in Rochdale. However, one Saturday afternoon, I decided to travel to Rochdale, to make some enquiries. The headmaster of one of the schools had certainly remembered her and had already given me what he thought was her address. But time had elapsed from the drawing of the logo and her family had moved house. When I eventually found the house, her father answered the door and thought I was the new curate. He welcomed me in and told me that Angela was out with her mother shopping, but I was lucky in that she was home for the week-end and that I would be able to see her. She returned with her mother and I had her guessing who I was.When I mentioned the drawing, she recalled having won the first prize. Since then, her family has been very friendly towards us. Mrs. Maxwell sadly died a few years ago. She was an exceptionally nice person and more than kindly disposed to our work. We still use Angela's drawing today and the logo appears prominently on the antimensia of our altars. It depicts the Cross of Christ on a helping hand, with rays of grace coming down from Heaven upon us. It is printed on the title page of these Memoirs and at the start of every chapter. It is also at the foot of this page.

Again, there is another reference to La Cenerentola by Rossini, in Leeds. This fits in well with my story about Angela Maxwell, because it was during the meal, after the opera, that I made the decision to incorporate the motto, 'Dum Spiro Spero' (While I Breathe I Hope) under Angela's drawing. I was accompanied by Terry on this occasion and we had retired to a Greek restaurant after the opera. When the waiter requested my order from the menu, I told him the item and then requested that I have my meal 'Hos Taxistos' which was the only bit of Greek I could remember ("as quickly as possible"). I don't know where the waiter had been educated but he replied, "Dum Spiro Spero," and I knew we had to have that as our motto. So those words are emblazoned under our logo and give us much inspiration and encouragement.

Some Interesting Folk . . .

12

IN the early '80s, Joan Lawson and Margaret Woods had gone to Pakistan to see at first hand the work the Sisters were doing in our Hospice there. They returned with a young lad called Yusuf. He had been a patient at our Hospice in Rawalpindi and the Sisters there thought that treatment in England might have some beneficial effect on him. As a youngster he had suffered from polio and he had become quite deformed. It was a great opportunity for us, of course, to be able to help someone like that in a practical way. Eventually we were able to get a bed for him at the Children's Hospital in Alder Hey, Liverpool. The doctors performed various operations on Yusuf and after two years, he was able to say goodbye to us and was able to walk. He lives in a village area, very near Gujaranwala in Pakistan and is still in contact with us. His English became quite fluent whilst he was with us and looking back on this experience, there is no doubt at all that we were the beneficiaries of the grace given to us through Yusuf.

It happened, that at that time, a young Pakistani girl, Marie Francis, had come over to England and was staying with us. We were able to put her in for her nursing certificate and she was able to care for Yusuf after he had had his operations and was recuperating with us.

All sorts of nice things were taking place at this time. We were able to greet Elizabeth Girot, who had worked so well for us in Colombia in San Bernardo del Viento. She had spent six years there.

We received our first appeal from Fr. Mekkunel for his work in India's state of Orissa. We had already started our help to India, by sending donations every month to Fr. Kattakayam in Karnataka, and Fr. Thumpayil in Kerala and that had been going on for many years. We did this specifically for the medical work, in which these Fathers were engaged. The same sort of help we gave to Fr. Jeyaraj in Madurai in the Southern Indian state of Tamil Nadu. All these priests are doing wonderful work for the sick in their parishes.

Then, our extensions at Thornton were being completed and there was a big function at the Apostolic Nuncio's house in Islamabad in Pakistan and we sent our greetings to the Committee over there.

Yusuf was becoming interested in the Cubs' organisation of his school. We went along at Christmas to see him in a play, dressed as a Roman soldier sitting in his wheelchair.

My Sister, Rita, retired from the Royal Liverpool Hospital in August 1984 and went to live in Hettinga House, our other Hospice, in Ormskirk. Tim and Roz Connery had volunteered together to go to Colombia and there is a note to check on the banks to see what the balance was. Actually, this was a daily occurrence but now and again, when things got too hot, a proper check had to be made.

Maria Luisa Vergara had come from Ecuador to stay with us, not only to improve her English, but to update her medical knowledge. In the past number of years, she and her family have given invaluable help to Fr. Frank Smith's work in Ecuador.

Then, Mary and Janet Ashcroft were preparing to leave for Honduras. Mary and Janet had both acted as nurses here and had been looking forward to the change of work in Central America. Both were good nurses and were a great assistance to us.

During this time, I made a trip with Filomena, to our Hospices in Central and South America and could not help but be impressed with the work which was being carried out.

1985 seemed to be a year of routine activities. We, of course, celebrated St. Patrick's night and the Feast of St. Joseph with the usual Annual Report on March 19th and the St. Joseph's Day dinner. There is a special mention in that year about preparing the tape for Holy Week and a note was included that Mary Carson must be the first to receive an Easter Egg. She likes those small ones with cream inside and every year Mary comes along to break our Lenten fast.

To make a tape for Holy Week takes a long time. I always include for Maunday Thursday, a part of Haydn's Seven Last Words of Christ on the Cross and on Good Friday I play the Taizé tape of Jesus Remember Me. Holy Saturday night is a bit more complicated, because I take the various parts of the Mass, Gloria, Sanctus and Agnus Dei, from recordings.

Filomena visiting our Hospice in Villa el Salvador, Lima

I recall Mumtaz visiting us in 1985 on one of his frequent visits to his son, Saleem, who lives in London. I have mentioned his wife, Mary, earlier on in these Memoirs. All of their lads went to our school in 'Pindi and were taught by the Mill Hill Fathers–another link with our 'Pindi Hospice.

Jack Blanchard did a lot for us at this time, organising a type of lottery through the C.Y.M.S., or, as it is now called, the Catholic Men's Society. Hettinga House celebrated the Feast of St. Joseph The Worker on May 1st and, of course, Terry O'Leary was the one to be requested to show slides on that evening which we all enjoyed. Then, in May, we had the funeral of one of our patients, May King, who was a neighbour of Ron Wharton. It was at that time Ron and his wife, Kitty, took a great interest in what I was doing in the Hospice in Thornton and Ron, in particular, became a special visitor. He was a Eucharistic Minister and was able to help me out in so many ways, preparing the requisites for Mass and assisting me with Holy Communion as I went around the patients.

Bernie and Mary Lash from America had volunteered to go abroad together for us. They were two people who became stranded in Bolivia. A nun came to see me about them. She had worked with them in Africa and was worried about them. I managed to find out the telephone number where they were staying and rang them in San Jose in Bolivia and they both were delighted to

95

work for us. They came over to see us before that, in order to become acquainted with our work and then they departed, after a few weeks, to the project we were working on at that time with Archbishop Ruiseco, in Cartagena, Colombia.

Quite a few notable visitors came to see us in 1985. We had the great honour of receiving Sister Lucille, our Matron in Rawalpindi. Fr. Frank Smith returned from Ecuador to celebrate his Silver Jubilee and he invited us to join him in St. Anne's, Crumpshall, on July 10th.

My cousin, Philip Endean, was ordained as a Jesuit at Holy Name Church in Manchester and it was nice to know that another member of the family had made it ! I already have two cousins as Bishops: Bishop John Rawsthorne, on my Dad's side and Vin Nichols, the new Archbishop of Birmingham, on my Mum's side. They missed me out ! Philip Endean S.J. has gone on to do some marvellous research work on Fr. Karl Rahner !!

The following month Rita went to Loch Lomond for a well-earned rest with Fr. Hughes and his relatives.

There are various references in 1985 to the number of places we have visited in connection with the establishment of our Academy. There is a note about visiting Winstanley Hall, near Wigan and trying to get some land on the shore at Freshfield. These ideas came to naught.

We had a visit from Fr. Jose Ortiz S.J. who is working as a doctor in our Hospice in Honduras. He came during the summer time when our patients departed for Blackpool for a few days change. I am pleased that he visited Blackpool with us, because when Dawn Connor came to me and asked me for a dance, I told her I wasn't up to it and sent her to Fr. Jose. That was about 9 o'clock in the evening and at 12 o'clock, he was still on the dance floor. He enjoyed it immensely.

Many notes were made for the planning of our Gala Concert to be held in 1987, like booking the Hall and preparing the programme. Gala Concerts take a lot of time in preparation, because you have to get four good soloists. The difficulty is getting them all to appear on the same night–it is not easy.

One of the nicest things to appear in my diary at this time was a little note from Thelma Merino in her own writing "Please come to 9, Paddock Close at 7.30-ish." It was usually a pleasant evening at Thelma and Frank's house. They invariably provided some nice food and a good tipple.

Fr. Hughes had invited my Committee to go and have dinner with him and every year on January 1st, Fr. Hughes makes this offer, which all of us take up gladly. One of the particular notes I had at this time was to preside at the funeral of Hetty, a patient who died in Hettinga House. More about her later.

Elementary, my Dear Watson ...

13

IN 1986, there were the usual comings and goings. It was a great delight to receive Gerry Tims. He lived at that time in Australia with his daughters. He was our first Hon. Secretary in Pakistan. He was a great man and guided us in many ways in our first days. Above all, he had been so very excited about our small Hospice in Rawalpindi and when he came to see the splendour of Thornton, he found it difficult to realise that we had come this far.

Bishop Kevin O'Connor came for tea in Jan of this year. He had been appointed by Archbishop Worlock to look over the phenomenon of the Imprint (described later) and we had great pleasure in showing it to him.

Two of our nurses, Kathy Gardner and Denise Heslip, visited Honduras to see the work of the Hospice in Central America.

There is a little note in August – "Cathy O'Keeffe is going to start today." She worked for us for over four years in Honduras, having received her Spanish studies from Terry O'Leary. She worked wonders in Honduras and very ably took over from Anne-Marie Rice who had completed six years in Honduras successfully.

1987 was to be our Silver Jubilee Year and the diary makes many references to remote preparations about printing the Silver Jubilee brochure and planning for the Gala Concert, which was to be held in October of that year.

From the jottings in the diary, I was busy getting ready, too, for the Wexford Festival, to which I went with Rita, Terry and Filomena, to listen to Rossini's opera, Tancredi–which is rarely performed. It was beautifully done and one of the soloists, Kathleen Kuhlmann, I managed to book as our mezzo-soprano for our Gala Concert. It was a lovely Festival, but the weather was not too kind. However, the scenery and the food made up for this deficiency. It was very interesting also, to mix informally with the singers and members of the orchestra.

On August 9th, Yusuf, who had come through his operations very successfully, had a farewell meal at the Blundellsands Hotel. We invited a lot of people on that occasion. I think all of the Committee attended. My Brother and Sister also came along for this great farewell occasion.

We had a patient at this particular time called Joseph Guidera. He was quite elderly and was very sick, but he smoked a pipe. When I went round to do the assessment on Joseph, we got on fine for the first five minutes, but he then started to light his pipe, right next to two huge oxygen cylinders. As I rose to make my way out of the room, he was busy assuring me that there was no harm in a lighted flame near the oxygen cylinder. I was afraid that he would blow up the whole house and I tried to tell him, that whilst he could put the house at risk, I didn't want to be subjected to the same fate and blown up. Joseph eventually came in as a patient and was with us for some time. He enjoyed the flowers and the lawns, but, above all, the night air. Many a night he would sit outside in his wheelchair, with a blanket round him, just enjoying the air. It was he who suggested that we call our new building La Casa de Los Pequenos Milagros de San Jose (The House of Little Miracles of St. Joseph). That inscription is above the front door of the Academy and we are reminded of Joe every time we read that little saying.

At this time I noted that we got our first ambulance for the Hospice here in Thornton, donated by Eddie Kane and his friends. Meanwhile I was busy ordering tickets for Rita to listen to Nana Mouskouri, in Southport.

Filomena and myself had the great joy and privilege of taking one of our nurses, Paul Martin, down to Harbourne, near Birmingham, to start his studies to become a Jesuit at Manresa House and we were making arrangements to visit Dr. Zugibe, a famous forensic specialist in America, so that he could study our Imprint.

The early months of 1987 are littered with the names of Jessye Norman and Samuel Ramey, the famous soprano and bass. I had an idea to invite them to sing for us at our Gala Concert later in the year. I didn't have high hopes of obtaining their services, because you have to book about five years in advance for either of them.

The name of a town in Sicily, Porticello Flavia, appeared regularly, as a reminder to me of taking on the role of Sherlock Holmes–the lads in Pakistan used to quip "SheerLuck Holmes". I thought this was quite good. There is an interesting story connected with this town in Sicily. A friend of mine had gone on for years telling me that she had never met her father.

One day, when she had some important documents out–I think they were marriage lines–I looked over her shoulder and saw the name of her father– Giovanni America–and that he was from this town of Porticello Flavia. Every atlas I looked through, I couldn't find it. Then one evening I was watching television–a holiday programme, I think it was–and the town was mentioned– a suburb of Palermo, the capital of Sicily. I thought, well, they must have a parish in that area so I wrote to the Archbishop of Palermo, to see if he could supply me with the name of the parish priest of Porticello. He did this and gave me a telephone number for the parish priest, Fr. Giovanni La Mendola. All this was part of what you might call "the operation" and my detective work seemed to be succeeding. My next move was to book the services of Miranda Smith, who used to come to the Hospice and still does every Sunday afternoon to help with the lunches. She is Italian and the thought came to me to use her as my interpreter. I went to my office with Miranda after Mass one Sunday and rang the parish priest of Porticello. I mentioned to him that I was taking him into my trust and that the matter was completely confidential. Yes, he did have a family called 'America' in his parish. It was a long shot, but it turned out to be conclusive. I therefore asked him to make discreet enquiries from the family about the names, particularly of uncles and their whereabouts at the present time. Very quickly he wrote to me and said he had visited the family and had seen the lady of the house. She had given him the names of her mother and father and uncles and where they were living at the moment. She could account for all of them. They would be brothers of her father. Some had died but there was one on the list called Giovanni and she just had 'Portugal' next to his name. Her mother was called by the same Christian name as my friend and I deduced this must be the family I was looking for. Quite excitedly I went round to her house and told her that I thought I had found out where her father's family lived. Stage three, of course, was to find out where he was in Portugal and particularly, whether or not he was still alive. My friend reckoned that if he were still alive he must be in his eighties by this time. She had been born in Spain, but had been brought to England as a baby. That was all she knew and her father had seemed to disappear. One day, she looked at an atlas and saw the town of Oporto, in Portugal. She knew her father had been connected with the fishing industry and logically she looked for a seaport. When she rang directory enquiries and asked whether or not they had a telephone number for a Giovanni America, they said they did have a number listed and so she rang him. After having asked for Giovanni, he came to the telephone. She expressed her excitement and told him that he was her long-lost father. There was a silence and then they began chatting. Within a few days, my friend and her husband had packed their bags and were on their way to Portugal.

I felt very chuffed that Sherlock Holmes had solved another mystery. It was a very satisfying feeling. My friends met Giovanni over the weekend a few times and my friend was absolutely delighted that after sixty-odd years, she saw her father for the first time. Afterwards she said to me, "How did you do it, Father ?" Unhesitatingly I replied, "Elementary, my dear Watson."

Comings and Goings

14

WHILE we were preparing for the 1987 Gala Concert, which was to be held in October, it was quite difficult to establish who our soloists would be, and indeed, which Choir would sing. I rang Brendan O'Dowda, the famous Irish tenor, and he put me in touch with Bernadette Greavey, the renowned Irish contralto. I explained the type of music to Bernadette, but she informed me that that was not her style of music and advised me to get someone else, although she would have been pleased to appear for us. As I mentioned earlier I had obtained the services of Kathleen Kuhlmann and she put me in touch with Patrick Power, the tenor. I then still had to find a bass and look for the choir.

I was lucky enough to contact Proinnsias O'Duinn, the chorus master of Our Lady's Choral Society in Dublin. I had heard previously some recordings of Our Lady's Choral Society with Sir John Barbarolli conducting them. Proinnsias agreed to do the Concert. I then arranged the packing of the music and sent it to Dublin. Fortunately, John McKenzie, from Australia, was staying with us and he had planned a trip to Dublin. He took most of the music over for me.

At this period, Rosaleen Faulkner was planning a big concert in the Civic Hall in Crosby, and she was in a terrible state of nerves at the thought of selling 400 tickets. She sold them all right, but then I began to wonder how I was going to sell 2,000 tickets for our Gala Concert in the Philharmonic Hall. I felt weak at the knees.

I noted that there was a large group of ladies who go to our Hospice at Hettinga House every weekend to do lunches. Beryl Puddifer was to be in charge of the arrangements for organising the rota of ladies which Jim

Culshaw had set up. They come along dutifully every weekend with no fuss or bother, get on with their work, and provide some wonderful lunches, but nobody ever seemed to say thank you to them. To rectify this we organised a night especially for them at the Aughton Village Hall. It was a great night I recall, with all those very kind ladies coming together to celebrate their own goodness basically.

We were studying the plans now for the Academy, and we wanted to achieve our overall aim: to have a purpose-built building with an holistic approach to the care of the dying. It had to be Christocentric. That meant that all the rooms were facing the little Chapel. The building would comprise also a Conference Room, a place where seminars could be held. But it was difficult to plan and the first designs which were drawn up, we changed completely.

I was discussing the nature of holism with our Nursing Superintendent Filomena. She submitted a statement to me about her view of holism which I thought was very accurate and contained some good theology. Her statement went as follows:-

"Human beings, whatever their creed or persuasion, possess a spiritual persona, one's innermost self which needs nourishment for health.

Love allows a spiritual persona to grow and develop or become fulfilled. Lack of love results in gradual stunting and even complete death of the spirit.

The body of an unloved, uncaressed baby does not thrive, as does that of a baby who is nurtured and loved.

If this is true of a healthy person, it is even more true of an ill person.

Relationship is preferable to service. One must encompass the other. Christians believe that God, who created all things, is love. That love was most manifest in the person of Jesus Christ who, before he died, instituted the Eucharist, which Christians believe is the fullest presence of God on earth, the source of Spiritual life.

The Eucharist reserved in the Tabernacle is the centre of healing, and this is the basis for placing the Chapel where it is surrounded by people each suffering in his or her own way, a microcosm of the suffering of Jesus, who we believe rose again from the dead, conquering forever death as we perceive it. Death is a change into a new life, the final healing. This is a mystery, not because it cannot be explained but because no human mind can plumb the mystery we call God. So we begin with faith and grace, which are gifts from God, to accept that there is much more than we can understand to the mystery of life, before and after death.

We draw on this belief in the complete love of God made manifest in the life of Jesus and draw on that love first ourselves as healers, nurses, tenders of the sick and communicate in love with the spiritual persona of the sick person.

When this is perceived, recognised and accepted through the day to day ministrations of carers, a reciprocal dynamic takes place; the sick person thrusts himself / herself to the carer and the best is drawn out of the carer by the dependent patient. An evident change is there and certainly in compassion much spiritual nourishment and consequent acceptance and healing takes place, if not of the body, certainly of the inner spiritual persona.

Healing is a personal encounter and exchange of God's love through the aware individual. It can only happen with the individual's willingness to relax and accept the love given.

Our Father who art in heaven, etc. takes on a new meaning.

Come and try it for yourself, you have nothing to lose but your incredulity."

I have often mentioned how the spirituality of St. Joseph's Hospice Association is based on our patients and their holiness with this aspect of holism in mind. It is difficult to understand the concept of spirituality, because it is an all-embracing term, but to identify it is more difficult. Perhaps one or two stories about our patients will help to give some sort of an explanation.

I have mentioned before, our first two patients, Eileen Gibson and Bob Kinder, both undoubtedly saints and both highly regarded by their nearest and dearest. Alan, Eileen's husband, used to come not once a day, but sometimes, two or three times a day. She used to sit in the corner of the lounge, observing and getting all the news, of course, from the various people who came to visit her. But she was able to carry her sickness in a very dignified way.

Bob Kinder was such a popular man. He had been sick for many years and always had his Bible at his side and was very receptive to religious activities. He received Holy Communion every day with great devotion. I remember the day he died. One of the nurses on the night staff, saw a beam of light coming into the Hospice and she thought it was a policeman with a torchlight. Having checked that there was nobody at the door, she felt it was time to see to the patients and she found that Bob had died. I always like to think that it was an angel, coming to take Bob's soul. He was so near to God.

Another patient, Lilian Blackshaw, often got very annoyed that patient Lydia Howell used to keep two tarts for me every weekend and she got quite angry with me for accepting them. Once, as I passed her, she shouted to me, "Enjoy your tarts." It was the only sentence she had uttered all week and every one of us was highly amused. Some very nice things used to happen which affected us all, as when the de Brandt girls were working here. They used to make delicious pancakes and after night duty, which would be the early hours of the morning, they would make chips and we would go down to Crosby shore and eat them.

I remember Tom Connor coming to see us, to request a bed, because his sister could not look after him. However, the thought of leaving home was too much for him and every day he would get a taxi to his house to see his sister. I remember that it was the Feast of St. Joseph and he had come down to Mass. He excused himself, just before Mass, as he wasn't feeling too well and he died shortly afterwards. A wonderful man, who died with great dignity.

Then, of course, there was a marvellous patient among our ranks, called Ernie Lee. Ernie had been very sick and had been expected to die about 14 years previously but he always enjoyed a good joke. One day he asked me the question, "What is the hardest thing in the world to do?" I knew I had to answer "I don't know. What is the hardest thing in the world to do ?" He promptly replied, "Give a black man a black eye" (or words to that effect). That was O.K. but the following day, I was taking the Bishop of Bamenda from Cameroon, on a visit round all the patients and as soon as Ernie saw him, he kept saying "Father, what is the hardest thing in the world to do ?" I had to go up to him and ask him not to ask me that question but he was convulsed with laughter at the thought of it. He wasn't confused but quite often could give vent to outstanding statements. They were usually full of good humour. He went with our patients to the Shrine of Our Lady in Lourdes. Ernie had to be taken everywhere because he was completely incapable of walking. In his own way Ernie was quite a devout man. But on this occasion in Lourdes he had been humped about here and there and, of course, felt compelled to join in the usual amount of prayers which had to be said. Having been taken to this particular spot or that particular spot he was eventually hauled up quite a steep hill and on enquiring where they were taking him, when they reached the top of this hill, Ernie in his own inimitable way said "Not another bloody church" and that was that.

Stan Kennedy was an ex-submariner and a fireman. His illness did not allow him to make any movement, so whenever you went to see Stan he would be inclined to say, "Would you just move that there" or "Would you just fetch me that." He became one of our 'Four Just Men' as a result. He used to wait patiently for me in the early hours of the morning to have a drop of rum with him. That was his favourite tipple and he always liked a good joke.

Bob Kinder was on our list to travel with the Jumbulance to Rome and I remember waiting with him for the special vehicle to arrive. We were making a joke about writing to the Holy Father and what I would say to him. So I jotted down a short letter in which I put something like "It's about time you made me a Bishop" which Bob thought was very funny.

I folded the letter and put it into an envelope and gave it to him. Then I thought that it might get into the wrong hands, so I changed the letter to an ordinary one saying that this is Bob Kinder etc etc, not thinking that Bob would be in any position to give it to the Holy Father.

Then as the Holy Father was doing his rounds in the big square of St. Peter's Basilica he stopped at Bob Kinder and there is a photograph of Bob presenting my letter to the Holy Father ! I thought afterwards that it was a good job I had changed the content of my letter, otherwise we would have all been in for a bit of a shock. Bob enjoyed his trip to Rome and counted it a great blessing that he had met the Holy Father. We have a photograph to prove it !

I remember Cyril Foley. He was a great man who came from the Portsmouth area. The Social Services had sent him to us and he arrived in Filomena's office with all his worldly possessions in a plastic bag. He came to interview us to see if we would suit him. Thank God he came to us because he was responsible for giving us so many happy moments. We didn't know whether he had any relations or not. So when he was dying I went through his little diary in case I could contact someone who knew him. He had always kept a photograph of a lady in a red dress and of two children on his television set. I tried many numbers from his little notebook but to no effect. Finally I rang one number and a lady answered and said that she knew Cyril and remembered him well. I told her that Cyril was dying and she came up immediately. She was the lady in the red dress. It was great to announce her arrival by way of a big surprise to Cyril. She stayed that weekend and Cyril died the following weekend. She came up for his funeral and proved the great friendship she had for Cyril. He was eternally grateful for her loyalty.

One of the nicest things to have happened to a patient was when Dan Howard was dying and felt very disconsolate. Filomena was on duty and she had tried everything, not only medically, but pulled out every stop in an effort to take his mind off his illness. She asked her twins to come along to visit him and when I arrived at about nine o'clock in the evening, I could hear strange sounds in the ward. The O'Leary twins were dancing their hearts out. Claire and Bernadette took Dan's mind completely off his illness and made him very happy, which was, of course, the whole object of the exercise.

We were always very hard pressed for cash. To my surprise a lady came into my office and said that she would like to give me a donation, but that I would have to come and collect it myself from her house. This I readily volunteered to do. The amount was £2,000 in cash and she was afraid to carry it with her.

105

She explained to me that she had always wanted to give me a donation and thought that when her house was sold, she would be able to do so. Her house was sold on the Feast of St. Joseph, so this was a sign to her that St. Joseph's Hospice Association should benefit from her kindness. The date she handed the money to me was May 1st, the Feast of St. Joseph the Worker.

There were other little stories, like the time I took a large group of people to Goosnagh near Preston. On the way back, one of the cars suffered a breakdown and about twelve people got into our other car. Quite a good introduction to Bishop Richter Prada from Peru. We managed to get home, although with a slightly squashed prelate !

Then there was the time when I was going to Manchester Airport and got a leaking radiator on the M62. I was in a great rush for the plane and I managed to stop on the hard shoulder because the fan belt had snapped. I don't know whether or not you've tried to flag down a lift on the motorway, but it is both dangerous and somewhat hazardous (quite apart from being illegal). I was able to be in time for my flight but left a rather disgruntled Filomena on the motorway, with the task of getting the car fixed.

Ron Wharton has been reading at Mass for me for many years. He has been coming since Mary King died about ten years ago. She was a next door neighbour. One morning, I think it was the Feast of Our Lady's Assumption, Ron was giving the first reading from the Apocalypse, where the dragon is waiting to devour the baby that is to be born. When Ron read this quote from the Scripture, Annie Barnes, a patient, was listening intently and when she heard these words, she said out loud in the Chapel, "...eeou !" and astonished us all. Annie hadn't been doing a lot of talking but she enlivened us with her exclamation and more than a ripple of laughter rang through our little Chapel.

This shows how mixed up one can become. John our Chairman was anxious that everything should be clean and tidy and had mentioned this to Shelagh Keating. Shelagh, daughter of our Treasurer, Jack Keating, asked John what he wanted to be cleaned. John was talking to her about the state of the flags outside the Hospice which needed cleaning badly. John said to Shelagh, "These flags are in a terrible state and need washing." Someone then called John away to see about something and when John came back he found Shelagh Keating at the top of one of the flagpoles. She had shinned up the whole way. John was surprised and enquiring what she was doing at the top of the pole, was told, "I am getting these flags down to wash them." When Shelagh realised she was at the wrong flags she and John went into tucks of laughter. Shelagh's laughter got the better of her. She laughed so much that she was carted off with a suspected appendicitis and when she got to the hospital, she in fact had to have her appendix taken out. A timely lesson for us to make sure we know the meaning of the words we utter !

Two Muslim Patients

15

W E have tried to face important aspects of prayer in our lives. Many retreats and days of recollection take place here. But I find one of the most helpful for this life of prayer exists in our monthly All Night Vigil before the Blessed Sacrament. A goodly number of people attend this and we rely on their prayers very heavily. Liz Kendrick and her friends have been stalwarts in this way. It is not only by their attendance but also by their organisational abilities because it is not an easy task to meditate for such long periods of time. They organise and arrange the hymn singing and various prayers. Our reliance on this monthly venture becomes real. It is difficult to learn how to live in the presence of God but this act of Adoration brings us into close proximity to the Divinity. I suppose in one sense it should be easy for those nursing sick people to live in the presence of God, but one can become so distracted with administration and organisation that it is good just to be with a group and to share that union with Christ with others similarly motivated as ourselves.

I must admit that in my position I am very often asked for prayers for a sick person and I find no better way of praying for them than by asking Our Lord, Our Lady and St. Joseph to make that particular person a member of the Holy Family and often ask for permission myself to be welcomed as a member. We couldn't get a better group of people to look after us.

There is a great feeling of home when you think of the love that must be constantly exchanged between Our Lady and St. Joseph and their Child. I wouldn't know how to become a member of that Holy Family really but it's nice to think that they have adopted you, care for you and look after you or anybody else that needs protection.

Other people who have given us a spiritual experience were two Muslim patients Moka and Wasantha Kumar. Moka came from what is now Bangladesh. His father had died and being the eldest son, his mother looked to him for support. He had been sent to us at Thornton by an enclosed Franciscan nun, Mother Monica, whose congregation I had been friendly with, in Pakistan. Moka had visited their Monastery many times and had been befriended by the Sisters. He was a Muslim but had not found it difficult to associate with the Sisters. He came to us with a very bad ear condition, which was put right by a great surgeon in Walton Hospital. It was an unusual exercise in ecumenism, for the surgeon was a Jew, Moka was a Muslim and we, of course, were Catholics. Thank God, everything went well. I remember Filomena going to visit Moka in Walton Hospital and as she went into the room she said "Hello, Moka" and Moka replied "Filomena, I can hear." These words were music to our ears, so it had been well worth the effort of finding the money for a ticket and accommodating Moka in our Hospice here in Thornton. He was a great lad and made many friends.

Wasantha was from Sri Lanka and had been in an accident with a bullock cart which resulted in his breaking his leg. Many doctors in Sri Lanka and in India had attempted to mend the leg but it became increasingly difficult to get him better. He went to the Catholic priest in his village, who made contact with us and we agreed to find a doctor who would make him better. It was a Mr. Simonis who said he would try to fuse the broken bones in his leg by a new method. Wasantha came to us at the Hospice in Thornton immediately after the operation, and then to recuperate spent the rest of his time at Hettinga House in Ormskirk. He came on crutches but was able to walk on to the plane taking him home. Just recently he telephoned me and told me he was doing well. Thank God for these two people. Wasantha was also a Muslim and both of these patients were a means of showing how much better it is when people get on well together, but how sad it can become when departures are made. Mary Carson recalled about Natividad and Hilda packing their many boxes to go home to Peru and taking them down to the midnight train. They were both very upset making their goodbyes and both were crying. When we asked them how they felt and told them that we were looking forward to seeing them in the future, Nati interrupted by saying, "My eyes are raining, Father" and that expressed it all.

The Imprint . . .

16

IN February 1981, I received a telephone call from a noted Liverpool consultant surgeon, Mr. Robin Downie. He enquired whether or not I had a bed available for one of his patients called Les. I said that there was a vacant male bed and that I would go to Fazakerley Hospital to see him. I did so and something quite remarkable happened.

On February 27th, 1981, Les came to us. He was suffering from a carcinoma of the pancreas. His doctors had stated that there was no further treatment possible for his condition and his prognosis was very poor. They gave him only two weeks to live at the outside. In fact, his stay in the Hospice lasted only ten days.

He hailed from Bootle and was 44 years of age. By nature, a pleasant man, Les had lived a simple life, was caring in his attitude to friends and neighbours and being a single man, had a deep filial devotion to his mother Hilda. There was nothing particular which marked him out from the ordinary man in the street. He had tried his hand at many jobs and had, like so many others in a depressed Merseyside, experienced many months of unemployment. He was never one to complain even when he became afflicted with this particularly distressing form of carcinoma. However, as the illness progressed, Les began to suffer from depression, when it became increasingly obvious that the doctors had nothing to offer him by way of a cure–or in fact could not discover any way of alleviating the nausea and listlessness from which he suffered.

When I was requested by Mr. Downie to visit Les in Fazakerley Hospital, with a view to accepting him as a patient in our Hospice, I did so willingly, not only because I had great admiration for the wonderful work of Mr. Downie, who laboured tirelessly for so many patients, but also because of the apparent hopelessness of Les' condition. That same evening, I went to see Les, with not a little trepidation—a usual experience for me when visiting a person afflicted with a serious illness. I found, to my great delight, that Les greeted me with a wonderful smile. Our meeting was not too prolonged and I felt at ease with his smile and realised my fears were unfounded. Les was delighted to accept my invitation to come to our Hospice and most wonderful of all, I detected no sign of the depression I had been warned about. That is not to say Les was not still depressed about his condition, but the relief on his face at the prospect of coming to St. Joseph's Hospice in Thornton made our first meeting an uplifting experience. I came out of his hospital room a different person—uplifted spiritually and thankful to God that He had given us a beautiful present in the person of Les.

I did not realise at that time how eventful a visit it had been, for this was the beginning of many wonderful happenings which were later to unfold.

When Les arrived at the Hospice, our nurses and staff did their utmost to make him comfortable. He asked for a Bible to read and then settled down to enjoy a bowl of jelly. I visited him shortly after his tea and was surprised to discover how well he was settling in. He remarked how pleasing it was to see such lovely trees in our garden and said how much he was looking forward to the Spring. He conveyed this same happiness to nurses and visitors alike; so much so, that many members of the nursing staff and their friends were electrified, just sitting with him and saying a few prayers. Here was a man, very ill, and, in human terms, helpless, yet he was able to have a profound effect on all with whom he came into contact. When asked why he had come to St. Joseph's Hospice, Les said, "I've come here to meet God."

A few days after Les arrived a group of people visited the Hospice to pray with the patients. They entered Les' room and asked him if he would like them to pray with and for him. He said they could and lay on his pillows watching them. One of the group, from St. Patrick's parish in Southport, recalls what happened next.

"After a while Les suddenly sat bolt upright, and looking towards the bottom of the bed, said, 'Oh my Lord, you are here. You have come for me ! But I, Les, have never done anything for you !' Then, looking at his hands, which were large for his size, he continued, 'These hands have done nothing for you, and yet you have come to me.'

"We all left the room quietly, deeply moved by the spirituality of a person who himself had said that although brought up a Christian he had not taken an active part in his faith during the latter years."

On Sunday, March 8th, Holy Mass was celebrated in the Hospice lounge at 7.30 p.m. Les was present, sitting next to the table which served as an altar. I recall how pleasant it was to be able to say Holy Mass surrounded by our patients. When Mass had finished, I tried a bit of leg-pulling, by remarking how awful the singing was ! The patients countered my remarks by stating how much below par my sermon was ! "Bloody awful" some of them said. They were probably right. We always enjoyed–and still do–a little bit of banter after Mass and on this particular occasion, there was quite a lot of laughter and noise. I turned to Les who was sitting near me, because he wasn't joining in the fun. I knew how sick he was. He was bent low in his wheelchair, until I spoke to him. "What do you think, Les ?" I said, trying to coax him into the general merriment. He lifted his head slowly and replied, "Father, I was enthralled." A silence descended on us all. Les had followed the action of the Holy Mass carefully and was overcome by the awesomeness of the Holy Sacrifice. He obviously was enthralled. Shortly afterwards, the nurses took him back to his bedroom and settled him down for the night. Poor Les looked so ill, yet he displayed a remarkable composure of mind and a dignity no sickness could destroy.

At 5.30 a.m. the night nurse in charge, Elizabeth Lavis, altered his position and made sure that he was comfortable. At 5.55 a.m. Les died. At that point, no-one could have guessed how important Les' death was to become. When other nursing duties had been completed, Les' body was washed and prepared for the undertakers who arrived at approximately 11.00 a.m. One of the nursing staff was detailed, immediately Les' body was taken away, to wash down the bed and the mattress cover, in preparation for the admission of a new patient.

She scrubbed away but found the task was taking much longer than she had first thought. There were some difficult stains which were proving to be particularly obstinate. Scrub as she might, they seemed to be indelible. Then, all of a sudden, she discovered that the mark she was attempting to erase was in actual fact an imprint of a hand. She immediately stopped and called in other members of staff to witness what she had seen. They were all astonished. Some time later I and other members of the Management Committee of Jospice were called in to observe this unusual happening.

For safe-keeping, I folded the nylon mattress cover and took it home. There it stayed for five years, wrapped in a plastic bag. From time to time, I thought about showing this phenomenon to experts of the Holy Shroud, but these were only fleeting thoughts and were soon supplanted, by what seemed to be more urgent considerations concerning our Hospices here in England and abroad. There were, after all, many visits to be made to our patients, financial problems to solve and the usual difficulties of running an organisation to be tackled. However, an article on the Holy Shroud in the Catholic Herald in

March 1986, made me resolve at last to show our Imprint to certain professors of forensic medicine, to see what they thought.

In 1987/8, these learned men experimented extensively and had unrestricted access to the actual nylon mattress cover. The results of their work turned out to be inconclusive. Three questions occupied my mind: What was the mark on the mattress, how did it get there and why did it happen? The far reaching problem of why it happened, would be beyond the scope of any scientist, but I had no doubt that the other two enquiries could be examined scientifically.

The experiments the scientists employed involved a wide variety of disciplines. All proved to be of no avail, despite the fact that the Imprint itself was made accessible to the best experts that could be found. They could feel it, take scrapings from it and examine the nylon texture, with the most up-to-date methods in microscopy. The Q.E.D. team from the B.B.C. went to great lengths over a period of six months to find the finest experts in the textile industry and leading figures in the medical world; again, to see if a solution could be found to the aforementioned questions, all to no avail. Also, Professor Frederick Zugibe, an accepted authority in forensic medicine in the United States and a student of the Holy Shroud for over 40 years, submitted the mattress cover to every possible test in his laboratory in New York, but finally acknowledged that to him, the Jospice Imprint was a conundrum. Professor Cameron of the London Clinic, and other leading experts, were similarly left perplexed.

Then in late 1997 an explanation of how the Imprint could have been formed was sent to me by American scientist Dr. Phil Callahan. His paper used phenomena called electrets. In 1995 he had attended a conference at Thornton on the Imprint, the Shroud of Turin and the Tilma of Our Lady of Guadalupe, and at the end I gave him a small piece of the mattress cover to use in his experiments back home at his laboratory in Florida.

Dr. Callahan related that electrets, which were discovered in the 1920s, are formed in wax under certain circumstances by heat, light and electricity. They can be likened to magnets, except that where a magnet has two opposite magnetic poles, an electret has two opposite electric charges, positive on one side and negative on the other. The mattress cover has on it a thin film of polyurethane, coated with rosin, a material on which electrets can occur.

Like magnets, electrets attract iron molecules. Dr. Callahan goes on to explain that sweat contains molecules of iron oxide, which would be attracted to the mattress cover and leave an image, similar to the process involved with photographic film. Such images are actually formed in darkness. In the case of the Jospice Imprint the darkness would be provided by the sheet covering Les. The image would not become visible until it was "fixed" by being exposed to daylight when the bed was stripped. In areas of the body where sweat occurs in abundance–the creases of the hand or between the fingers–the image left on the mattress cover would be particularly strong.

A lot of time has been spent in these scientific investigations but if it makes one person believe in God, it will have been time well spent. However, perhaps one could be permitted to depart from the hard technological sophistication of scientific experiments and be allowed to use a more gentle approach, in trying to solve the conundrum of the Jospice Imprint. The brief of science is limited to what can be experimentally, or empirically verified. Is there a place for Faith, or some other non-scientific concept, on which to base our reasoning ?

It is interesting to note the similarities between the Holy Shroud and the Jospice Imprint. They are both imprints; the only two known to medical science. Both have images which are adsorbed on to, and not absorbed into, their respective fabrics. Both images occurred at the time of death (or resurrection). Both happened at a time of trauma.

Jospice Imprint contains the image of the face of a man, and like the Man of the Holy Shroud it can be seen only by taking a photograph of a negative image. The story of the first photographs of the Holy Shroud is well documented. The figure on the cloth was found to be a negative image. In the case of the Jospice Imprint, a similar factor was noticed. When one examines the area of the face on the nylon mattress cover, only the jaw area is apparent and some matted hair. When this area is photographed and developed, an ordinary positive result is obtained, as would be expected. However, when a photograph of the negative of this photograph is taken and developed, the whole face is revealed. What is more extraordinary is that this face does not seem to be the face of the patient as we remember him ! The face, of course, was lying on a pillow. For this image to penetrate on to the mattress cover, it would, of necessity, be required to go through a pillow slip, a pillow, the under-covering of the pillow slip, through a cotton sheet and then to fix itself indelibly into, or through, the very thin layer of polyurethane which lies on top of the mattress cover.

There may be many other points of similarity between these two imprints, which still have to be discovered and which would make the comparison of one with the other even more interesting. Could it be that both images occurred in the same way ? With regard to the Holy Shroud, despite many years of research, no scientist has yet been able to offer a suitable answer in this regard. The Holy Shroud has been recently carbon-dated, to find out the age of its fabric. The three laboratories, where the tests were carried out, came up with medieval dating, although many scientists today dispute the results of these experiments.

On the other hand, there is no difficulty in dating the Jospice Imprint–March 1981 ! Since the Holy Shroud and the Jospice Imprint are the only two medically recorded imprints of a human body, it would not, I think, be unreasonable to suggest that the causation of one, is similar (or the same?) as the other. Further, it would seem that both defy ordinary physical laws and are of an essence which is obeying the natural laws of causation.

If these two examples of an imprint are sui generis, would it be pushing a point of comparison too far to say that they are not only imprints which bear comparison with so many similarities between them, but that they are imprints of one and the same person ! Obviously, people would think this type of speculation to be beyond any reasonable thought; but if it were the case and in some supernatural way, Christ did manifest Himself on the morning of Les' death (and we know Christ lived in the first century!!!) the dating of the Holy Shroud itself might no longer be in doubt. After all, Christ is present, crucified again in every suffering person. So, is this speculation really out of order ?

'I have to make up in my own body what still has to be made up by Christ on the Cross.' *(St. Paul, Colossians).*

All this seems, I know, to be far-fetched and stretching the bounds of reason to the ultimate, but at least it is worth a thought. A million similarities do not make one sameness, just as a million probabilities do not make one certainty. Hence, any exercise in comparison is fraught with an untold number of pitfalls and one is left in the world of speculation only. However, the Jospice Imprint is so out of the ordinary, that it deserves a speculation or two!

What is certain is that we have here in Jospice a piece of nylon material which will keep students of the Holy Shroud occupied for many years to come. Whilst we all realise that we do not need the Holy Shroud as proof of Christ's resurrection, we may have been sent, through the Jospice Imprint, a supernatural phenomenon, which may be an aid in highlighting the veracity of the Holy Shroud and all that is implied in it, for the benefit of a very materialistic, unbelieving and cynical world.

As Hans Werfel said at the end of 'The Song of Bernadette':.........

"To those who believe in God no explanation is necessary;

To those who do not believe in God no explanation is possible."

At a recent prayer group meeting, Bernard Mangley, for whose cure we were praying, reminded me of the first time I had shown him the mattress cover.

He and his wife Ann had invited me to have lunch with them in Southport. This was a few months after Les had died. Ann's uncle Eugene, a Christian Brother, was interested in the work of Jospice and they had asked me to bring the mattress cover with me.

The cover was laid on the hall carpet and Bernard told me that as Ann's uncle traced the outline of the Imprint with his hands I suddenly exclaimed, "I see the significance of this. See the hand, it's the most clear part of the Imprint. Now look at my badge . . . . it's the same hand. That is God's hand and He is telling me that I am not to worry, that his hand is in my work." Fr. Maurus Green O.S.B., thought likewise when he saw our Imprint.

Early in 1998 I received in the post a copy of Ian Wilson's latest book entitled 'The Blood and the Shroud.' Ian is the author of the 'Turin Shroud', the authoritative book on the Holy Shroud which is kept in the Cathedral in Turin. This new book is a very scholarly investigation of this phenomenon. I have on many occasions requested Ian's advice regarding our Imprint. He visited our Hospice on May 1st, 1986, when I exhibited our Imprint publicly for the first time. I remember it was the Feast of St. Joseph the Worker and after Holy Mass a group of us gathered round to look at our mattress cover and we realised how blessed we had been. I was delighted that in this new book our mattress cover had been given a mention and that Ian had included a photograph of the hand as imprinted on it. Ian has always kept in contact with us and has kept us informed about the new books he is writing.

First   Gala   Concert

17

ARRANGEMENTS were still busily being made for the 1987 Gala Concert which was to take place on October 31st. I have various references to the conductor and a gentleman called Herbert Handt. It was quite a job tracking him down but his was the only name I came across in connection with Rossini's Messa di Gloria. Through ringing this one and that, I managed to track him down to a small town called Lucca in Italy where he was busy organising a festival. He gave me the name of the publisher of the Rossini Mass. He had himself done a lot of research in putting the Mass together from some rather old manuscripts and soon we had copies of the Mass for distribution to the choir.

We were so fortunate that year because good friends David Newton and Mr. Waterworth, who were directors of Everton Football Club, put forward our name to the Charity Shield Committee. Everton had been playing Liverpool that year at Wembley and we became the proud recipient of a Mini Bus. My Brother Arthur and Archie Downie went along to collect it and they had the great privilege (for them) of driving around the pitch at Goodison Park in front of many thousands of people. There was an unnerving experience for me too about this time. I had to go to collect a television set through the kindness of David (the same gentleman) and I remember getting a big cheer from the Everton crowd before the start of the match.

1987 ambled along quite normally with references to our first retreat given by John Murphy, a local deacon, and I have a note about a Mr. Leyland and a Mass to be said for him and all our legators who are so important to us.

There are one or two aide-memoires about getting my Tango orchestrated for the Gala Concert. I wrote the Tango when I was in my second year Theology in Mill Hill and that was that. I hadn't thought about it again, but as we were preparing for the Gala Concert I thought: Why not get the Tango orchestrated ? I contacted Proinnsias O'Duinn the conductor and he simply said, "Send me the music." I thought Our Lady's Choral Society could do 'oo's or 'ah's as a background to it. He telephoned me to say that he wanted words, as it wasn't the custom for Our Lady's Choral Society to accompany with 'oo's and 'ah's. We had a Committee meeting that same evening and we scrambled together some words and within a couple of weeks Proinnsias O'Duinn had come up with the harmony for the choir and everything was ready for rehearsal. Ken Hesketh did the orchestration. He was a student at the Royal College of Music and a very clever musician. As well as doing my Tango he orchestrated my Dad's Mass and the parts we were going to sing–the Benedictus and Agnus Dei–and also my Dad's Ave Maria. Whilst all this was happening I came across Lees' Our Father which we decided to include in our Mass and after many phone calls I contacted the conductor who had made the recording of this piece. He lived in Holland and his name was Arie Pronk. He sent me the orchestration. It is a wonderful piece. The harmonies are very delicate. It does express, as I brought out in the Gala notes, the sacredness of the Our Father as it was Our Lord Himself who composed the words and this sentiment the music brings out.

It was at this time too, having done a funeral at Ford Cemetery, I looked into the Church there called The Holy Sepulchre which seemed abandoned. There was a cement mixer in the middle aisle and I turned my eyes on the beautiful statues and Stations of the Cross adorning the church. As the church wasn't locked up I thought I might as well remove them all before anybody else did !! So I went back with a lorry to Ford Cemetery. The caretaker said I could take the statues and the Stations of the Cross if I wished. The statues I got painted and put into our Hospice in Thornton. But the Stations of the Cross were very big so I had them cleaned and made our own Stations of the Cross in our beautiful grounds. They are a lovely memory of all the people who have died in our Hospices.

We tried to make the most of our Silver Jubilee year of 1987 and many functions were put on all leading up, I suppose, to the peak of our excitement in the presentation of our Gala Concert followed by a special Silver Jubilee Mass at SS. Peter and Paul's, Crosby, on November 1st, the following day.

The diary is littered with little notes about this singer and the other, where they were going to stay, and who was going to entertain them. The first ones to arrive were Kathleen Kuhlmann from London, Proinnsias O'Duinn, John O'Flynn, our bass-baritone, and Canon O'Sullivan from Dublin. Fil and Terry picked up Kathleen Kuhlmann and I put the other three into my car at Manchester Airport. We all made for the Adelphi Hotel where there was a special meal laid on for them in the French Restaurant. Brendan O'Dowda, meanwhile, had made his way with his family to Hettinga House in Ormskirk, where they were to be accommodated. Maura and Liam O'Leary, my friends from Cork, went to the Adelphi and we had to keep popping from one to the other to make sure everything was satisfactory for them. On the evening of the concert itself it was great to see Patsy Ruttle and her friend from our Dublin group dashing into the hall at the last minute.

The first rehearsal was on October 30th at the Philharmonic Hall and for one horrible moment I thought that I had hired the wrong music or that the music I had hired would be in the wrong key ! All sorts of possibilities ran through my mind. It was a very exciting moment. The programme we planned was quite an ambitious one, very tuneful and full of musicality. The Kyrie was from Rossini's Petite Messe Solennelle. The Gloria was from the Missa di Credo by Mozart. This was followed by Gounod's Sanctus from the Mass of St. Cecilia which led into Lees' Our Father. Then we had my Dad's Benedictus and Agnus Dei from his Mass of the Sacred Heart. This was followed by Cesar Franck's Panis Angelicus, O Rest in the Lord from Mendelssohn's oratorio Elijah, Inflammatus from Rossini's Stabat Mater and we rounded off the first part of the concert with Rossini's Cum Sancto Spiritu from his Petite Messe Solennelle. It was performed so well I could hardly believe my ears.

The second half of the concert was a little trickier and slightly more complicated. We opened with Rossini's William Tell Overture and that was followed by the aria Largo al Factotum from the Barber of Seville, the duet from The Lily of Killarney, The Moon Hath Raised Her Lamp Above, and from Balfe's The Bohemian Girl, Suzanne Murphy, our soprano, gave a beautiful rendition of I Dreamt that I Dwelt in Marble Halls. After the trio from Faust we had some Irish melodies sung by Brendan O'Dowda. These were expertly done and then we were all able to join in with the Jospice Tango. For the final work I chose the Gloria in Excelsis Deo from Rossini's Messa di Gloria. Then Mgr. Vincent Hughes read the Jospice Prayer and gave us his Blessing and we all sang the Jospice Hymn to conclude the concert.

Everyone who attended the concert enjoyed it but the singing wasn't over yet. We all retired to the Adelphi Hotel for a first class meal and a few drinks. Our Lady's Choral Society did not seem to be tired and started a sing-song which went on until four o'clock in the morning. I then went home myself as I had to be at Hettinga House early that morning to say Holy Mass for Brendan O'Dowda who was going back down to London. Brendan asked if it would be possible for him to sing for the patients when I was taking Holy Communion to them. Brendan decided to sing Lord for Tomorrow and Its Needs. He started off very well, but he got a surprise when Sebastian, our Old English Mastiff, joined in. When Brendan started to sing, Sebastian came in with a big howl. Our little congregation was in tucks of laughter. Brendan was amused as well. Sebastian composed a little poem afterwards which went as follows:

Dear Uncle Francis,

Did you enjoy my performance last week,

When at Mass, by the Altar I lay,

I was having a doze when you left for a while,

And there's something I really must say.

The voice that I heard was so lovely, but strange,

Not at all like our music you see

And I felt such an urge to sing a duet

I rolled over and joined in with glee.

No one else sang a note, so I just cleared my throat,

And tried to sing louder and louder

Then I opened my eyes and to my surprise

I was singing with Brendan O'Dowda.

Best wishes and tail wags

from Sebastian.

I met up with the soloists and choir later that day at SS. Peter and Paul's Church, Crosby, where we had a special Mass at one o'clock. The choir sang the music from the Mass which they had sung the previous evening. Suzanne Murphy and Patrick Power sang the Panis Angelicus with the appropriate obligato, then after Mass we made for the Blundellsands Hotel for lunch. After an enjoyable lunch the choir started to sing again and sang for about an hour. They then got into buses and went to both our Hospices to sing for the patients. Finally the buses took them back to the ship in Liverpool. There was so much music that weekend that one was left a little stunned at the way it had all happened. Some of it was planned, of course, but some of it again was impromptu but no less enjoyable. A wonderful weekend and a marvellous way to commemorate the Silver Jubilee of St. Joseph's Hospice Association.

Silver Jubilee Recording
and Our Lady's Wing

18

ABOUT this time my diary notes tell me that Ken Dodd gave us an hilarious evening at Ormskirk Civic Hall. Also a note was made for me to contact Sister Bernadette Horvath in Hungary (the nun who gave me the holy picture of St. Joseph all those years ago in Pakistan). There is also an aide-memoire to contact Sister Joan Cole who was a Poor Clare nun in her Arundel convent. She and her husband had been supporters of ours for many years. Her husband died and she volunteered to join an enclosed order. She used to write many heartening letters to us and it was a great pleasure to be in contact with so many wonderful people. There was a sad note at this time about the death of Eamonn Andrews who had been friendly with us since the time of This Is Your Life.

An awful lot seemed to be happening abroad as well as at home. Fr. Kattakayam, Fr. Mekkunel, Fr. Jeyaraj and Fr. Thumpayil were doing their work which we support in India. The Peruvian ventures were going well. Fr. Frank Smith was looking after hordes of people in Guayaquil. Cathy O'Keeffe and Clare Sheridan were working hard in Honduras and our Guatemala Hospice was getting under way with Berta Mejia Medina and helpers.

There were very encouraging reports also from Pakistan. Sisters Lucille and Josephine had done wonders in Rawalpindi and we can thank God that at the end of 1987 everything was going fine. It was difficult on the financial side, but that was nothing for us to be surprised about because that was our usual situation. We were, however, managing to find our way from week to week.

We came into 1988 with the hustle and bustle of preparing our first video, called 'The Irrepressible Spirit'. Kate Flynn from John Mills and Co was writing her script and work on our extension to the Hospice in San Jose was being completed. Our Lady's Wing opened on the feast of Our Lady of Lourdes on February 11th. The ceremony was attended by Fr. Godfrey Carney and many other priests who were supporters of ours.

There is a note that Cathy O'Keeffe came back from Honduras on holiday and I asked her to pay a visit to our Hospice in Rawalpindi. She had a wonderful time there, where she met Sadiq, Alice and their daughter Rita who took Cathy up to Ayubia, where she caught more than a glimpse of the Himalayas. It was marvellous to be able to link up our Hospice work, particularly that taking place in Central America, with our tasks in Rawalpindi.

After Our Lady's Wing had been opened we then began preparing our first record to celebrate our Silver Jubilee. It was to be a record of Hymns and Christmas Carols. Once more we had to find good soloists and a good choir. The choir was easier this time than the Gala Concert because it was made up of the Capriol Singers who are mostly people who live in the district of Crosby. The four soloists were more difficult to come by. Rosa Mannion was our soprano. Rosa used to work for us when she was 14 years of age as a member of the St. John's Ambulance Brigade. She was with us for some time then all of a sudden she seemed to disappear and I lost trace of her. She had gone off to study music at my old University in Glasgow and she had won all sorts of prizes and gold medals. She then went on to appear with Scottish Opera and various musical societies and by 1988 was an established soprano. She willingly came to give her services for the recording. Stuart Kale was our tenor, Richard Robson was the bass and Angela Hickey was the contralto. The work involved seemed to be as hard and just as arduous as that of the Gala Concert but we managed somehow despite the theft of the music from the back of a car. At one point we thought all the music had been lost but we were able to redeem most of it. Particularly attractive is the Novello arrangement of the Adeste Fidelis which is rarely heard these days and the beautiful Christmas carol Sleep, My Saviour, Sleep by W. N. Hedgcock. The exercise was well worth it.

I used to go and see a lady at this time called Mona Boyd. She had turned 90 and although she was in a rest home we thought it would be a good idea to bring her to our Hospice in Hettinga House. Her husband had died a few years previously there. She was not a Catholic but for many many years she had intended to become one but had never got round to it. I got a call one evening when her husband was dying and I went along to give him the Sacrament of the Sick. He was still conscious and so he was able to receive Holy Communion. Mona was very dutifully at his bedside. Whilst there I said to

Mona, "You've been intending to become a Catholic for a long time now, there's no moment like the present." In answer to my questions she said that she acknowledged everything that the Catholic Church taught and believed it strongly. So I baptised her and gave her husband what turned out to be his last Holy Communion and gave her Holy Communion as well–her first. There was just sufficient time before Mr. Boyd died for Mona to lean over him and say, "I have just become a Catholic, dear." He then died peacefully and she was extremely happy and felt secure. Later Mona became one of our patients. She was a great artist and painted many pictures for us. She was in our Hospice for a number of years and then died herself. Both of them were instrumental in giving me an uplift of faith for both were great examples of practical Christianity.

During this same month of May there was a big concert in the Civic Hall in Ormskirk. It was put on by the children from St. Bede's School in Ormskirk.

The B.B.C. were still asking us at this particular time about making a film for the Q.E.D. programme. This was in relation to the Imprint which I have mentioned above. The B.B.C wanted to do a programme on it and to link it up with the Holy Shroud of Turin. It was many months in the making and demanded an awful lot of our time, being interviewed and the like. As usual the Q.E.D. programme left the problem up in the air. No conclusive solution was found.

On the subject of the B.B.C. there is an enjoyable programme called "Anything Goes" put out every Sunday by Bob Holness on the World Service from London. It is a popular programme and having heard it a few times (broadcast at 3.30 every Monday morning) I thought it would be quite in order to make a request for our girls in Honduras. So I wrote to the B.B.C. in London and put in a request for Josef Locke singing I'll Take You Home Again Kathleen because one of the girls in Honduras was so named. He played it and later I checked with the girls whether or not they'd heard it and they said they had. I suppose this was another way of communicating with our Hospices abroad !!

Some Interesting Events

19

THE Crosby Ten, which is an annual marathon performed by a group of runners round Crosby each year, gave us a cheque from their sponsored run. I noted too that Fr. Allah Ditta had written to us. He is the priest who runs our other Hospice in Pakistan in the town of Layyah. He has made tremendous strides among the Christian population there. His parish is surrounded by Muslims, of course, but the little area that he takes care of is Catholic and so we felt at this time an obligation to care for him and his small Hospice which consists of a few nurses and some rooms to care for people who are sick. He has referred many cases to us and thank God we have been able to send him the funds to pay for operations on his patients.

On September 13th a gentlemen called Colin Miller came to me and asked me to be the subject of a Desert Island Discs programme which he was arranging for the Moor Lane Methodist Church in Crosby. I readily accepted to be the castaway and I had great fun in choosing my list of records. I remember starting the programme with a march by Sousa, Semper Fidelis. That was followed by an overture by Rossini, from the opera The Barber of Seville and next I had Gounod's Sanctus, from the Mass of St. Cecilia, my Dad's Ave Maria and a great favourite of mine The Cat Duet by Rossini. Also included were I Wanna Go Home by the Beach Boys and James Last's arrangement of Irish songs. My book was on St. Thomas More, whom I admire so much, and as far as I can remember my luxury was a book of photographs to remind me of the many happy occasions of my life as a priest.

Another joyous occasion this month was attending the wedding of An Saen who got married to Johan Vanderveld in Belgium. She had volunteered to work for us for some time in Thornton and had made great friends among our patients. So she invited myself, Terry and Filomena to her wedding in Brussels. In this month, too, I had great pleasure in marrying Janet Ashcroft, who had worked for us in Honduras, to Bill Jackson in St. Helen's Church, in Crosby. Janet and her Sister Mary have always kept in contact with us and they both did excellent work for us abroad.

I was invited to attend the Silver Jubilee celebrations of Sister Mary, a nun from Park House who very often pops in to visit the Hospice. Then I note that on November 30 Monica and Leo as the Crosby Entertainers put on a concert for us in the Civic Hall. As usual this was very enjoyable.

In December of this year I have a note that Anne-Marie Rice finished working with us in Honduras and Thornton. Anne-Marie had done wonderful work in Honduras and had made many contacts for us there.

Looking through my diary of 1989 I concluded that it was a bit of a mixed year. We started off traditionally with an evening in Fr. Hughes' parish at Lowe House in St. Helens on January 1st. I recall that it was a very enjoyable evening as it is every New Year's Day.

Then all of a sudden we found ourselves celebrating the anniversary of the opening of Our Lady's Wing at Thornton and we had John Murphy holding his day of recollection for the Legion of Mary.

I went to see a young lady called Imelda Priestman from Crosby. Imelda had been told that she could have a heart and lung transplant and was waiting for an ambulance which was to take her down to Harefield Hospital for the operation. I got round to her house before the ambulance took her away and I was able to anoint her. Thankfully her operation was a success.

Stephanie McKenna and Siobhan Browner appeared for their interview for Honduras, Sister Marion had returned from Peru to visit us and a great lady, Mrs. Seeley, told us of the work she was doing for us in Kirkby and District. We, of course, felt very grateful to her for all the fundraising she did for us. Then in July I baptised Rosa Mannion's baby in our little Chapel of San Jose. It was a great event and endeared us even more to Rosa and her work. In July Kate Daley and Eileen McKay started our Morning Prayer Programme. I was always anxious to have the Prayer of the Church as part of our activities. These good ladies provided the incentive to others to say the Church's Prayer every day.

Our Pakistani friends, Sam and Saleema Qasir, I invited for our Annual General Meeting on November 19th. It was nice to see them again. Sam had been a member of our Management Committee and Saleema had done night duty for us. They both had strong Rawalpindi connections and with our Hospice in Pakistan.

Leo and Monica, I note, put on another concert for us and I recall the quite stunning fancy dress show outside Sainsbury's on Saturday December 23rd.

On the 26th the Consolata Seminarians came to stay with us at Hettinga House and enjoyed their sojourn with us as part of their Christmas break.

We opened 1990 in the customary way of saying Midnight Mass and invoking all our patrons to guide us through the rigours of the year and to thank God that the reports from the overseas departments were good. Sister Mary Dornan took charge of our Hospice in Rawalpindi and Fr. Allah Ditta had only good news for us despite his difficult circumstances in Layyah. We continued supplying him with donations for particular patients and he was very gladdened by the way his project was going.

Sister Patricia McGlynn, whom I remember taking on many years ago in Pakistan, came to visit us at Thornton. She hadn't been keeping very well, but at this time she said how much better she felt. She comes from a famous family. She and her four sisters are dedicated Franciscan Missionaries of Mary and her two brothers are priests, one of whom is the Abbot of Nunraw Abbey near Edinburgh. After her mother died her father thought that he would try his vocation and entered a Cistercian monastery. So it was a great pleasure to receive Sister Patricia. She has appeared in a few of our advertisements, particularly the one with the baby found in a dustbin in Rawalpindi. She was astonished to see our Hospice here in England and was full of praise for it. Our South American ventures were going well and our girls in Honduras and Guatemala were performing wonderful tasks.

Some Anecdotes

20

IN February 1990 our world was shaken by the announcement that a new road was going to be constructed outside our grounds at Thornton. This was the first time that we had heard about the Blue route and how it was going to affect the vicinity of our Hospice. A small group was formed which was going to attack the plan put forward by Sefton Council. It took five years and quite a few pounds to win the battle. But if the plan had gone through, our tasks in the Hospice at Thornton would have been seriously disrupted. Our work had to go on and funds still had to be raised to keep our heads above water. We were helped in this by a donation from Our Lady's Church in Formby and a sizeable collection from St. Anne's Social Centre where a cabaret was put on for our benefit. Deyes Lane High School made us their charity for this year and I was requested to go along a few times to speak to the students in the school. Their efforts were outstanding. I am continually surprised and amused by sponsored silences in schools !! These star pupils did their best in so many ways.

We received the sad news of the death of Gerry Tims in Australia and a member of our Management Committee here in Crosby, Jim Allen, also died. Jim was a fine man and looked after our interests at Hettinga House with great circumspection. It seemed that every moment of every day he was doing something for Hettinga House or for one of the patients. He would share our trials but always expressed his amazement on the ways we had of keeping the Hospice going. He took a very active part in our Management Committee and was often concerned about the approach to our spiritual progress. I suppose most evenings he went to a Prayer Group meeting and was always in attendance when I said Mass at Hettinga House. So his death was a big blow to us and we still miss him very much. We are all blessed with various gifts from God which we try to use to the benefit of others. As a Committee member Jim amused us by his sense of humour and above all by his gift of mimicry. He did this with the tone of his voice or the look on his face.

He was completely hilarious. We have to thank God for this. Jim was constantly at the bedside of patients and was able to communicate with them. They found a great friend when Jim went to see them, joking, laughing, making light of the more serious things in life and this was a great blessing we all enjoyed.

In 1978 I had written a paper on the need for our Association to have a place which would be serviceable for us to practise holistic medicine. I arrived one afternoon at my office and went straight to my secretary who was capable of putting down immediately everything I dictated.

Margery Baden got my words down perfectly and I dictated for about 25 minutes. In that short space of time I was able to direct my thoughts to this holistic aspect of caring. The dream of having a special Hospice for this holistic approach to nursing care seemed unrealistic because we had no extra finance to establish such a building at that time.

However, in 1990 we were left a large legacy by a Mr. Maroukian. He lived in Crosby, and although we had never met he had admired the work I was doing. His generosity meant our dreams could now come true. It took until the summer of 1992 to plan and erect the building, and on June 26th, the Feast of the Sacred Heart, we had the solemn opening.

One of my ideas which didn't get off the ground was the Hooley. O'Leary is a great name so I thought it would be wonderful to collect all the O'Learys, as many as possible throughout the world, to have a Hooley here in Thornton. I got all the O'Leary names from directories and books of that kind and during the summer of 1990 I wrote letters to them stating that it would be marvellous if the O'Leary family, or tribe if you like, could get together and contribute to the cost of building and running the Academy. We would fly them over from the United States or Australia and the cost of this we could defray by the donations that they would hopefully give. But as I say, the idea didn't get off the ground, much to the relief of my Management Committee. It was a good idea though.

Our minds were distracted from this rather outlandish idea of the O'Leary Hooley by attending a very pleasant reception put on by Louise Frazer and more particularly by going down to London to attend Terry Seasman's ordination. This was very important for us because Terry had studied extremely hard for eleven years. We admired him so much for this. He had been a nurse at the Hospice in Thornton for many years, so we looked on him as one of our special products. He built up deep friendships with our patients and staff. Although we missed him when he went away to the seminary, we wished him the best of luck in his new endeavours. He was ordained on June 2nd by Cardinal Hume in London. A number of us from the Hospice, including my Brother Arthur, went down for this special day. The following weekend, on Sunday June 10th, Terry came to the Hospice and celebrated Holy Mass with me. Kathleen Bucher put on a good reception for him. Terry had been brought to us by two members of our Committee, Jack and Colette Keating. Terry's mother had died and he was ill at ease with his job. So we gave him a big white coat and told him he was a nurse and that he could live with us. He had a room in the attic. This was the only available space we could offer him as living quarters. Believe it or not, when he went down to the seminary he was put in the attic there too. He was a bit homesick and had yearnings for the attic in Thornton, incommodious though it might have been.

June was a very busy month. There were celebrations at Herbert House, Freshfield, for some Mill Hill Fathers' Jubilees. Bishop Malone came to visit us and the usual talks were given to Professor Sells' students. A special breakfast was put on for our examiners for the English National Board nursing course. Kathleen Bucher did us proud again and we got permission to supervise our own 'Care of the Dying' course.

In order to gain some prestige for our Hospice in Ormskirk we had lunch with Dr. Horsley, Dr. Underwood and Dr. Stuart Meehan from the local health board. The idea was to build an extension at Hettinga House to complement, as it were, the palliative care teams which were just coming into being. Unfortunately, nothing came of this meeting.

We received the sad news that Sadiq Masih had died in Rawalpindi. He was the man who had helped me so much when Mrs. Jacob was dying. He and his family were great supporters.

In January 1991 Richard Maude of Yorkshire Television came to visit me. He was instrumental in making part of the series called The Witness for ITV and he thought a focus on St. Joseph's Hospice would be a good idea for one of his programmes. This was a surprise to us, an agreeable one in a way, because allowing professionals to do a job like making a film is worthwhile. It doesn't cost anything except a lot of one's time. That is something which is so important because time is a very difficult commodity to ration.

Shortly after Richard Maude's visit we had quite a long visit from Fr. Liam Hayes, an Irishman who brought with him his Bishop from Argentina, Bishop Giaquinta. The Bishop was asking us to build a hospice for him in his diocese where they made the film 'The Mission'. We had no funds to build a hospice so we decided to finance one or two of his friends to become nurses. However, Fr. Liam managed to get funds to build a Cheshire Home and I believe that is now flourishing.

Before we could turn round we found that we were celebrating the fifth anniversary of the Rosary on Wednesdays. Ron Wharton, Archie and Helen Downie with their friends come every Wednesday and have a Eucharistic Service, say the Rosary and offer special prayers for those who are sick. They go to both Hospices, San Jose and the Academy. Hettinga House also provides the same service from Jim Holland. These services are very helpful not only for the patients but also for ourselves. At this time we found we were hosting meetings for the Huntington Society. The Huntington Society consists of a group of people whose relations or friends are stricken by this horrible disease and they come together in a spirit of friendship to exchange views and have talks from specialists. For their first evening here we gave them a slap-up meal and Leo played on the piano for them. Once again it was a great evening.

At this time I received a letter from a Sister Dorothy from Bury about the opening of the Hospice there. This project really took off from a talk I gave in Bury some 15 years previously and at last the building was ready to open. I went up to have a look round the new building and was pleased at everything I saw. Then on March 10th we began the novena to St. Joseph, a very popular devotion for us all because we realise how much we are indebted to him. We need that constant intercession and we must familiarise ourselves all the time with St. Joseph's part in our Association.

Having celebrated the 20th Anniversary of our group in Sudbury we turned our attention to a little ceremony of turning the first soil on the site on which the Academy would stand. We had a special Mass on that day, May 1st, the Feast of St. Joseph The Worker. We all trooped out to attend this turning of the first soil which I myself performed. It was a great occasion and helped us to become more involved with the new project.

There were other things to celebrate in the May of 1991. We had John O'Leary's wedding in London. John is one of the sons of Fil and Terry. After the marriage ceremony we retired to a hotel to rejoice with him and his new wife Meryl. John now lives in Madrid and is often host to his family when they visit Spain. Then there was the ordination of Juan Manuel in Mexico. We sent him our congratulations as he was a helper with us both in Thornton and in Hettinga House in Ormskirk. He now works as a parish priest in Mexico. Then on the July 31st we had a meeting with John Rooney our architect, and the contractor from Tomkinsons, and the Academy work started in earnest.

Soon after that four Punjabi Sisters from Pakistan came to visit and had lunch with us. Tina Quispe went back to Peru and then we were soon celebrating the fifteenth anniversary of Honduras. Shortly after this the portacabins arrived so that work on the site of the Academy could begin on August 27th.

I have a little note in my diary that Margaret Hughes, one of our cooks, borrowed my book 'Full Tilt' by Devla Murphy. I met Devla Murphy in the early '60s. I had been invited round to dinner at the house in Rawalpindi of Beghum Shahid Hamid. She had a special guest coming and had invited me round to meet her. Unfortunately, I was late and everyone was seated before I arrived. I made my apologies and was requested to sit near this lady. After everyone had retired from the table there was just the two of us left. I asked Devla how she arrived in Pakistan, by boat or plane. She told me that she had come by bicycle all the way from Dublin. So we got chatting and she enquired from me among other things about the possibility of a Christian marrying a Muslim. I told her that in the Rawalpindi diocese the Bishop would give a dispensation on special grounds. It was a beautiful starlit night and very hot, so we retired to the patio and continued our conversation. I invited her round to the priests' house the next day in 'Pindi City. She, unknown to me, had been making notes for a book she was writing. Many months later this book arrived in 'Pindi and my name duly appeared. So it was odd that when Stephanie McKenna, one of our Honduras nurses, visited Pakistan, someone had given her a book to read on her travels. When my name appeared on a certain page, Stephanie couldn't believe her eyes because it was I who had sent her to 'Pindi. Fortunately I acquired a copy of the book. Margaret Hughes heard of it and borrowed it. It was a long time before I got it back !!

Our minds were taken away temporarily from the Academy because on September 5th four girls departed for our Hospice in Honduras–Christina McNamee, Kathy Caulfield, Annette Armstrong and Diane Sorrell. It is always exciting when our nurses depart for foreign shores. Not only do we have to find the money for the tickets, but a host of things to remember. There are always medicines to take out and gifts for the other girls.

The following month we got news of Peter Carter's indisposition and Filomena and I made tracks for Spain, where he was on holiday, to pay him a surprise visit. Despite the circumstances it was a pleasure to see Peter and to be able to offer Mass for him in Spanish in the hospital ward. Thank God Peter had his operation in Santander and it was so successful that he could take his position on our Management Committee again.

Also that month we had a surprise visit from Archbishop Jose Ruiseco from Cartagena in Colombia. We did the usual things like visiting Hettinga House and taking him round various points of interest, one of which was Chester Cathedral by which he was captivated.

At this time too we had a special Mass for our Secular Franciscan Order and the E.N.B. 931 course on the 'Care of the Dying' was started for our nurses by Dorothy Whitehead.

Oh dear, so much was happening at this time. This brought us into November. We had had a new conservatory put on to the Coach House beside the hydrotherapy pool and a complete refurbishment of the pool had been arranged. It is beautiful to watch so many patients using the pool and the enjoyment it gives them. The Coach House and the pool are magnificent amenities for which we thank God. Over the years so many hundreds of people have been able to use this particular facility.

The names of Neil Brown and Jackie keep cropping up in the pages of the diary. I met both of these people when I was in my third year at University. I remember Neil giving me a special prayer book before I departed to Pakistan. Neil for his sins was doing geology like myself and I used to invite him and Jackie to come with me when I was inspecting outcrops of rock. Jackie was very kind. Every weekend she would make potato cakes or, as they say in Scotland, tattie scones. They were delicious and I used to look forward to her weekly supply. Some years ago I learned that Neil had died suddenly. Later Ian MacNicol, another friend from the University, told me that Jackie had got married a second time. I was anxious to meet her again. Through the kindness of Ian MacNicol, who found her new address, this became possible. Neil and Jackie were lovely people and a great example to me and others at the University. I remember well how Neil came to my Mass in the Sisters' Convent in Great Western Road and took me through my work before the examination. He knew his stuff well. Possibly I learnt more in the half-hour after Mass than I did in the whole year. He made sure I knew how to dot the 'i's and cross the 't's in my map work and in my identification of fossils and things of that nature. I expressed my sorrow to Jackie about Neil's demise because we had been good friends. In March 1993, on the tenth anniversary of Neil's death, I went to Glasgow and had the great privilege of saying Holy Mass for both of them.

Further Meanderings

21

FOR many years Fr. Hughes bought me a desk diary, usually a Collins, and he always put in a phrase or two at the beginning of the diary to inspire me in my work for the coming year. Sometimes he wrote in Latin and sometimes it was in Spanish to challenge my efforts of translation, but for 1992 he had written in English and it reads

" 'Be patient; in time an egg will walk'

(an African proverb).

with best wishes at the start of the Academy project"

The egg I suppose was the Academy !!

On January 24th 1992 many of us went down to the ordination as Bishop of Fr. Vin Nichols in Westminster. Since he is my cousin I felt quite honoured that the Holy Father had chosen him for this office. His brothers Peter (from Australia) and John were present. It was nice to see the three of them together.

We were pleased, too, that we were now able to get a bishop to open our new Academy and Vin consented to do this for us. I gave him a present from myself and Rita, my Sister, of some paintings of Little Crosby, a village next to Thornton which is still Catholic going back long before the Reformation. These were particularly pleasant paintings and had a special point because Vin's mother and father were associated very closely with Little Crosby and I recall walking there with his mother, Mary, to Midnight Mass one year on Christmas Eve.

Then on the January 29th, Jane Hough, who had been a nurse with us and had gone on to be a doctor, spent some months at our Hospice in Honduras. My diary tells me that I was worried about our Mud Hut in Rawalpindi and to contact Bishop Pereira in order to save it from being taken over or knocked down. This Mud Hut is our shrine, if you like, the place were Mrs. Jacob died. The area is now in Anglican hands. Very recently the Anglican Bishop of Lahore did listen to my request to put in motion a measure to preserve this Mud Hut, so we are all pleased.

When I went back to Pakistan in 1985 and arrived in St. Mary's compound where the Mud Hut is situated, I was warned that the person who at present occupies the hut was going to make a strong appeal to me to allow him to stay in that dwelling. It wasn't for me to say yea or nay, but his defence was that when I was parish priest of that area I gave him permission to live there. I can't remember telling him to do that, but apparently when he tells authorities this, it is a strong point in his favour. I am pleased that he is there because it preserves the building and nobody can knock it down willy-nilly.

We celebrated in due fashion the 10th anniversary of Hettinga House on February 9th. A few of us went down to Sudbury for an evening celebration on February 22nd. We always make a special effort to accept the invitations given by Sudbury because they are such a strong group, very devoted and very loyal to our Association and in fact make a significant contribution to our funds every year.

The work abroad, thank God, was proceeding smoothly and Rachel Birch informed us how well the work in Honduras was going, of all the advances they were making, and about her plans for a new Hospice building in San Pedro Sula.

The 11th anniversary of the death of Les was on March 9th which we duly commemorated and soon it was time for me to send off my telegrams for St. Patrick's and St. Joseph's Days. There are certain friends of our Association with whom one wants to communicate particularly on these two great days. For example, Sister Margaret Carr in Karachi, who was one of the nuns who cared for Mrs. Jacob in the very early days, hails from Killibegs in Donegal. Every year I send her some shamrock. It takes quite a time to dictate these telegrams and more have to be sent out for St. Joseph's Day !!

However, it is nice to greet all our Hospices on this great Feast of St. Joseph because he is the one who is responsible for all the work that is carried out. On March 14th I gave a talk to the Christian Democrats. I am one of their very early members. I think my membership number is 250. There are many thousands of members in the organisation today.

Having celebrated St. Joseph's Day with a big dinner and my Annual Report we had another celebration to attend in Maghull Social Centre. Barbara and Charles McCoy, along with Anne and Ian Hill, put on a big function on our behalf. At this time I was having meetings with Richard Maude and Barbara

Twigg in relation to the television documentary The Witness. Easter was fast approaching so our Easter appeal had to be prepared for the special house-to-house collection. Meanwhile the television people were wandering around all the time and we had to accommodate their wishes by having our photographs taken here and there. The actual film was quite successful. It is rather a strange experience to have one's work publicly portrayed. In fact, one feels a bit of a fraud. Somehow they manage to portray the happiness of the operation but are unable to communicate one's worries and troubles.

A happy event was to follow. A Mr. Patrick Curry had written to me saying that he wished to have accommodation with us as he felt he was getting old and needed someone to care for him. Some years previously I had gone to Mr. Curry's house after his wife Agnes had died. He gave me a cheque for ten thousand pounds which was from his wife's estate. He had no wish to keep it since her death and had looked through the Universe for a place to send this money. At that time we had a tiny advertisement in the Universe. It was so tiny that you could hardly see it; but his eyes fell on this advert and it prompted him to invite me to go to collect the cheque at his home in Manchester. I brought Patrick over to the Hospice on April 7th and he stayed with us a couple of years until he died. A very generous man was Patrick and an extremely good and prayerful example to all. His Catholic faith was so secure that it gave him a closeness to us. He made further donations in gratitude for having been so well looked after.

In the meantime, my cousin, Fr. Willie Russell, was poorly in Herbert House in Freshfield. He was a retired Mill Hill Father, who had done sterling work in Uganda and as a Chaplain in the R.A.F. For all this work he got an M.B.E. My Sister and I went to see him. He was 92 when he died in August.

We seemed to be all of a sudden into May and Bring Flowers of the Rarest time sung by Canon Sydney MacEwan. It is a beautiful hymn and Canon Sydney gives it such a meaningful rendition. The words are well chosen for the month of May and every May 1st we play it at both our Hospices in Ormskirk and Thornton.

The Academy Opens ...

22

OUR thoughts in 1992 were centred on the smaller details in preparation for the opening of the Academy: things like stained glass windows and which scenes we would have depicted in them. I know St. Thomas was a favourite, as he was the patron saint of Pakistan, although when I rang the Pakistan Embassy to confirm this, they had no idea who was the patron saint of their country. Then there were all the invitees to list for the opening date of June 26th, the Feast of the Sacred Heart.

But before that date we had to celebrate a few things like the fourth anniversary of our little Hospice in Layyah in Pakistan, the funeral of Ann Leary to attend and Sister Bernadette's birthday in Hungary to honour, which I do every year through Interflora. My own birthday was on June 18th and Joan Kirk, a great friend to whose husband I used to take Holy Communion, had her birthday on the 19th.

My Brother at this time was very sick and, sadly, on June 21st he died. In my diary it reads "Arf died this evening, a great man." My Brother was buried from SS. Peter and Paul's Church on the Thursday morning and the Academy was opened on June 26th the following day.

Bishop Vin Nichols thoughtfully made a special mention of Arf before Holy Mass began. There was a huge attendance which came for the opening of the Academy and we were glad to welcome Dr. Mumtaz Husain who was able to recall our first days in Pakistan. Mumtaz was in charge of the Combined Military Hospital in Rawalpindi and I often consulted him when I was starting our first Hospice in his country. So it was appropriate for him to be present at the opening of the Academy.

There were quite a few priests at this opening Mass. Fr. Paddy Doyle, from Ireland, Mgr. Vin Hughes, a great friend of mine for many years, and Fr. John Taylor, who had been Chairman of our Hospice in Rawalpindi, Canon Casey a great friend of the Hospice for many years and Fr. Joseph Jones, who was a student with me in Mill Hill and was now working for the Mill Hill Society in Ireland.

St Joseph's Hospice. The Academy

Bishop Nichols cut the tape and we were open. He gave us a very inspiring sermon during the Mass and then went round every room with his Blessing. Bishop John Rawsthorne, also a cousin of mine, graced the occasion with his presence and gave an excellent talk too. Fr. Maurice McGill, Superior General of the Mill Hill Fathers, was pleased to attend and also gave us an inspiring speech. We are very grateful to Fr. Maurice for the kindnesses he has shown over the years. Fortunately for us, the occasion was videoed by Eric Durkin who for many weeks was busy making copies to send out to the special guests.

On July 7th I gave a talk to Professor Sells' students from Liverpool University and then had time to rejoice in the thirty-sixth anniversary of my Ordination on July 8th. Jacobs the famous Cream Cracker factory in Bootle presented us with a cheque and on July 18th I married Mary Ashcroft to Danny Hamilton in St. Mary's Church, Little Crosby. Mary was one of our nurses who volunteered to go to Honduras with her sister Janet. I had already married Janet to Bill Jackson, a few years previously. Mary moved up to Glasgow and is now living there.

Little Cathy Venton came for her interview at this time. I use the word 'little' advisedly. She seemed to be about four feet nothing ! Cathy did great work for us in Honduras. She had a great passion for reading books, a habit which stood her in good stead in her time in Central America.

Shortly after this I celebrated Mass with Canon Jimmy Collins for his Jubilee in St. Joseph The Worker in Kirkby. Jimmy's sister was a patient with us and it was a great pleasure to travel with her to Fr. Jimmy's church for this special Mass.

Billy Butler was putting on a show for us in the Civic Hall in Crosby and I have notes to remind me to make some programmes of words and music for the sick and one of my notes reads: 'Never got round to it'. What I had intended to do was to contact the B.B.C. to put on a programme, weekly or monthly, for the sick and to play requests for people who were ill. Maybe there's time to do it still. Perhaps now is the time to get round to it.

A pleasant diversion was to go to Settle to a summer house of one of Rita's friends. Settle is a beautiful spot in Yorkshire and on a journey there one sees some of the most beautiful scenery in the country.

By August 16th a new tabernacle donated by John and Mary Carson was placed in the Academy. It was of a special design by Robin McGhie incorporating the Mogol Arch and within it the Celtic Cross to show that Christ had died for all men. The altar, which was built and donated by Terry Sarsfield, also had the Mogol Arch inscribed on it. It is a nice link with our Pakistan Hospice and our contact with the Muslim world. I had the great joy of celebrating the first Holy Mass at our new altar. Believe it or not, despite everything that was happening my thoughts were moving towards Christmas.

There was a note in my diary which tells me to contact Fr. Piers Grant-Ferris O.S.B. who mentioned to me that a relation of his kept llamas and I wanted a llama for the Pageant on Christmas Eve. As it turned out the llamas were not available and I had to go to a circus in Liverpool to obtain these shortly before Christmas Midnight Mass.

Rita's birthday was on August 18th which we celebrated with due acclaim. Then I was off to Belgium to marry Kirsten de Brandt to Patrick van Bruyssels in Brussels. Mr. de Brandt informed me that he wanted me to conduct the wedding but the thought of doing it in Dutch or Flemish made me apprehensive and I telephoned Mr. de Brandt that I would probably be late for the wedding and it would be better to get the parish priest to perform the ceremony. When Fil, Terry and myself arrived outside the church there stood Mrs. de Brandt. We were late.

Everyone had gone into the church including the bride and groom. Mrs. de Brandt came towards me and took me by the arm and said, "You are going to marry my daughter." So I hastily went to practise my Flemish with the parish priest. He was very accommodating. We had most of the readings in Flemish and the actual marriage ceremony in Flemish too. I gave the sermon in English as most of the people there understood English and the Canon of the Mass was said in Latin. Thank God I got through the ceremony. I was surprised that Filomena and Terry didn't congratulate me on my linguistic ability !

On September 1st a Mexican girl called Angelica joined our staff as a nurse whilst she was studying engineering in Liverpool. Ann and Louis Coelho, who had been supporters of our Association for a long time, came to visit to present a cheque to us. Events seemed to increase considerably in the October because we had a Knights of St. Columba retreat on October 11th and on the same day we had our Annual Rosary Rally. Hundreds of people came from local parishes to say the Rosary with us and Leo Connor played suitable hymns to Our Lady.

On the 18th we had a retreat for the Union of Catholic Mothers from St. Gregory's parish, Lydiate, and on the 31st we had a Day of Recollection. So we prayed for the many graces we needed and encouraged as many people as possible to join us in these functions.

Sabrina and Fatima

23

WE had been busy at this time preparing for our little girl Sabrina to arrive from Pakistan. Because of her lack of English it was necessary to ask one of my friends, Sam Qasir, in London whether or not his daughter could come up and spend some time with us. Sybil duly came on November 9th and on the 10th Sabrina arrived at Manchester Airport.

We met her there on her own, sitting in the waiting room, crying and very upset. Filomena made some remarks to help her get over her bout of crying and I remember buying her a big Toblerone. It worked and she ate the whole bar !

She had travelled with an American lady from Rawalpindi to Manchester and British Airways had taken over from there. It was an odd experience meeting up with her. We realised with difficulty she was one of our own girls, quite literally because when she was six months old we, as an organisation, had adopted her. Poor Sabrina was suffering from a congenital handicap which forced her to come to us for operations. She must have felt terrible herself because she kept asking for Sister Mary and the Hospice in Pakistan. She had no concept, of course, of how far she had come, or where Pakistan was in relation to Britain and so these first few days were very crucial but also very special.

We marvelled at her attempt to learn English and she adopted her own words and expressions to signify what she wanted. She felt really lost so we took her to our hearts which was the only thing that we could do. Arrangements had been made through Dr. Irene Desmet to fix up appointments with Mr. Rickwood who was a consultant in Alder Hey Hospital in Liverpool. I took Sabrina to see him and he arranged for her first major operation.

Fortunately at the time we had working for us a nurse called Fatima Perera from Sri Lanka. She was at hand to give succour and help and the two of them went into Alder Hey Hospital, both very apprehensive as to what was going to take place. Thank God the operation was successful and Sabrina was returned to us with the prospect of having a further operation in a year's time. It was wonderful to see how Fatima adapted herself to the role of mother and has acted in that capacity ever since.

Sabrina had come on a year's visa but she needed a new visa to stay with us for further medical help. With the necessary letters from Alder Hey Hospital we got an extension for Sabrina for a further year, the first of many one-year extensions we had to obtain. The second operation took place in 1995 and, thank God, was very successful. This was a relatively new operation involving microsurgery.

All of us were very concerned, but Mr. Turnock, a new consultant, performed minor miracles and everything, thank God, up to the moment has been working well. Fatima, naturally, has to keep up her attentive attitude and, as Sabrina grows up, has to be even more careful. Sabrina started school at St. Mary's primary in Little Crosby, doing well and taking part in most of the activities, even sports events. She is now at Holy Family school in Thornton.

Miscellaneous Events

24

ON November 14th 1992 Fr. John Doran, Vocations Director for the Mill Hill Fathers, brought four lads from his group who are intending to become priests to work at Thornton. It is a good introduction for these lads to the seminary life. It takes a few years to prepare them well to adapt themselves to the rigours of the seminary !

Towards the end of November I booked six seats for the Barber of Seville at the Empire Theatre in Liverpool. We enjoyed this performance and had a meal afterwards in the Academy.

An important activity in the December of this year was to accept an invitation to open the site of The Woodlands hospice in the grounds of Fazakerley Hospital. As usual I felt nervous because all the big people from the Sefton Health Authority were present and I remember muttering something about a symbiotic exchange between patient and nurse to give people my idea of the holistic approach to the caring of the sick. I really didn't have to do anything except say a few words and declare the ground open and wish the medical team success.

But before that I had been in Sudbury at Rosemary Turnbull's house. Both Rosemary and her husband Paul are very supportive members of our Sudbury group and it was a great joy to meet all our helpers down in this southerly outpost of ours. They have remained so loyal and put their trust in us completely. We have to return and acknowledge that trust by doing our best for them all.

Thornton Parish Council under the leadership of Charles Coles came to have their meeting in the Cardinal Vaughan Library in the Academy, which they normally do once a month. It is nice to meet up with our local parish councillors.

The Air Squadron in Enbutt Lane presented us with a huge hamper for Christmas and we looked forward to the Capriol Singers coming to the Hospice on December 20th. Then there were the usual festivities for Christmas and we had our live Crib as is our custom every year. We commemorated Bishop Hettinga's anniversary on the 26th and then finished the year with Midnight Mass on December 31st.

In 1993 we had a surprise visit from Professor Jack Scarisbrick, the founder of the Life organisation. It was a great pleasure to talk with him and learn how widespread the Life organisation had become in Britain and his plans to build a Life Centre in Liverpool.

But we had a few funerals in January about which we were all very sad. There was May Russell who was married to my cousin, a lady called Kathleen Stannanought who very kindly had left us something in her will and the funeral of auxiliary nurse Billy Grieveson who was very close to us and particularly to the O'Leary family. Billy had been with us shortly before he had died but unfortunately had not conveyed to us his inner feelings. He was a good lad. I conveyed the news of his death to Catherine O'Leary who was at our Hospice in Honduras. She and her family had befriended Billy on so many occasions and she was very sad when she heard of his demise.

On a lighter note the Norah Christina School of Dancing put on a show for us at the Crosby Civic Hall which was an outstanding success. Norah has done so many functions for us and we are very grateful to her for her many kindnesses.

On February 9th I went down to Bristol to say goodbye to Mr. and Mrs. Quadros whose daughter had a house there. The Quadros family had decided to emigrate to Canada and I had the opportunity of showing them our latest video. I also showed them a copy of 'This Is Your Life' in which Mrs. Quadros herself took part. They were a contact, of course, with our Hospice in Rawalpindi because they were on my first Committee there.

We also had another type of contact with Rawalpindi in the person of Carmen de la Pena from Spain, as she was the niece of the first matron of our Hospice in Rawalpindi, Sister Maria Dolores F.M.M. It was nice to receive Carmen and have her associated with our work and I was surprised to find how alike she was to her mother's sister, Maria Dolores. Sister Maria Dolores was a very spiritual person and like the other F.M.M.s was very devoted to her work. We were so blessed when she was appointed to look after our first faltering steps in Rawalpindi in those early days.

On the 13th 'The Cream of the Barley' band raised £1,400 for us at St. William of York Church in Thornton due to the enthusiasm shown on our behalf by Fr. Vin Fedigan.

On a different tack I gave a talk, believe it or not, to the School of Advanced Motorists at the Royal Clifton Hotel in Southport and they promised to help us in our work.

Then on the February 20th we had our first preparatory meeting for our next Conference in the Aquinas Hall. I had wanted the Aquinas Hall in the Academy to be the venue for seminars and talks on religious aspects of our Catholic Faith. Peter Garrett from the Life organisation and his brother Gregory helped Filomena and myself to work out a programme.

Our Conference was called 'Cradles to Graves'. It needed a lot of planning time. We were fortunate to choose very good speakers. David Alton M.P. opened the event by giving us a very enlightened talk on the value of life and the horridness of abortion. Mr. de Brandt from Belgium provided us with a very reasoned talk on the attitude of the Church in Europe to abortion and euthanasia. The two Garrett brothers contributed with a prayerful meditation and Peter Garrett stressed the part that the Life organisation had to play in the fight against abortion and euthanasia. Filomena O'Leary treated the topic from the family point of view and John Carson gave us a brilliant resume of the day's talks. We had Holy Mass and an evening of entertainment which everyone enjoyed.

We said goodbye to Marie Rawsthorne and Catherine O'Leary on May 17th and wished them well on their second tour to our Hospice in Honduras, both excellent nurses. They were able to deal with the problems which any organisation has in Central America and they did it very competently. Joining them, on her first tour, was Catherine's younger sister Elizabeth. At this time Nina Arpino from our Sudbury Group had died and Filomena and myself represented the rest of the Management Committee at her funeral on June 4th.

We came back to help Fatima prepare little Sabrina for her first Holy Communion on June 25th. Once more we were thrown into the realm of rejoicing with the 'Evening of Midsummer Madness' on June 23rd and a function put on by the Round Table at the Greyhound in Ormskirk. On August 4th Mother Raymond, who had been instrumental in getting her sisters, The Franciscan Missionaries of Mary, to work for us in Rawalpindi, was 100 years of age.

By way of diversion we put on our Strawberry Fayre on July 10th. It was a great success. That same weekend the Secular Franciscan Order came here for a day of prayer and retreat and Fr. Hughes gave another retreat for his parish here on July 31st.

At the beginning of August we welcomed Sidonie Puech from France who had been very friendly with my Brother Arthur. She had come for a week's holiday to stay in the Hospice and we enjoyed her presence with us.

Sadness tinged our activities again with the funeral of Margaret Killourhy, a very saintly person. Her husband Michael bore his sadness very bravely. He always used to tell us the story of how he once played professional football with Stanley Matthews and Tommy Lawton. His biggest claim to fame, however, was when he took a penalty at Anfield against Liverpool and missed the goal completely. He told me that the ball had hit the 'O' of Bovril on the hoardings behind the goal. He got a tremendous cheer, of course, for having missed the penalty. He is always welcome here and I get him to tell the story to many of my friends.

On August 16th, Dr. Ged Corcoran officially took up his post as a consultant oncologist. We thought it would be a good idea to start his posting with a special Mass for him in our Chapel in San Jose.

Soon after that I went up with Rita to my cousin Celia in Leeds to celebrate Rita's birthday and the fact that they hadn't met up for such a long time. It was very appropriate that the film Fantastic Facts was shown on television that evening. This featured our Imprint and Richard Maude, whom I have mentioned previously and who was married to my cousin Celia, provided expert commentary on the production. Fiona Armstrong presented the programme.

Our eyes were focused on the 17th when John McKenzie from Australia came into town. We booked a table at the Blundellsands Hotel and enjoyed his Australian twang. John became a great friend and has always kept in contact with us. Dr. John Hayes, a good friend of the Hospice, died and his funeral was on the 25th

For a change I took a group to the Empire Theatre for a performance of the Pirates of Penzance performed by the D'Oyly Carte Opera Company and after the show returned to the Cardinal Vaughan Library to enjoy a nice meal. A fitting way to round off the evening.

October opened in a very lively fashion with a magnificent ceilidh put on in the Academy by Pat Savage. But our thoughts were saddened at this time by the death of one of our patients in the Academy, Charles Monaghan. Charlie had been the manager of the Westminster Bank in Crosby when I had started my work at the Hospice in Rawalpindi. He helped to guide me through the first stages of our fund-raising. It was to him that my Mother gave the first donation to our Association, from a coffee morning, of £86. I was in regular contact with him when I was in Pakistan and it was good to know that we were able to help him in his last days. The circle had turned round fully.

On October 1st 1996 I got a great surprise. One of my friends whom I have mentioned on quite a few occasions, Charles Evans, (he is the one who has done all the big marathons for us) presented me with a little gift, which he said was from his wife Lynn. I registered my thanks with him and he said:

"Do you know what is in that jar?"

I said, "No",

He said, "That is St. Theresa's Jam."

It was the feast of St. Theresa. He was telling me that his wife had a great devotion to her, as St. Theresa was responsible for her conversion to the Catholic Faith. Charles had been married to her for eight years and for some reason or other she had a habit of praying to St. Theresa (the Little Flower, that is–not Avila). One morning she got a surprise when she opened the front door. It was in December and very cold and there on the doormat were two rose petals. She immediately thought of St. Theresa and brought it to her mind that this was a sign for her to make the final decision. She became a Catholic shortly after and every year on St. Theresa's feast day she makes this special jam, of which I am proud to have a jar. It is nice to have presents of this nature which bring a lot of joy into one's life.

Looking at my diary for 1993, I see that in October we went down to the funeral of Marguerita Freely who had been the leader of our Sudbury group for a number of years. She was very fond of our Association and raised many thousands of pounds on our behalf. We expressed our condolences to Gerald and the family.

David Moorhead brought students from the local school and I showed them a video and gave them refreshments. A novel form of entertainment was put on in the Academy, when a Bolivian group came to give us an evening of South American music. We all enjoyed this and we were glad to be able to give our support to these Bolivian singers and dancers.

I went up to Durham to the funeral of my cousin Nell Endean on October 29th and on the 31st we commemorated the sixth anniversary of our Gala Concert at the Philharmonic Hall by playing the video of the whole concert. It was most enjoyable and very refreshing.

Then we said goodbye to Fatima and Sabrina. Sabrina went back to Pakistan for a holiday because I was anxious for her not to lose her Urdu and to become acquainted again with her friends in the Hospice, whilst Fatima went to her own country, Sri Lanka, to be with her family over the Christmas period.

Una O'Dowd left for her work abroad and we were back once again with our Christmas preparations. Fr. Pat Harnet put on a retreat for the St. Mary's College boys on December 10th and another retreat was held by John Mannion, the uncle of Rosa Mannion, the soprano. The Georgian Singers from Maghull came to sing carols for us and our official carol concert was given by the Ormskirk Town Band on December 21st.

Once again we had our Christmas Pageant which was enjoyed by all and once more we commemorated with a special Mass for Bishop Hettinga on the 26th, his anniversary. With the usual Midnight Mass on December 31st the year was brought to a close, and we looked forward to the next year.

If one were to make a list of the number of people associated with St. Joseph's Hospice, you could gauge from it that the number of birthdays which we have to celebrate is enormous. With a staff of about 90 together with members of families who are associated with us, we get a birthday nearly every day !! 1994 brought its usual cluster of celebrations and funerals. Helen Taylor in Hettinga House was 90 and Fr. Johnny Bull celebrated his 90th in Freshfield.

But beating them all was Mr. John Cody, who lives in the same avenue as myself. He was 100. There hasn't been a time when I have not known Mr. Cody. When I was a youngster I used to see him coming along Enfield Avenue on his bicycle on his way to work. He is a very staunch Catholic and as far as I can remember, he used to go to Mass every day in SS. Peter and Paul's Church in Crosby. He is a great man who is not only a gifted musician but a wonderful painter. He did many pictures for us. There was a recording made a few years ago of the Bohemian Girl and my Sister Rita bought it for him. Today he plays it very often with great enjoyment. We put on a special party in the Academy for Mr. Cody's birthday and when the party broke up at midnight he was the one who was still on the floor and still dancing. Mr. Cody has been a great example to all of us and we thank him for his great generosity. [As these Memoirs were being completed in the spring of 2000, he was still going strong at 106 !]

We had Fred Bates's Golden Wedding as well to celebrate. Fred has grown flowers for us for a number of years and has won many prizes for them. It was good to rejoice with himself and his wife Monica.

Joan Lawson, who had been working in the Hospice for many years, decided it was time to retire and we gave her as good a send off as we possibly could. She was a very devoted nurse and made a special point of caring for each one of our patients. Again a marvellous example for us to follow. A Dr. John Clements, who had worked in our Hospice in San Francisco in 1975, came to see us. He was very worried about his father and asked if we could accommodate him. It was nice to meet John once again.

It was at this time that Rachel Birch's father died. He had been associated with many projects in his home parish in Macclesfield and we sent our sympathies to his wife Margaret. They had encouraged Rachel so often and for so long when she worked for us in Honduras.

The Catholic Men's Society had their annual meeting in the Cardinal Vaughan Library and the Secular Franciscan Order had a special Mass and celebrations on February 15th. We were pleased to hear that Jenny and Roger from a local hostelry had, for a fourth time, collected a lot of money for us and I went along to receive this personally and once again had another photograph taken.

Peter Deary made contact with UMIST at the University of Manchester and we took the mattress cover along to have some spectrometry performed on the Imprint. As we guessed nothing spectacular came from this meeting, although the scientists put it to every test available to them.

On March 4th Fatima came back from her holiday and on her way back picked up Sabrina in Pakistan. At Manchester Airport, Sabrina refused to speak English to me and spoke only Urdu. It was a bit difficult trying to remember nouns and verbs from my Urdu vocabulary, but after one or two days she began to speak English again . . . much to our relief.

We were able to celebrate at Hettinga House the fact that Ruth Hislop had been 20 years with us as a patient. Ruth had come on really well with us. When she was first admitted she had a great interest in watching wrestling and every Friday night she would go along with her husband to the Stadium in Liverpool and see a good wrestling match. She walked with difficulty and always needed help. My favourite task was to do the tango with her from the lounge to the dining room, which she always seemed to enjoy.

Frank McGreavey in Our Lady's, Formby, once again organised the Catholic Men's Society to present us with a big cheque for which we were extremely grateful.

There was also a big function put on by Maureen O'Boyle at the Railway Pub in Ormskirk and St. Benet's had a hot pot supper in the April.

The Associates of the Sisters of Mercy came to us for an afternoon of prayer and on a lighter note we had another very successful ceilidh put on by Pat Savage in the Academy.

This brought us up to our May Procession which took place on May 1st and the Secular Franciscan Order had a conference on May 7th followed on May

12th by a special Mass commemorating the anniversary of Edel Quinn, whose cause for canonisation is being promoted by the Legion of Mary. Fr. Hughes brought his parish to us for a Day of Recollection on May 14th and on the following day the Union of Catholic Mothers from St. Gregory's parish came for a short retreat.

However, we were all saddened by the sudden death on May 19th of Dr. Marie Cleary. She had been our consultant for 20 years and everyone felt a great sense of personal loss. I celebrated the Mass for her funeral in SS. Peter and Paul's, Crosby.

John McKenzie, our friend in Australia, requested that an award be made in memory of his mother Dorothy McKenzie. The first winners were Val Soens from Hettinga House and Paula Claro from Thornton. This award is made every year for the best non-registered nurse, and the most caring nurse, and these two nurses had worked very solidly with us.

There was a big celebration, too, for the centenary of SS. Peter and Paul's Church, Crosby, in which I was invited to participate. I was baptised in SS. Peter and Paul's, confirmed there and I said my First Mass there with my Mum and Dad present together with all my family and friends. Mum and Dad were pillars of the Church and it was great to be able to celebrate their memory as well as the church. In the late 1930s, the B.B.C did a couple of broadcasts of an evening service and Benediction from the church and I still have letters of appreciation which were sent to my Father expressing the joy of the listeners to the music of these evening services.

On June 10th we had a healing Mass organised by Fr. Jimmy Collins. This was a special event from which we all drew a lot of spiritual satisfaction and contentment. On June 18th we said goodbye to Marie Cambray, Anne McGovern and Clare Leonard to Honduras to join the very successful team there. Meanwhile there was a lot happening in Guatemala, where our Hospice was thriving and Fr. Frank Smith in Ecuador sent us his usual faxes thanking us for the customary help we give him in Guayaquil.

Fr. Francis came to sing for us on my birthday and I note on July 19th I said goodbye to Cath O'Leary, who was returning once again to Honduras, and to Maureen Keane who was proceeding to Guatemala. They are two great girls. God has blessed us with some very noble people to carry on the work started so many years previously.

But among the usual crop of sad events and happy moments, we had the funeral of Thelma Merino, the wife of Captain Frank Merino, one of our office staff. Thelma had been our chief fundraiser and had often performed minor miracles for us. Also the funeral of Patrick Curry took place. Patrick had been a great friend of St. Joseph's Hospice, so it was an honour to say his Requiem in our Academy.

This sad note was compensated by Charles Evans and his grandson Jamie doing a sponsored cycle for us to Our Lady's Shrine in Walsingham. As usual both of them raised thousands of pounds. At this time I went down to Cold Ash, in Berkshire, to see Mother Raymond, the former provincial of the Franciscan Missionaries of Mary, who was 101. I was delighted to see that she remembered me from our first days in Rawalpindi. She was a real 'mulier fortis' and all the sisters were scared of her when she became hot-headed. She had a very manly booming voice. I got on famously with her and it was a great happiness to welcome her on her occasional tours to Pakistan. A convert to Catholicism, she had a great devotion to the Blessed Sacrament.

Sabrina started school at St. Mary's, Little Crosby, which is an idyllic village, and in the little school there were only 80 students. This school my mother had attended when she was a young girl. Sabrina settled in quite quickly despite the fact that she had to work in English. But Fatima guided her and was always at her side to assist her in difficulties.

We had a big meeting with Holy Mass and discussions for the Legion of Mary and the Crosby physiotherapy group had a special day in our hydrotherapy pool and gave lectures and demonstrations. We said goodbye to Cathy Pearson, Cathy Venton, Lucy Murray and Liz Long to Central America. The Secular Franciscan Order spiritually supported us again with their celebration on October 3rd of the special 'Transitus'. Not to be outdone in prayer, the Walsingham Association held their retreat in our Academy and we commemorated the anniversaries of Eamonn Andrews and Francis Xavier Quadros who had emigrated and died in Canada. 'Curly' (as they used to call him) Quadros was one of our principal Committee Members in Rawalpindi.

We continue to pray for 'Curly' and other deceased members of our Committee: Jim Allen, Gerry Tims, Dr. Marie Cleary, Derek Smith, John Pinto, and Sylvester Gulfam. Without a doubt they have all been protecting us. The example they gave us was superb and they are still helping us from above.

It was getting near Christmas and we had a lot of work to do once again, as we do every Christmas, preparing to distribute our Christmas cards. The hubbub of Christmas is always quite dramatic preparing for the Pageant for Christmas Eve night–finding Our Lady, St. Joseph and the baby Jesus, the llamas, the donkey and making a host of other preparations, so that Christmas Night will be very memorable. Thank God it always is and turns out well.

We had been preparing for our Second Gala Concert in the October but a minor complication arose when I had to go for an operation in Fazakerley

Hospital and it became evident that I wouldn't be available for the Gala Concert in October and so it was postponed. Recuperation in Park House, Waterloo, under the care of Sister Kevin, made a new man of me.

One can easily forget the people who come on a regular basis to pray with our patients and to offer their prayers to God on our behalf. Marian Maher and her husband Peter, Maureen Blain and her husband Peter, come along every two weeks and have been responsible for a large spiritual input which keeps our work in being.

At the beginning of January, 1995 we thought of Misha our faithful friend. She had died the previous January. We recalled what a beautiful Irish wolfhound she was and how our patients loved her.

Caroline Horsley came on January 9th for her interview, and she went on to do wonderful things for us in Central America. Caroline has a very special gift for administration and has great organising ability. There is something very extraordinary about her. The usual 'Splosh and Nosh' took place in the Coach House and the hydrotherapy pool. Joan McNeil, the wife of Malcolm, and one of our regular Rosary Group, sadly died and we had her funeral on the 25th.

Meanwhile we were busily preparing ourselves to welcome the Missionary Banner of Our Lady of Guadalupe. The Image of Our Lady had been going around the country and we were very proud to be the only place in the Liverpool area to be host to her on February 7th. It was a wonderful day. Holy Mass was celebrated and Fr. Carney and one or two other priests gave lectures on this wonderful vision of Our Lady. She certainly attracted us to do her work more earnestly, as she has inspired so many people in Central and South America. Her apparition to Juan Diego in 1531 is very maternal and she brings us her Son Christ in a very loving way. I placed all of our work in Central and South America under her tutelage because her protection is the only way by which we can beat the evil of deprivation and hunger. The thousands of people who come to her Basilica in Guadalupe show a very distinctive type of faith.

Then we heard the great news that a good friend of ours, Bishop Rubiano of Cucuta, had been appointed Archbishop of Bogota in Colombia. We sent notice from our Management Committee of our congratulations to him and we hope that he will keep an eye on our Colombian ventures.

Grainne O'Hara and Clare Leonard left for their work in Central America and Niamh Killilea arrived on February 25th for her interview. March opened with a donation from the Freemasons, the first of quite a few presentations from this organisation. On March 19th we had our usual Annual General

Meeting on the Feast of St. Joseph and I gave my Annual Report as is the custom on that day.

On April 7th I left with Filomena to visit the Mother General of the Franciscan Missionaries of Mary in Rome. The reason for this visit was to try and find some nursing Sisters for our projects in Peru. Soon after this we visited their Provincial House in Lima requesting their Provincial to send us Sisters. Unfortunately they had no nursing Sisters they could spare and we came away feeling rather helpless and hopeless. But to enliven our hearts Cath O'Leary and Carolyn Barber came back from Central America to take a holiday from their work in Honduras. I had an invitation from Sally and John Kilbride to go to the ordination of their son Thomas in Glasgow. Sally and John were friends of mine from Glasgow University and they have often sent me cheques and donations. I also had the good fortune to meet Mary and Ron Laycock when at University. Ron's Liverpool accent was a delight to hear. He and Mary became great friends and were very good to me. I made a lot of good friends at University but alas, there are many with whom I have not had any contact, except for the occasional bouquet of flowers which I send to Alice and Bruno Felletti. A great pity because all these friends were very good to me. On April 22nd Dr. Louise Bates came for an interview expressing her wish to work in our Central American ventures. She had studied some Spanish at school and this came in handy for her in her work for us abroad.

St Joseph's Hospice, San Francisco Peru

151

The Alzheimer's Society presented us with a cheque on April 26th and then on April 29th Ruth O'Leary, a daughter of Fil and Terry, married Stephen French from Glasgow at SS. Peter and Paul's Church in Crosby and the reception was held at the Aquinas Hall in the Academy. We welcomed so many people to this celebration and despite our Sassenach accents we were able to give Ruth and Stephen our very best wishes.

We held a day of prayer with Tony Hickey from the Medjugorje Centre in Manchester. His lectures were very incisive and very prayerful and had quite an affect on us all. Then the Catholic doctors graced us with their presence for their annual Mass and dinner. A film of our work was shown to them after their repast and they seemed to have enjoyed their evening.

Symbiosis and more Interesting Events

25

IN the care of the sick and the dying the word 'holism' is often used. We have tried to produce this holistic attitude among our staff and patients so that the symbiotic approach is effected.

Everyone knows what the principle of symbiosis is. When a friend, doctor or nurse goes to a patient, they go not only as qualified people but also as themselves and the patient responds in the same way they are greeted. The nurse may bandage cuts and bruises but she won't do anything for the inner person if the only thing she brings is her expertise. But it is the whole person of the doctor, nurse and carer which the sick person will respond to in a whole way. It is very difficult to teach an holistic approach these days. I suppose that has always been the case, but to elicit acts of spiritual endearment from one person to another, there has to be a well-grounded, spiritual prayerful input. Some people come to the sick to be refreshed and they bring with them the armoury of prayer.

And so we have regular meetings of the Secular Franciscan Order and the Serra Society who come to us every two weeks. The Legion of Mary meets every Friday in St. Joseph's Room. The local Cursillo movement–part of a worldwide organisation which meets for prayer–is encouraged to come to us on the first Wednesday of every month and they have Holy Mass and a talk. Every Monday afternoon Bernard and Marie Coyne, along with Malcolm McNeil, organise the Stations of the Cross. We are very grateful to them for this.

The Cenacle started to meet in 1995. In one of the messages to the children at Fatima, Our Lady requested us to make the first Saturday of each month a time of prayer which was to include Holy Mass, Rosary and Confession. She promised us great graces. The Marian Movement for priests, which now includes the laity, is a movement dedicated especially to pray for priests and the peace of the world. Thank God, we have a very flourishing group.

Nearly every day of the year there are seminars and conferences for the local health authority and I hope that in some way the spiritual atmosphere of our work sinks into the people attending them. Not only do we have a Crucifix in the Aquinas Hall but statues of Our Lady and St. Joseph look down upon participants and this can only be good.

The little chapel on the first floor in the Academy and the chapel in our main building in San Jose, ensure us that Christ has His own room in our Hospices. He must be part of our work. The main problem, of course, is that His Presence is often forgotten and we do not give sufficient thought to His being among us. In actual fact He is always present in a special way at the bed of a sick patient. When a person dies, one kneels down and says a prayer for the one who is sick. But the moment of death is a very special happening when God becomes present in a particular way. I often feel that having prayed for a patient at one moment, the next moment the patient has gone to God and one finds oneself praying to them to ask them to help us, a piece of spiritual blackmail if you like, entertaining the thought that if we cared for them here, the first thing they do is to look down on us, protect us and pray for us in Heaven.

We have to learn by experience. The majority of people would take little heed and would term the foregoing as gibberish, but it is true. Our love for a sick person transcends all bonds, even death itself, and every person who dies takes our love to God. God is always present in His love but we rarely tell Him of our love. There are just three words needed. 'I love you'. I think that is the secret of the peace which comes upon a dying patient. When love is present it becomes stronger and more effective than the physical medicine that is being taken.

The highlight of our celebrations in May 1995 was the VE Day celebrations – 'The Stage Door Canteen', which was organised by Anne Smith. She and Derek, both Committee members, had looked forward so much to this evening and had made many preparations for it. Derek's untimely death on March 17th had denied us his company and it was to his memory that the evening was dedicated.

The Serra Society of the North of England held their annual meeting with Holy Mass and a buffet in the Academy. They all seemed to enjoy it. The students from the University came for their usual talks and the Associates of the Sisters of Mercy held their retreat on May 21st.

At this time we were all hard at work preparing for the delegation which was coming from Holland. They had asked us to help them prepare to build a hospice in Holland. The Dutch people are at the forefront of the euthanasia debate, so we decided to do our utmost to entertain and talk to them the best way we could. Nurses from Thornton and Hettinga gave talks and lectures and showed videos of our work, both here and abroad. I was very proud of our staff for the way in which they tackled the problems of speechifying because it is not an easy thing to do. But we tempered our talks and discussions with good meals, a few drinks and an evening at Highfield Hall, in Northop, North Wales. Thanks to Molly Miller for her magnificent reception.

I was able to give a version of 'Hup Holland Hup', a popular Dutch ditty which I remembered from my days in Roosendaal. They all seemed to enjoy it. This day also happened to be the 41st wedding anniversary of Filomena and Terry, so a good night was enjoyed by all.

It was at this time that we were preparing for our Conference on St. Joseph 'The Silent Witness'. Again we had good speakers, especially Fr. Pat McDonald, who stepped in at the last minute. He spoke about St. Joseph's noble calling. The conference went down very well and we concluded the evening with a programme of Desert Island Discs. I interviewed Chris McKay and he gave us a nice selection of music and showed us a video of 'The Famous Liver Building' where he was a director.

Our conference on St. Joseph was no sooner finished than we had our first meeting for another conference, this time on 'The Imprints'. We needed to do a lot of research on this conference because we were trying to compare our own Imprint with the Holy Shroud of Turin and the Image of Our Lady of Guadalupe.

On June 14th I was presented by Joe Coyne with an unusual chess set cleverly made by the pupils of Chesterfield High School, Crosby. It now has a place of honour in our Cardinal Vaughan Library.

Then on June 17th we had a special Mass for Freda and Bill Pimblett who had been connected with a patient in San Jose and they wished to celebrate their Silver Wedding anniversary. They thought it would be fitting to hold their festivities where their relation had died. We held a special Mass for them during which they exchanged their marriage vows again. We gave them a fine evening meal and they and their families enjoyed the night thoroughly. Neither was a Catholic so it was nice to be with them all.

We were due to commemorate the third anniversary of the opening of the Academy. We had a special Holy Mass followed by an enjoyable buffet and I invited Norman Cresswell to be our castaway on the Desert Island. Unfortunately his record requests didn't correspond exactly to the records I played. The amplification system wasn't working very well but Norman took it all in his stride.

Jean Keenan returned to Guatemala after her holidays at home and we celebrated Eunice Kinder's 80th birthday. Eunice and her sister Jean often come to the Hospice. Their brother, Bob Kinder was one of our first patients. Their mother spent her last years with us.

All our prayers at this time were centred on Sabrina when she had her major operation on May 9th. She came through her operation very well. Every day we thank God for sending her to us. She is that important link between ourselves and our first Hospice in Rawalpindi. Another of our patients reached the magic age of 90. Her name was Mamie Carroll, a great lady. We pulled all the stops out to make it a nice birthday for her. I don't think she realised exactly what was happening but she seemed to have enjoyed herself.

It was time now to say goodbye to Rachel Norwood, Caroline Horsley and Sister Emily. Sister Emily was from Uganda and belonged to an order established by Bishop Brandsma. She was on sabbatical leave with us and so had little hesitation to volunteer to work at our Hospice in Guatemala. I am sure she must have been the first Ugandan nun to have entered Guatemala, because we had terrible trouble over her passport. Eventually she got to our Hospice and did great work there, despite the fact that she had no Spanish and everything was so strange for her.

A view of our Hospice in Tambo, Peru

We were delighted around this time to receive Carmen Pari, a girl from Lima, Peru. She re-established our ties with our Hospices in her country. The Callao Hospice and the one in Villa El Salvador impressed Filomena and myself when we visited them in March of this year and we were delighted to see the amount of people they were able to treat. The majority of Peruvians live in very difficult circumstances, so one can imagine the horror and fear of anyone who is very ill. Both Callao and Salvador gave that service of which we were proud.

New Stations of the Cross were placed in our chapel in the San Jose Hospice in memory of Derek Smith. His wife Anne was very pleased. We were saddened once more by the death in June of Margaret Brady who had been a patient with us for many years. She had been sent to us by Mother Teresa's Sisters in Liverpool and made our Hospice in Hettinga House her home. She was a very prayerful lady and a great example to us all.

We received a visit from Jim McKinnon, a classmate of mine from Mill Hill days. He was accompanied by an economist, who tried to teach us how to convert begging into borrowing but our auditors were not having anything to do with it, so we did not proceed with his scheme unfortunately. I say 'unfortunately,' because when 'Mac' (as we used to call him) got an idea, it was usually a good one. He was very good at Theology and Philosophy, but he was especially renowned for his expertise on the piano without being able to read a note of music. The harmonisation of his left hand was very good. It was a rare gift which he had.

After the death of Dr. Marie Cleary, in 1994, we all felt very bereft because she was such a wonderful doctor, as I have already indicated, but we were grateful in 1995 for being able to secure the services of Dr. David Flanagan, who was already involved in our work and who also had been to our Hospices in Honduras and Guatemala. I asked Dr. David to join our Christmas Pagent as a shepherd. He did a wonderful job. Thank you, David, for all your kind ministrations to us all.

157

Some More Memories ...

26

ON July 5th the Union of Catholic Mothers held a hot pot supper in the Academy after attending Holy Mass and then on Saturday July 8th, the anniversary of my Ordination, a very successful 'Strawberry Fayre' was held, to which hundreds of people came. In Thornton when we celebrate this day we don't call it a Gala Day as they do at Hettinga House, it is 'The Strawberry Fayre' and gets that name because Helen Downie, so many years ago, had the first one in her big garden in College Avenue, Crosby. That was very successful and so it is repeated every year.

Jack Moran, a good friend, spurred on by Tony and Gwen Brown, had called round waiting an opportunity to show the video of his sponsored walk to Lourdes. He showed it to my Committee. Then on July 27th he took off for Lourdes, by plane this time from Speke Airport, and I went to see him off. Shortly after that on August 3rd, we had a leaving Mass for Cath O'Leary and Carolyn Barber and the parish council had their usual meeting in the Cardinal Vaughan Library.

I noted that the inauguration of the League of Friends took place on August 9th. Dorothy Hughes and her friends had been helping at St. Mary's College, Crosby, and wanted to keep the group together, so they had volunteered their services to us. They have made possible the refurbishing of Hettinga House, costing many thousands of pounds, and our thanks are due to them. This group meets monthly and has been responsible for so much good work.

On August 15th a special Mass was said on behalf of all those who suffered in Hiroshima and Nagasaki in Japan. A special V J Night was held in the Aquinas Hall and on August 18th my Sister's birthday was celebrated by enjoying a narrow boat trip along the canal, through Halsall and the beautiful Lancashire countryside.

August 25th saw myself and Filomena off to Negritos, Peru, for the Silver Jubilee of our Hospice there and we made visits to our other Hospices in Peru, Honduras, Fr. Frank Smith in Ecuador and then on to Guatemala and Mexico. It was a great privilege to go and celebrate Holy Mass once again in the Basilica of Our Lady of Guadalupe and a great blessing not only to be near the image of the Apparition of Our Lady but to witness the faith of the Mexican people. Thousands and thousands were at the Basilica and I couldn't get over how devotional the people were and how intent their vision was on the Holy Mass. The main celebrant of the Mass was a Bishop who had special responsibility among the Mexican Bishops for Third World work. His English was very good and we had a good chat. Unfortunately the taxi driver stole my camera and so the shots I had taken in Guatemala, Honduras, Ecuador and the Basilica itself were lost. A great pity, really.

Our Hospice in Negritos, Peru

On September 3rd Hettinga House had its Gala Day and we were still busy preparing for the conference on 'The Imprints' which was to be held on September 16th. We had our usual array of speakers but in addition to them we had Dr. Philip Callahan who was an expert on the Apparition of Our Lady of Guadalupe. He had been given special permission from the Mexican Government to do scientific work on the Tilma, Juan Diego's garment on which Our Lady's image is visible. He is a brilliant scientist and was able to explain to us the connection between the Holy Shroud, our own Imprint and that of Our Lady of Guadalupe. Apart from being a very good scientist he is also a very devotional man and impressed all of us deeply. He had a meeting with Chris Heneghan, the son of Kevin Heneghan whose article on the Holy Shroud I had read many years ago in the Catholic Herald. Chris was writing a special account of our Imprint for publication and Dr. Philip was able to assist him.

I have a note in my diary to send flowers to Mrs. Sylvester Gulfam. It was the first anniversary of her husband's death and we wanted to reassure her that we would remember to pray for him. Sylvester was an outstanding person in Rawalpindi and a great Catholic. We wanted him here when we started our project in Thornton, but he had a wonderful job offered to him in the United States together with a visa. He studied hard and was ordained a deacon in the Chicago Archdiocese. I had known Sylvester from the beginnings of our Hospice in Rawalpindi and if one were looking for a leader among the Christian community, Sylvester would be one's choice. His mother and father were very poor but he had taught himself how to build houses and built a very nice place for himself near the Holy Family Hospital where he worked. The people all looked up to him and expected great things from him. He did achieve wonderful things, principally, I imagine, because of his spiritual outlook on life.

At this time Kay Walsh, who lived in America and who had worked for us for some time in Honduras, took off again to join our girls in their work there. Kay is quite a remarkable lady. She must be in her early sixties but despite the extremely hot climate in Honduras, she still volunteers to go and work for us once a year. One meets very few people of that ilk.

During this time Fr. Frank Smith came home for a well-earned rest but sadly his brother died during his stay at home and some of us went over to Manchester for his brother's funeral. Frank went back to Ecuador shortly after this on November 3rd to continue doing his stupendous work.

Rachel Birch, who had worked so well for us, got married to Dr. John McKay on October 7th. They had invited me to their wedding, but the Sudbury group had decided to visit us on that day and I had to be here to welcome them.

On October 11th, Niamh Killilea, Clare Leonard and Dr. Louise Bates left these shores for Central America and we bade them farewell at their leaving Mass. We were busy at this time preparing our special day of celebration on December 12th for Our Lady of Guadalupe but we had to pack in quite a few events before then. For example, the Wizard of Oz was being produced in our Academy and there were all sorts of rehearsals for that.

Fr. Frank Smith with Maria Luisa and helpers outside our Hospice in Guayaquil, Ecuador

We had been busy with getting our Gala Concert prepared and had the soloists, choir and orchestra ready. But on having a meeting with the Philharmonic Society we discovered that the choir and orchestra would not be available at the same time for the date in October we had planned. This was an oversight. So the Gala Concert was transferred to February 17th, 1996 and we had to start all over again getting soloists ready and ordering the required music. I was grateful that they had transferred the date because I didn't feel that we were prepared sufficiently for the event. So we left it in Our Lady's and St. Joseph's hands to arrange the concert for us.

Meanwhile The League of Friends were organising a dinner at the Blundellsands Hotel which we all enjoyed very much. What a great group they are.

In the November of 1995 we were busy selling our Christmas cards, calendars and diaries and preparing for our Foundation Day gathering on November 19th in the Blundellsands Hotel. As usual we celebrated with Holy Mass and a first class meal which was enjoyed by about 180 people. John Carson gave us his customary report of events which had taken place during the year and Filomena toasted the health of St. Joseph's Hospice Association in reply to John's speech.

The following day, on November 20th, Ros Taylor and Maureen Keane left for their work in Guatemala. December '95 opened with the North West

Annual Meeting of the Catholic Men's Society. On December 8th we had a special Mass for the Feast of the Immaculate Conception and the 'Hour of Grace' was held between 12 noon and one o'clock. The Rosa Mystica Group was responsible for this and again more prayers were said for us.

Then on December 12th we celebrated the Feast of Our Lady of Guadalupe with Holy Mass and a special video and a lovely meal. We prayed that Our Lady would keep near us and be always anxious to help us. On December 16th we had our usual Christmas Carol Concert with the Ormskirk Town Band and many people came along to the Aquinas Hall to sing their Yuletide songs.

On Christmas Eve we had our Christmas Pageant with Our Lady on the donkey with St. Joseph leading. We had llamas as usual and I have a note in my diary that this Christmas was very, very enjoyable.

Kathy and Peter Brannan, two great friends, held their Golden Wedding on December 26th and we once more commemorated the anniversary of Bishop Hettinga's death with a special Mass at Hettinga House.

Philip Daley our printer had his 40th birthday on December 30th and many of his friends took part in the celebrations and had a great night. My diary notes that on December 31st we had Midnight Mass to say farewell to the old year and to pray for graces and blessings in the New Year. There is a big 'Deo Gratias' at the end of the page on December 31st to thank God for all His Blessings.

There is a great feeling of satisfaction after our Christmas Pageant. Our Lady and St. Joseph and the baby Jesus have played their part well. The llamas and the animals have come and gone home and there is a great sense of quietude which has descended over the lawn at San Jose. This is always a special moment for me when hundreds of people have come to hear Midnight Mass and eventually gone home after a drink or two. The peace is superb. When everything has gone well you feel a great sense of security and happiness. You are left on your own in front of the outdoor Crib and you know that Christ has been born and has brought His peace to the world. I always feel a sense of anxiety to express my faith fervently enough to say thank you to the Christ Child who has been born for us.

Our Second Gala Concert

27

ON January 1st we had our usual enjoyable meal in Our Lady of Lourdes Presbytery hosted by Mgr. Vincent Hughes and then our thoughts turned to the big event of 1996. This was the Gala Concert to be held in the Philharmonic Hall on February 17th.

The Gala Concert is intended to bring us all together to celebrate the work of St. Joseph's Hospice Association both here at home and abroad. In order to make it a Gala occasion it is necessary to have all the ingredients there to make the evening a real Gala performance. And so our concentration and attention were given to the soloists who were about to perform for us and the choir and orchestra. The conductor, of course, holds everyone together on an occasion like this.

We were so fortunate to be able to have as our conductor Professor Ian Tracey who is not only an expert organist but holds a senior musical post in the Anglican Cathedral and is also organist to the Liverpool City Council.

Rosa Mannion was our soprano. Rosa was a St. John's Ambulance Brigade cadet when she came to work for us at the Hospice as I mentioned before. She was just 14 years of age. Rosa then seemed to disappear and I didn't meet her again until one afternoon she came out of SS. Peter and Paul's Church just as I was going in for a visit. She told me at that time that she had been to my Alma Mater in Glasgow and she had received a Gold Medal for singing. She went on to higher studies and was so successful that she was able to make her debut at Covent Garden in 1993. She has made many recordings and is recognised as one of the country's leading sopranos. She has appeared in La Traviata at The Coliseum in London, and in a Promenade Concert in the Albert Hall in 1997 she was a soloist in Schubert's Mass in A Flat Major.

Della Jones was our mezzo-soprano–she is a famous Rossinian singer. She was born in Neath and studied at the Royal College of Music and has won many prizes including the Kathleen Ferrier Memorial Scholarship. I had chosen a difficult aria from The Italian Girl in Algiers by Rossini so I was delighted that we had obtained the services of a first rate Rossinian singer.

For our tenor we chose John Mitchinson who also had studied at the Royal College of Music. One of his principal tutors was another favourite singer of mine, Heddle Nash. For many years John has appeared on the concert platform and at major musical centres throughout the world, especially in oratorio and in recitals. At present he is the head of vocal studies at the Welsh College of Music and Drama. How fortunate we were to have such a great singer.

Our bass was Michael George who had already established himself as one of Britain's most versatile bass-baritones. He was a major prize winner at the Royal College of Music.

To complete our singing group we had Brendan O'Dowda, the famous Irish tenor. Brendan had been heard by Count John McCormack and was recommended by him to study with Dr. Vincent O'Brien. Under their guidance Brendan's career took off, broadcasting on radio and later on television. He has always been in demand as a singer, particularly in Percy French's music and other Irish melodies, so we were pleased to have him as our Master of Ceremonies.

The choir was the Royal Liverpool Philharmonic Choir. It was in excess of 130 voices and, of course, there was the famous Royal Liverpool Philharmonic Orchestra. I had many chats with Anthony Lewis Crosby, present chief executive of the Philharmonic Society in Liverpool, and under his guidance our concert was assured of success.

We had quite an ambitious programme. As in 1987 we kept more or less to the same format and had a Missa Mosaica. The first part of our concert celebrated the fact that the Holy Mass has been the cornerstone of our work and I chose the musical settings of the Holy Mass, a Mosaic if you like, taking various parts of it set by different composers.

The Kyrie I picked was from Mozart's Mass No.12, a special favourite of my Mum and Dad. It was also played at my first Mass in SS. Peter and Paul's Church in Crosby in 1956. Then I chose the Gloria In Excelsis Deo from Rossini's Messa di Gloria which is quite a difficult piece to sing and needs an expert choir and soloists. We directed our minds in a celebratory hymn of praise to the Holy Trinity and we did our best to show God our anxiety to give Him the praise that is due to Him. This was followed by a delightful Offertory piece called Gloria et Honore from the Missa Sancta by Weber.

When he composed this particular melody Weber was very down with ill health, but he managed to contrive this beautiful piece for soloist and choir which helped us to express our feelings and love for our Creator.

This was followed by the pièce de résistance, the Sanctus from Gounod's Mass of Saint Cecilia. I remember my Father, who was the conductor of SS. Peter and Paul's choir in Crosby, sending me out when I was only nine or ten years of age to various members of the choir to make sure that they turned up for rehearsal. One particular night he said to me "Son–will you go and tell Charlie Sutton to make sure he attends the rehearsal because we are singing Gounod's Sanctus." I was serving the 11 o'clock Mass the following Sunday and paid particular attention to the opening bars of the tenor solo as my Dad had told me.

I remembered the melody having heard it just once and many years later on my return from Pakistan I saw a recording in Rushworth's in Liverpool of Gounod's St. Cecilia's Mass. I bought it, came home and very quietly put the gramophone needle on the part which recorded the Sanctus. I hadn't heard the melody since that time in SS. Peter and Paul's Church but I recognised it as soon as it was played on the record and knew I had found the piece I had been looking for. It recalled for me the joy my Mum and Dad expressed about this lovely music.

John Mitchinson entertained us with a wonderful rendition of this piece and the choir gave a noble performance. This was followed by another favourite piece of mine, the Our Father by Lees. This setting of the Our Father, for me, depicts the solemnity of the words and the prayer itself. These were Our Lord's own words and His own prayer and this melody brings out in a very solemn way the sanctity of these words.

Then we moved forward to the Benedictus and Agnus Dei composed by my Father in the late 1920s. They were part of his Mass of the Sacred Heart. My Dad, of course, was organist of SS. Peter and Paul's Church in Crosby for 30 years, as well as being choirmaster. He had an extensive knowledge of Sacred Music which he passed on to me, my Brother and Sister. The final Dona Nobis Pacem of the Agnus Dei is written in chords of grandeur and the choir gave of their best.

After the action of the Holy Mass we sat and listened to Rosa Mannion and the choir giving an attractive rendition of the Laudate Dominum from the Solemn Vespers by Mozart. The point we noted in this piece was the soaring notes of the soprano which lifted our hearts and minds to God. We listened to

This was followed by Sleep, My Saviour, Sleep, a beautiful composition by the choral and the orchestral accompaniment with its singular harmonies, ensuring for us that peace which only Christ can give.W.N. Hedgcock. My

Sister had a recording of this carol made many years ago by Isobel Baillie and Heddle Nash and our soloists sang it beautifully.

Then the soloists and choir prepared for our next item which was my Dad's acknowledging Our Lady's role in our lives. In this hymn we praise her as the Ave Regina. This is an antiphon dating back to the fourth century Queen of Heaven and of Angels, asking her to show us her Son.

Then to bring the first half to its conclusion I chose the Cum Sancto Spiritu from the Messa di Gloria by Rossini. The striking contrapuntal fashion of the notes in this piece leads up to the glorious Amen. The music leaves us with a great sense of joy at having given to God the praises which are due to Him. This particular item provided us with a very exciting conclusion to the first part of our concert.

The second part of our concert was entitled Operatic Pearls and Emeralds. This was a good opportunity to produce the 'Irish Ring' which consisted of the Overture to The Bohemian Girl, by Balfe: the duet, The Moon Hath Raised Her Lamp Above, from the Lily of Killarney, by Benedict: and Scenes That Are Brightest from Maritana by Wallace. These three operas, The Bohemian Girl, the Lily of Killarney and Maritana have common ground, in that two are by Irish composers and the scene of the third is set in Ireland. These represented three lovely Emeralds for us.

Then we were on to the Pearls, the first of which was Der Vogel Fanger Bin Ich Ja from The Magic Flute by Mozart, Rossini's famous Cujus Animam from his Stabat Mater, the magical aria Pensa Alla Patria from The Italian Girl in Algiers by Rossini and La Vergine Degli Angeli from Verdi's The Force of Destiny. Verdi had the gift of expressing vocal melodies that enriched harmony and orchestration. Both Della Jones and Michael George plus the choir and orchestra did it full justice. It is a most beautiful piece. Then Brendan O'Dowda came on with his Irish melodies, a few more Emeralds–Love Thee Dearest, The Castle of Dromore and Phil the Fluter. Brendan put in a very clever Latin version of Phil the Fluter. Believe it or not, an Irish priest on the Missions in Africa said it would be quite a challenge to translate Phil the Fluter into Latin, which he did extremely well. 'Hilaritas praestabat in Philippi chorea', for example, was the final line.

After these gorgeous melodies we settled down to listen to my Tango which I had composed when I was a student in Mill Hill. The music and words were written out in the programme. Ian Tracey our conductor was wonderful. It was all great fun to join in and he incorporated everyone, soloists, choir and orchestra into a very exciting version of the Tango de San Jose. I am sure this is the only Tango called after St. Joseph !!

After the Tango we had our special Jospice Prayer and sang our own hymn which was again taken up so well by the singers, orchestra and organ. Mgr. Vincent Hughes then gave us his Blessing. In order to have a very fitting and exciting way to conclude this Gala Concert I included the very stunning piece In Sempiterna Saecula Amen from Rossini's Stabat Mater. What a wonderful night we had. Everyone enjoyed themselves and then we made our way to the restaurant in the Royal Philharmonic Hall and presented some commemorative plaques to the soloists and enjoyed listening to our favourite pianist Leo Connor. He entertained us by his expert touch on the ivories. I managed to sing some verses of my usual ditty to the melody 'Much Binding in the Marsh.' It was a last-minute composition but it went down well. Everyone was much taken by the night. The choir and soloists enjoyed one another's company and looked forward to the next Gala Concert, not knowing when that would be. As it happened we went through the whole enjoyable experience again two years later, and as these Memoirs were being prepared we were getting ready for the Third Gala Concert on March 21st, 1998 in the Royal Philharmonic Hall.

Some Reflections on Birthdays
and Launching a Record

28

FROM the end of February to July is a long time and thank goodness it was long enough to prepare ourselves mentally and physically to celebrate the birthday of Terry O'Leary who was 70 on July 27th. His family came from the ends of the earth to be with him. There was Ruth who came down from Glasgow, Anne-Marie popped over with her three children from Warrington. Bernadette, who is fairly near in Manchester, arrived. Patricia and Elizabeth came from Madrid as did John with his wife Meryl and their two children. Paul made the long trip with his son Terence from San Francisco, (the one in California). Claire was in Crosby already but unfortunately Catherine O'Leary was in Honduras, and could not make it.

They were joined by a whole host of friends and neighbours. For about three weeks they all seemed to do nothing but eat ! It was lovely to see them all, as I have known them since they were children and I was made very welcome to join in the family group.

We celebrated the occasion in the Hospice with a special Holy Mass and an evening of entertainment, at which both Terry and Filomena sang and I gave my usual ditty to celebrate the event. We thank God for these celebrations because Terry and Fil and their family over the years have been so helpful to us. It was our way of expressing our 'thank you' to Terry in particular on this day, for the way in which he has taught Spanish to all of our girls before they venture on their journey to Central or South America.

We have been very blessed by them all. Please God that will continue in the years to come.

Despite all these celebrations our different prayer groups had their meetings to make sure that our prayer life was on a strong basis and we thank them very much. They gave us also an opportunity of thanking Our Lord, Our Lady and St. Joseph for the way in which they took care of us throughout the year.

There were various other meetings which were of importance. I have highlighted just the principal ones which were part and parcel of the life of our Hospice, trying to fulfil the needs of those who are sick and overburdened with illness. And so we looked forward to the meeting of the Fuchsia Society in the beginning of September and to all those people who have chosen our Hospice as the venue for their annual meetings. We looked forward to this one with a sense of joy which the flowers, I am sure, gave to us and all of our patients.

The week before the Fuchsia Society met, we had the inauguration of Sean McGuire's new record of Irish folk music. This was another first. He chose the Academy for the launching of his record Hawks & Doves after being approached by Julie and Gerry Baden, two of our Committee members who were friends of his. Both made great preparations for this launch and we were delighted to welcome Sean and his orchestra, mostly comprised of youngsters, to whom he had been teaching the fiddle.

They were quite experienced in as far as they had already given a number of concerts and Sean himself, while touring the United States, had even performed in the White House. Julie and Gerry obtained the services of their friend Bernard Mangley, whom they asked to be the compere.

I felt very strange not having launched a record before, but took comfort from the fact that my name was O'Leary and I was able to regale the audience with the sense of pride with which I wore my name. It was an opportunity to tell my listeners of how St. Patrick went to my ancestor and asked permission to preach the Faith in Ireland and I told them the story of how the King's daughters Eithne and Fidelma both became saints. Maureen, Sean's wife, formally introduced the members of the orchestra to us and then Dr. Mairead, from the Institute of Irish Studies of Liverpool University, explained to us the appropriateness of launching an Irish record in Liverpool.

She related some startling facts about Liverpool's connection with Ireland and that in the mid-eighteenth century, 850 families in Liverpool spoke Gaelic as their first language. Of course Percy French, the famous Irish poet and musician, was buried in Formby, not too far from Crosby, and a singer rejoicing in the name of Signor Foli was really an Irishman. He trained as a tenor in Italy where he achieved great success. His name was Foley but for Italian audiences it suited him to spell his name Foli. He too is buried on Merseyside.

I expressed my appreciation to Patsy McCabe, the pianist of the orchestra, who accompanied the music so deftly and with great precision. I was put in mind of the B.B.C. Northern Ireland Light Orchestra under its conductor David Currie who used to perform regularly on B.B.C. Radio and played the jigs and reels with great gusto. Bernard Mangley, our compere, gave us delightful renditions of Irish songs.

Mr. Tom Kelly and his wife Catherine, from the Irish Embassy in London, and Dr. Eamonn McGuinness, the senior gynaecologist in Dublin, came along as supporters. It was a day of culture. Sean is a virtuoso on the fiddle and both he and his school of players performed wonders. The concert in the evening held many treasures for us and everyone without exception enjoyed the day and the record was truly launched. Gerry Baden caught it all on video and it does one's heart good to be able to view it again and again. The Irish jigs and reels always hold their popularity if performed well. They arouse a great spirit of fervour and love for the ancient Gael.

Shortly after this magnificent concert, we found ourselves busy again organising another event to celebrate the eightieth birthday of one of our notable supporters, Archie Downie. We were all anxious to make the night a successful one and Helen his wife and all their family came to celebrate. There was John, Paul, Michael, Stephen, Andrew and Martin and their wives and children. Archie has many friends and Helen his wife had extended her invitations quite widely to cover all of them. Archie didn't know anything about this celebration until his entrance into the Aquinas Hall and was surprised to find his family, some of whom had come a great distance to wish him a Happy Birthday.

We had Holy Mass for Helen and Arch and their family and after Mass the Liverpool Scottish Pipers came to entertain us. Archie takes great pride in the fact that his forebears were from Scotland and the Liverpool Scottish played their hornpipes and reels in the accustomed fashion.

The Celtic element of the afternoon was well founded and before we had the birthday dinner the piper played in the food. We sat down and enjoyed the party and the entertainment which followed. I did one of my famous ditties to commemorate the event which I am sure Helen and Archie and their family enjoyed.

Coping with Death
and Bereavement

29

PEOPLE often say to me – "How do you cope with bereavement and loss, Father?" I usually reply along the lines that everyone without exception suffers at one time or another bereavement, sadness and a sense of loss. As human beings we value our closeness with members of our family and the friends we have made in the course of our lives. The friendship we experience acts as a security net into which we can fall when adverse circumstances assail us. Even with animals we build up a sense of love and affection which some of us treasure dearly.

I had a gorgeous Irish wolfhound called Misha whom I have already mentioned. She was getting very old but had done her duty so diligently as a Hospice dog (a very special vocation) and given joy to all our patients, their relatives and friends. My Brother was particularly fond of Misha and took good care of her. They were great friends and several times a day walked through our beautiful grounds. They were a true source of comfort to one another. Sadly my Brother died a few years ago.

In his last days of illness, Misha took up her station next to his bedside knowing that something was wrong. Her loyalty was so steadfast and true that even the highest consultant in the land or the most fiery matron would not have been able to make her budge from her post. Although the situation was a very sad one, this outward expression of loyalty and trust was something of great beauty.

Misha's grief had begun sometime before my Brother's death and one could perceive the nobility of grief shining through this relationship of one man and his dog.

On a higher level, of course, is our human situation with grief and bereavement. The sense of bereavement, more often than not, has its onset when a mortal illness has been diagnosed, rather than at the final demise of a good friend or relation.

People grieve in various ways and for different reasons. There may be regrets for not having done the right things or for not having made the right protestations of love. One can experience deep sorrow for past wrong-doings. Even deeply religious people express their anger with God for visiting on them a sadness and a sorrow which they feel they don't deserve. In a case of sudden death, bewilderment can hide all other emotions. Very often one hears, "I was speaking to him only yesterday ....", "We had arranged to go for a drink tonight........." No wonder then, in helping a person to come to terms with grief, it is difficult to sort out the confusion which exists in a person's mind. The one bereaved is left pondering on the special relationship they had with a loved one or a friend. The mind tries to analyse this relationship in a confused way. Did we love the deceased as we should have done ? Did we offend in any way ? Is it now too late to reconcile the wrongs we have done and how genuine is our sorrow ? Can we make amends to ease our aloneness–and is it possible to make ourselves whole again?

After death has taken place we no longer can speak to a loved one. No longer is it possible to experience an empiricism to satisfy our grief. The sense of sharing and confiding to our loved one has gone. The mind does not know how to cope with the unreality or the wilderness into which we have been thrown. What is the point of living? For the purposefulness of life has suddenly disappeared from our vision. It seems impossible to cope with the vacuum which now exists but which was once full of joy and love.

Shock of bereavement shakes us to the core, possibly because we are all of a sudden confronted with a notion of eternity and the uselessness of material things. The awesomeness of God's presence becomes very meaningful. Where has our loved one gone to ? It is at times like these we thank God for our Faith and wonder what it is like for those who do not believe in God!

During my 38 years of Hospice work, sharing in people's grief, I find the notion of living in the presence of God the most comforting thought to offer to the bereaved. I explain that there is, after all, no finality about death. We were born to die to go to God and to be happy with Him for all eternity.

If God is present with us, as He surely is, then our loved one who has died and for whom we are yearning is now with God and is therefore also very present now with the bereaved, in a more intimate way than any physical experience in the past. I often encourage people to pray and to talk to their deceased loved ones. The realisation of the presence of God within us helps to assuage any excessive grief, despite the very natural feeling of personal loss.

For example there was Eileen who had great difficulty in swallowing to take away her thirst. "I wonder if Our Lady has any iced water in heaven ?" she kept saying shortly before her death. We assured her that Our Lady would give her everything she wanted in heaven. Sometimes we think of Our Lady and St. Joseph as mythical figures, but they are real people and I'm sure they will greet those who die with a great warmth and love that we cannot appreciate. Our Lady knows what real grief is–as she attended her Son when He died on the Cross. So she knows all about grief and bereavement.

The prayers we say with the relatives who suffer the sad loss of a loved one are so beautiful, consoling and joyful. We pray that the angels may take the deceased into paradise and we ask the martyrs to give them a great welcome. Most importantly, we commission the choir of angels to be on hand and to burst forth into heavenly song.

Very often we find that the expressed grief is changed into joy. Death is the final healer. One moment you are praying with the relatives and with the dying patient. The next moment when death occurs something wonderful takes place. Then is experienced the reality, in the words of the old song ('My Grandfather's Clock'), that 'the spirit is plumed for flight' and God is present in a very special way to introduce His loved one to the heavenly hosts.

Apart from the very natural personal loss, the relatives of a deceased person can experience a great joy and happiness which is a reflection of the radiant happiness passed down by their loved one who has now entered into eternal bliss. Some patients prepare themselves for the angelic throng long before they die. In the Academy at Thornton we have the great privilege of having our patients' rooms looking directly on to Our Lord in the Blessed Sacrament, thus enabling them to feel more acutely the presence of God. Margaret, one of our patients who died recently, very often said to me and to many of her visitors – "I've nothing to worry about, Father. He is there, Father ! We are wrapped in His love !" This anxiety to be with God took away the sting of grief from her husband and family.

Our principal effort in counselling and comforting the bereaved is to take away the tenseness of a sorrowing situation by sharing the burden of bereavement or lightening the pain of loss. This is chiefly obtained by a spirit of prayer and sometimes by an expression of lightheartedness. Long before the patient dies there should be a continual embracing of the patient and of relatives and thousands of smiles, hugs and kisses exchanged. Very definitely a hands-on operation !!!

Not so long ago I had a classic example with a lady called Henrietta–a stalwart of the Orange Lodge in Liverpool. Her family was steeped in the history of King Billy and the Battle of the Boyne. When I admitted her she was bewildered by so many statues and holy pictures. The Holy Mass relayed on the internal television network was the last straw. As I passed her bed when distributing Holy Communion, she made it known in no uncertain terms that she didn't want even a blessing and so I would just wave to her with my left hand as I passed by.

After a week or so, she sent me a message requesting that I give her a blessing when I next passed her bedside, which I duly did. She had a very extended family who were also staunch supporters of King Billy. The time came for Henrietta to die. I was sitting with her holding her hand, as she appeared to be in extremis. "I feel like a spare part just sitting here, Henrietta," I said. "Why, Father?" she replied. "Well, there is so much I could give you," I said. "Like what ?" she mumbled. "Well, like bringing Christ nearer to you by giving you His Sacraments," I suggested. "Go ahead and get on with it," she ordered.

I knew the family would be visiting in their droves at any moment, so I nipped down to the Chapel to get the Holy Oils and the Sacred Host, I managed to anoint her and give her Holy Communion just as her relatives were arriving. Then I whispered into her ear a few appropriate prayers, kissed her and felt overawed at God's goodness. Her relations knelt down reverently and preserved a hushed silence.

One good turn deserves another I thought and so I bent over very close to her ear and began to sing in the softest of tones the well-known Orange anthem The Sash My Father Wore. Immediately she smiled from ear to ear. As we got to the second line of the song I found the decibels of sound increasing and by the fourth line we were all raising the roof with fists punching the air in rousing chorus. Then we all exploded with laughter at this very unusual happening. One had to admit this wasn't the most conventional way of making a thanksgiving after Holy Communion ! But it worked. Henrietta died joyously and peacefully. One of the relatives was heard to exclaim, "Good Grief." It was indeed ! . . .

After I had recounted this story, a well-known Catholic journalist, Norman Cresswell, said to me, "That's all very well, Father, but do you ever doubt ? Is God on the other side of the bed ?" This question was a very real one, so I told him about one or two of my experiences.

The first of which was quite scarey. I was knocked over by a lorry in Great Western Road in Glasgow. I had just completed my Degree examination at Glasgow University and, as a change from books, decided to have a bike ride to visit some friends. A priest colleague, Fr. Louis Purcell, had recently been given a new bicycle and he suggested I should try it out that morning. Within five minutes I was lying on the wet road. The front wheel had got caught in a tram line and I lost my balance.

As I lay helpless and disorientated I noticed a big lorry bearing down on me. It all happened in a matter of seconds. In that short space of time so many things crossed my mind including the telegram my Mother and Father were to receive about their son's death. Should I make an Act of Contrition ? It was all happening. I am going to die ! And then the thought wrongly crossed my mind that to do so would be to give up completely and I was determined to fight this one out. As the lorry came up to me I threw out my left leg against the bumper and was turned over. My head lay next to one wheel and the bicycle lay very twisted under the other. Rather stupidly I suppose, I felt my heart to see if it was still beating to reassure myself that I was alive–so surprised was I and relieved.

Oddly enough on reflection, I realised that there was no time to be afraid or to doubt that I was on the point of meeting my Maker. A sudden accident was one thing, a long drawn out illness is another, when one's faith in God can be sorely tested and tried. Invariably when a patient has asked me about life after death and pointedly said: "Do you believe in God, Father?" I always answer, "Yes, of course I do." I say this, I suppose, to keep my credibility as a priest and for the patient's own reassurance. But when I retire from the patient's bed I always have to make an act of faith myself and usually head for the Chapel to wrestle this one through. Why do I do this ? How do I know God is at the other side of the bed ?

There have been times when my own feelings can get really mixed up and one is left pondering, 'How do I know?'

I recall sitting with a patient one morning in the early hours and feeling quite useless in helping her to settle down to sleep. May was totally restless. When I admitted her she was quite fearful of her condition. The nursing team gave of their best, but no matter what we did for her, the poor girl just could not settle down to sleep. She had received all her medication with little effect. My constant prayer for her was, "Our Lady and St. Joseph, please let our patient May settle down to sleep."

But after one full hour nothing happened and May still tossed this way and that. My prayer became more desperate. "Please, Our Lady and St. Joseph, let May settle." Still no effect. I wanted to say to her – "Look, May, Our Lady and St. Joseph are here with us so don't worry." I wanted to say this with conviction. It is so easy to tell a patient, "I'll keep you in my prayers," and then go off to do another job. In the circumstances I could not do this, because I became worried myself since my faith in Our Lady and St. Joseph was being slowly shattered.

So I popped down to our own small Chapel to pray for the strengthening of my own faith. If Our Lady and St. Joseph were present, then why didn't they act ? After all it wasn't any huge favour I was asking. As soon as I began to pray, a horrible, terrifying thought came into my mind: "Is Christ truly present in the Blessed Sacrament ? Of course He is," I thought. "Yes, but how do I know that ?" Despite protestations of belief, I still felt a little unsure. The logic being that if He were present, then Our Lady and St. Joseph must exist too. Then I realised that I believed only because Christ had told us that He is present under the appearance of Bread and Wine–and therefore, I believed.

Freed at last from these horrible imaginings I could at last go back to May and say with conviction, "Our Lady and St. Joseph are with us, May, let us pray to them" – and my patient immediately settled down. That exercise in faith was to rear its head again many times and my rather turgid act of faith would follow. This was very unsettling and I began to say to myself that there must be an easier way of praying about my faith.

Without exception a patient will immediately spot it, if I were to show the semblance of a doubt and, of course, I couldn't speak to a patient if I didn't believe wholeheartedly that when I prayed I firmly believed what I said and that God was on the other side of the bed. Happily, my dilemma was sorted out by just praying "Lord, I love you" because that affirmation covers every difficulty.

Judy Garland, a super artiste, in Summer Stock conveys in one of her songs a very direct approach to God being on the other side. As she slinkily slipped through her chorus of male admirers she sings, "Come on, come on get happy and chase your cares away.. Wash away your sins in the tide, it's quite peaceful on the other side.... The sun is shining, the Lord is waiting to take your hand." With confidence and verve she expressed her message in very clear terms with no shade of doubt in them.

Even if I had the vocal excellence, it would be rather strange to sing Judy's song to a dying patient, although it might be possible with a person who belonged to another culture and whose faith was strong. Nevertheless, words of encouragement are needed when chatting with dying patients and not a few psalms are quite apposite. One of my favourites is:

"O rest in the Lord wait patiently for Him

and He will give you your heart's desires"

which Mendelssohn used with great effect in his oratorio Elijah. The psalmist unites in a few words the sentiments of the dying person and those of the family gathered around the bed and he is saying God is on the other side.

The moment of death is magic and majestic. It is the moment each one of us has been waiting for through all our years. Not only is it the transitus of a soul to God, but more importantly, God comes to collect the soul of His loved one and once again heaven and earth unite and the Lord is waiting 'to take your hand.' One moment you are praying for a patient–saying slowly the Hail Mary and the next moment the patient is being welcomed with Mary's open arms along with St. Joseph and the choir of angels–and choirs must sing and are rejoicing in song shouting, "You've made it !!" The martyrs come to welcome you to take you to the Holy City, the new and eternal Jerusalem.

"Be patient if He hasn't come yet," you might suggest or you find yourself saying, "Remember, it's manners to be asked !!"

If there is time and opportunity it can be very fitting to dispose the patient's mind along these lines. And then invariably a death can be an act of celebration both for the patient and his family and friends. I recall a young patient called Brenda who was afflicted with a very serious illness. She had battled through many operations but had realised that she did not have long to live. Near to her was another patient named Sue Hodge who was in her late twenties and who was dying. As we attended Sue and were saying our prayers, Brenda got out of bed, moved us gently apart and placed a kiss on Sue's forehead, whispering to her, "Don't worry, Sue, I'll see you soon." We stopped our prayers, simply amazed by this act of faith that God was on the other side and they would be united in Him.

Some Turning Points
...and some more Dogs

30

I AM often asked: "What were the turning points in your life, the really important meetings which you have had ?" I invariably reply my family and my Management Committee with whom I meet, if not daily, then at least once a week. They continue to provide me with inspiration and energise me in my task of running an organisation which, thank God, is flourishing and growing. I must include the hundreds of staff who have been under my control. They have all been so loyal and good. Our dogs, too, have played a not insignificant part in easing our way forward. But all things considered I have to make mention particularly of my family, my Mum and Dad, my Sister Rita and my Brother Arthur. They have guided me in so many ways. God places you into a family and you are received with love and kindness throughout your life and under God, I am grateful to them for nurturing my vocation to the missionary priesthood. I recall Mum and Dad being so delighted when I said my first Mass. The sacrifice of the Mass was so important to them and I am still inspired by their devotion and fervour.

I wrote to the late Mother Teresa in 1962 when I was starting off the Hospice in Rawalpindi, receiving no reply from her until 18 months had passed. Relations between India and Pakistan were not good at this time and it was impossible to send or receive post. A letter eventually arrived written in her own hand.

I had asked Mother Teresa how to make a beginning and where she got her funds from. Briefly her answer was not to worry about money and to place one's trust in God and He would look after everything. I took that bit of advice and keep thinking of her words day by day.

As time goes on the cost of running the Hospice Association becomes much greater, and as I write it amounts to something like £40,000 EVERY WEEK. But Our Lord looks after us and Our Lady and St. Joseph protect us and so we stumble from week to week financially. We have had some very hard times, as our previous treasurer Jack Keating and his wife Colette will aver. Many weeks, in order to keep the bank balance, I have exchanged cheques with Jack when the cheques themselves weren't worth anything. Crossfiring I think they call it. It was necessary to adopt measures like this in order to keep the work in progress. Jack and Colette understood exactly how hard pressed we were for cash and it was marvellous to feel that they understood our difficulties.

The prize for patience and complete understanding must go to our bank manager, Mr. Peter Lythgoe from the Nat West Bank in Crosby. He seemed to suffer our hardships and difficulties and, thank God, somehow managed to pull us through.

There were many horrendous times when I had to go to see our bank manager and request a loan. The difficulty was that one was not looking for hundreds of pounds but thousands. A lot depended on the understanding of our situation by the bank manager.

It was never easy and I often wondered how people like Mother Teresa were able to found so many Hospices or institutions of that nature throughout the world. To take one example, the air fares were very expensive and there were some years when there were many nurses who had to travel. Not only was it necessary to sponsor this activity, but huge expenses had to be faced in collecting medicines and equipment to send abroad.

As you can expect there were many sleepless nights in trying to solve financial problems and so it might seem odd that proper thanks are due to John Bailey, our local bank manager from the old William and Glyn's Bank in Waterloo. He had plenty of time to prepare his answers for me when he saw me walking into his office because he had no doubt in his own mind what I was going to request of him. I would put forward the figure I was wanting in my best fundraising manner. His eyebrows would shoot up and with a smile he would say, "Of course not, Father," or he might take another tack and say, "Yes ! But when will you pay me back ?" or "What collateral can you offer ?"

I remember one occasion when I couldn't offer him anything but I did mention the possibility of donations and on purpose overestimated the collections of our flag days and pub crawls. "But", he would retort, "that won't cover anything, what else can you suggest ?" I would mention St. Joseph as the best collateral. I recall him receiving my answer with a wry smile saying, "My boss, the area manager, wouldn't wear that one," but he nevertheless would accede to my request. I certainly had the feeling that if I hadn't mentioned St. Joseph, he would be troubled in his own mind because he knew that prayer was an essential part of our operation and that prayer meant donations !

On the whole it is surprising how continually smooth our relationships were, particularly when I mentioned the spiritual involvement. If he hadn't co-operated, goodness knows where we would have been today !!

I have to mention Kathleen Bucher's dog Muffin, who keeps us happy and makes our work flow. Whether you like it or not you have to accept the good wishes which a dog offers you and on so many occasions I've seen Muffin in every part of the building with a concentration, of course, on the kitchen because that is where Kathleen works. I like to think of Russo, who is known in these parts only to Filomena and myself because we met him on guard duty outside Carmen Pari's house in Lima. He is a big chap who would scare the daylights out of any intruder.

On the more gentle side we had Pindi. I met him on the Landing Stage in Liverpool early one morning at about two o'clock. I was waiting for one of our nurses to arrive from London and the train had been delayed, so I suggested to Filomena that we go down to the Landing Stage as it would be cooler.

There was nobody at the Landing Stage apart from ourselves, or so I thought. Then I heard steps behind me and wherever I went this dog followed. Eventually I went back to the car and then I saw the little dog staring at Filomena in the face. She opened the back door and said, "Come on in." We hadn't gone very far when we found that the dog had been sick in the back of the car. He wasn't very well and needed caring for. So Pindi that's what we called him (after Rawalpindi of course) stayed at the O'Learys' house and made great friends with Mamie Carroll who was staying there. A marvellous little fellow was Pindi, with all the tricks of the trade. The times he pretended to be ill ! He would raise one paw and limp along the road to attract our attention. There was nothing wrong with his paw, he just wanted us to say hello to him and not to scold him for being out.

Then there was Sebastian, a huge fellow who weighed about 12 stone. I mentioned him before. He was an Old English Mastiff. People were afraid of him. He was our guard dog at Hettinga House and made great friends with my Sister Rita and Marie Wills who was doing marvellous work for us as our social worker.

In Thornton we had Misha our Irish Wolfhound. I got her from Preston and brought her back to our San Jose Hospice in Thornton. I was playing a record at the time called Mise Eire and so her name became Misha. Ted Cleary comes very often in the evenings with Rita. Ted was the dog of Dr. Marie Cleary who, sadly, died in 1994. Rita collects him every night to bring him up to the Hospice in Thornton, to give him a run which they both enjoy thoroughly. One or two of our patients have biscuits ready for him when he visits and he knows where their rooms are.

I should mention Emma who comes to Midnight Mass on a Friday. Emma's claim to fame is that she is a great 'hoover' and any food that has been dropped on the floor she will gather up for us. Dogs make everyone so happy and they are able to express in their own terms the reflection of God's love for each one of us. I know they have their own vocation but they are able to express their feelings where humans fail.

Apart from the dogs not a few humans have had vital roles in my work. Peter Carter, who speaks fluent Spanish, and his wife Celsa have served us so well with all the legal aspects that we have had to grapple with. Peter has the facility of writing brilliant letters which have eased and indeed solved my problems in so many ways. As our solicitor, Peter's incisive mind always detects the dubious point with precision. We are pleased to have him.

I have mentioned Bishop Hettinga on not a few occasions but it was his valiant efforts for the Church in Rawalpindi which gave my vocation new life each time I met him. He was a marvellous missionary and a very good man. Not only did he build houses for the poor people in Peshawar but he became the first Bishop of Rawalapindi and started projects in the educational and medical fields. A very determined man, he was a great spiritual leader and gained one's confidence immediately. He built up a great relationship with the Muslim leaders in Pakistan at that time and in so many ways brought great credit to the Catholic Church in that country. He was helped so often by Fr. Paddy Byrne and Tess and May Flanagan who taught in St. Mary's Academy. I used to think it was very funny when reading the list of teachers at the school. It went Byrne, O'Leary, Flanagan, Flanagan, Brady. Five people with Irish names teaching in a Muslim school !

Thank God we have been blessed with many helpers. I am thinking of Bernard Chubb who started our Sudbury Group. He set the pattern for that group which still meets regularly and has so many supporters. For many years Judith Meredith took over his role. Marguerita Freely, ably assisted by her husband Gerald, carried on the same spirit of the group and this was later taken over by Loraine Maguire, a wonderful worker. In similar fashion Eliza Lopez and her sister Carmen started our group in Allerton and Patsy Ruttle did the same for us in Dublin so well.

You can imagine how many thousands of letters leave my office every year. For devoted service I have to thank Rita Rogerson and Eily Cropper, Harry Nichols (Archbishop Nichols' father), Pauline Farrell, Bunny Attridge, Terry Rooney and Wilf Heslop and a host of other people. That secretarial tradition today is carried on by Wyn, Barbara, Val, Sue, Pat, Marjorie, Moira, Cathie,

Frank Merino, Joan and Stan (in the Academy) and a thousand others including Jean, Josie, Pauline, Therese, Maureen, Angela, Cynthia etc, etc. I am thinking too of Mr. McVey, Mr. Stannanought, Fr. Ames, Fr. Pilson, Sister Agnes, Sister Petronella and Canon Walmsley from SS. Peter and Paul's Church, Crosby, who all took a part in forming my character and Sister Francis who prepared me for my First Holy Communion in 1937.

My mind also goes out to Fr. Mekkunel, Fr. Kattakayam, Fr. Thumpayil and Fr. Jeyaraj spearheading our work in India. We have always been impressed by the medical work which these priests do in their areas and look forward to receiving their reports. Their apostolic spirit constantly enlivens us to support them in their work.

On the nursing side high standards were set and maintained by Filomena, Maureen Grieveson, Joan Lawson and their friends, ably carried on today by Margaret Culshaw, Margaret Woods, Gail McKay and their teams. In fundraising the League of Friends are very active under Dorothy Hughes and Jean Hassit and many outstanding events have been staged by them.

Mexico, some Final Reflections, and the Third Gala Concert

31

IN September 1995 I had the great privilege with Filomena of going round our Hospices in Central and South America. The highlight of my trip was my visit to Our Lady of Guadalupe in Mexico.

I had arranged to meet a gentleman by the name of Alejandro at Mexico City Airport. I was dressed very obviously as a priest and was extremely surprised when no one came to meet me. I stayed on about an hour and a half waiting for him and then I sat down and said a prayer to Our Lady to let this impasse pass because without Alejandro I would not be able to visit the places he had designated. Filomena guessed I was saying a prayer and she told me that Our Lady would organise everything for us in some way.

We summoned a taxi and went to the Cathedral to see if anybody there had a clue as to how we could get in contact with Alejandro. This took quite some time and by six o'clock that evening neither of us could even guess at what to do. I still had to say Mass and I asked Filomena to request the nearby parish for permission to say Holy Mass but she was informed that unless I could prove that I was a Catholic priest, no parish priest would allow me to say Mass. I had my passport but no other documents as I rarely ever carried my celebret with me. After further refusals we decided to take off to Alejandro's office connected with Caritas Mexicana. It was a Saturday, pouring with rain, and the office building was all shut up. However the taxi driver spotted a night watchman on duty and we got out to talk to him. He said there was a priest in the building and that we could speak with him. Fr. Guillermo came down. He knew Alejandro and telephoned all his friends to see if they knew of his whereabouts. The poor taxi driver was still waiting for us an hour later. He said that it didn't matter and he was not charging us. In the end without success, I asked the priest would he find a place where I could say Mass and give me his telephone number to show that I was bone fide. He directed me to a church a few blocks away.

The Hospice in Nezahualcoyotl, Mexico City

Filomena went into the church first and found that inside there was a high class wedding in progress. We thought it was going to take another hour at least until the priest had finished, before we could explain who we were and what we wanted. Filomena came out of the church and beckoned me to follow her. I went in and had been in the church only ten seconds when a lady came up to me and spoke in English. She asked me, "Are you a Catholic priest ?" "Indeed I am," I replied. She then said, "Would you come and say Mass for us?" I said, "Willingly. I've been trying to do that for the last three hours or so."

Filomena came over and I asked her to find out the circumstances. Two other ladies who joined the company explained that a young lad, Cristiano, had been killed that morning. His car had gone into a wall and he had suffered fatal injuries. His body was in the funeral parlour where his mother and father were praying and wanted Mass. Apparently the permission I sought was very exceptional. So we went round to the priest's house and found a priest who said he would phone the Bishop and get special permission. We waited half an hour until he came back and informed us that the Bishop had said that it would be in order for me to say Mass in the funeral parlour. The priest then presented us with the requisites for Mass.

The ladies took us in their cars to where the body was lying and it was a strange experience to go in and offer our condolences to the mother and father. Then I said the Mass for Cristiano and gave a short sermon. Filomena did the readings and translated my sermon although I was able to say the Mass in Spanish. It was a very sad occasion and they requested that I return the following morning to say Mass, which I did.

After Mass I then went to the Basilica of Our Lady of Guadalupe and concelebrated Mass with a Mexican Bishop. It turned out that he was the Bishop responsible to the Mexican hierarchy for projects like the one I was hoping to start in Guadalupe. I was able to have a chat with him and then went back to the hotel to find that someone had successfully made contact with Alejandro who had requested to come and see us. He did so and we had a very fruitful meeting at which we decided to open a Hospice in Mexico City near Guadalupe, on land which had been assigned to us in Nezahualcoyotl. We are doing this one in conjunction with the Society of St. Vincent de Paul and a lot of hard work has been put in to make secure the project which we had outlined to Alejandro. Our Lady was certainly looking after us and the impasse was no longer there. She has her own way of doing things. The manner in which she did this one became a bit complex but, thank God, our Hospice opened in September 1997 and is now flourishing.

Writing Memoirs, or meanderings as they inevitably become, are difficult in recalling the day to day happenings in the life of a priest. A priest has so many responsibilities to carry out. It becomes hard to know what to highlight and what not to.

Every Monday afternoon I make a practice of having a game of snooker with my friend Mgr. Vin Hughes. It may seem quite a trite matter to some people but it is a serious business with us and every game we play is a needle one. We are as bad as one another and I suppose this deficiency in our skill creates the excitement of each game.

Over the weeks we are more or less 'even stevens' and our anxiety to pull out the better shots in the snooker game is quite intense. But the exercise is good, in as far as it takes one's mind off the worries and cares of our work as priests and both of us find it very enjoyable. We only play for about two hours and manage to fit in maybe five frames. But it is amazing how this little exercise of knocking balls around a table can give one a new lease of life and strength to fulfil one's duties. I like it when Mgr. Hughes has played a particularly stupid shot after which he always says, "I need my head examining." My usual reply is, "I'd keep quiet about that, otherwise you will find some men in white coats coming to take you away !" Or alternatively, when I have performed a brilliant shot I might say, "What do you think of that ?" His riposte usually is, "Concedo omnino," an echo from our philosophy days in the seminary. Sadly Monsignor died March 14 2000. A great loss to me personally and his many many friends, may he rest in peace.

In the summer of 1996 I said my goodbyes to Pauline Whitehead, one of our nurses who most certainly had imbibed the aspects of holism. It became evident on observing Pauline's visits to patients that she would not only take into account the medical history of the patient but the finer things of life as well. Her attitude was very noble and on so many occasions she was able to provide total relaxation to a patient. We will miss her.

If it is not possible to witness the work physically, as in the case of our representatives abroad, you can gauge an attitude by reading their letters or faxes. Our little team in Peru has overcome insurmountable problems. Daniel Valdezan and his wife Monica, Stella Kirkland, Jean Keenan and Anne Bowers have returned remarkable results. Their bravery is to be commended. Also our teams in Pakistan under Sister Lucille, Honduras with Catherine O'Leary, Caroline Horsley, Marie Cambray and Dawn Connor, Ecuador with Fr. Frank Smith and our team in Guatemala under Naomi Hassan, Jessica Adair, Alison Bogues, Toni Finnigan, Jill Stockwell, Mere Finnigan, Mary O'Sullivan, Dr. Heino Hugel, Isabella Sanchez, Amaia Sarasti, Manuela Friedli, Rebecca Flanagan, Anne Armstrong, Diane Sorrell, Helena Clavijo and Sidonie Puech not forgetting, of course, our wonderful helpers in Nezahualcoyotl under Sister Lygia, Sister Edith, Sister Lidia and her Vincentian Sisters and all those in our other stations.

Louise O'Donnell and a group of medical students had a bed-push from the medical school in Liverpool to our Hospice in Thornton. They collected along the roadside and visited as many public houses as possible. We gave them a great welcome and thanked them for their generosity.

The same girl recalled an occasion when she went out to South Africa as a medical student and was posted to an orthopaedic clinic to assist the surgeon.

One day as she was chatting to him, the door opened and his wife walked in. The surgeon was going to be very busy, so he told Louise to go and have lunch with his wife. Louise was telling her of her experiences in Honduras and then all of a sudden this good lady exclaimed on hearing my name, "I know him. I met him so many years ago in Rome." Patti–that was the lady's name–was so excited that she wrote me a letter which Louise brought back to me. In it she mentioned that her husband insisted that she wrote that letter because he was as flummoxed as she was.

I remember her well. I had just come back from my interview with Mother Peter, the Mother General of the Franciscan Missionaries of Mary, when I was trying to obtain nursing Sisters for our first Hospice in Colombia, at San Bernardo del Viento. After I had received permission to build a Hospice in South America from Bishop Mahon, I immediately sallied forth to Rome. When I had finished talking to Mother Peter, I went back to my hotel in Rome because I was returning the next day to Liverpool. Naturally I was overjoyed that Mother Peter would allow her Sisters to work for us and by way of thanksgiving, I suppose, I popped into the Basilica of St. Mary Major, where there was a Mass in progress. The congregation sang a few hymns. I knew the melodies and followed the singing, but in English. The sound of another person giving the English version of the hymns was from a young lady in the next pew.

When Mass had finished I walked through the Basilica and stood on the steps wondering where I could get a meal. The same young lady was standing next to me. I was embarrassed because I only had a tiny bit of money left in my pocket and I told her that I would like to take her for a meal but could not afford to pay for her. She said she was thinking the same thing but she also had very little money. We walked over to a hotel and had to choose from the menu carefully so that it would be within our means.

During my meal I mentioned what my plans were for a Hospice in South America and this young lady seemed to be impressed and said that she would join up. She was a nurse and felt like doing that type of work. I was quite astounded that I had already not only obtained the services of some religious Sisters but also had my first volunteer. The lady left her address with me and told me that she was on her way home to America. Later I received a letter from her saying that she had changed her mind and was going to get married to a South African doctor. She did so and within a short time she became Mrs. Von Bormann. I was disappointed, of course, that she had had a change of mind but I was delighted that she had remembered me from all that time ago. She has a grown up family now and she seems to be very happy.

That was an enjoyable experience which was totally different from the supermarket entrepreneur who, on being requested for a donation, shouted at me to get out of his hair or another gentleman who tried to instil a great fear into our patients that the bailiffs were coming in to close the Hospice down. This particular man was very obnoxious and it was diabolical the way in which he tried to scare us all by ringing up bank managers, our printers and various other people in an attempt to cut off our credit. It needed the police to shut him up. I am thankful to them for doing so.

You need good friends when times are hard. We experienced grave times during the period of the three-day week in 1974 when funds where very low. But the likes of John Miller and his wife Mary would give us a boost–two excellent people whose faith and trust were very ardent. They could pull you up by the bootstraps and make you feel more confident to go on.

One of the special facilities we have at the Hospice is the hydrotherapy pool which is organised by Brian Farquhar and his team. Hundreds of people have availed themselves of the opportunity of using our hydrotherapy pool and local doctors often advise their patients to make use of it. There are about a hundred sessions a week, and if well enough, our own patients can enjoy a swim in the heated waters. It is a facility which brings many people great happiness.

Radio comedian Rob Wilton used to tell in his own inimitable way a very funny story about the time he went to a funeral of a friend. It was pouring with rain and very cold and as they were standing at the graveside old Joe was standing there also and Rob Wilton turns to his friend and says, "I don't think it worthwhile old Joe going home."

This story I recalled when I went to the funeral of a great friend called Cory Matthew at SS. Peter and Paul's in Ormskirk. As we were standing at the lych gate of the church, the old verger approached the coffin. His cassock was at half-mast and he was carrying a thurible as he stumbled towards us. He looked for all the world like the Hunchback of Notre Dame. As he shuffled along in his big boots I turned to the funeral director Harry Cookson of Leech's Funeral Services and said, "I don't think it worthwhile for him to go home." At which remark the funeral directors doubled up with laughter.

We went forward to the grave and the funeral directors were still laughing. As we got to the graveside, they were about to lever the coffin into the grave when the three on one side of the coffin slipped and fell over a mound of soil at the side. It was difficult to compose ourselves but I think Cory would have enjoyed the situation. A great man was Cory. He used to own the house which is now Hettinga House in Ormskirk. He always made us very welcome and was a thoroughly good sport. You were happy after meeting him because of his attitude to life.

The same goes for my relations whom I hadn't met for some time. It was the occasion of the funeral of my cousin Winifred. Her daughter Celia and her son Paul made Rita and myself feel so welcome and gave us a wonderful reception. I concelebrated the Requiem Mass with Bishop Vincent. It was simply a great joy to be with them all.

We always make a point of making our outside Christmas Pageant something memorable. Mary Carson recalls the time when it was certainly so for her. The role of the Archangel Gabriel has always been taken by Filomena. She puts one of my more voluminous albs on and takes the baby, well wrapped up, to a position behind the Crib before the procession.

Mary Carson was calmly recalling the story of Christmas over the microphone when all of a sudden this big white figure seemed to appear from nowhere and she got quite a shock. She did not realise that Filomena had been hiding behind the Crib with the baby and it was when she pronounced the appropriate passage that Filomena appeared in order to lay the baby in the Crib. When that is done all the lights come on and Our Lord has been born. It is then we all gather round the Crib and sing Silent Night. It is a beautiful moment and a very prayerful one for all of us.

On December 12th 1996 we had a great celebration in honour of Our Lady of Guadalupe. The famous mezzo-soprano Della Jones came to sing for us. Della has a very engaging personality and it was with great excitement that we listened to her singing for us at Christmas time. I have mentioned her before in these notes as one of our star soloists at our Gala Concert in the Royal Philharmonic Hall in Liverpool earlier in the year when she sang a famous aria from The Italian Girl in Algiers by Rossini.

Our concert took the form of a celebrity concert with audience participation and the backing of the Capriol Singers. We have lingering memories of her rendition of Gershwin's Summertime and the Negro spiritual Oh My Baby. The Holy City and Bless This House were outstanding, as well as her offerings of two Spanish songs. We enjoyed the services of a fine accompanist, Michael Baden, and an inspired conductor, John Emery.

We had a good selection of Christmas Carols in which the Capriol Singers made a notable contribution, and the third part of the concert was rounded off with Della leading the whole audience with songs like Moonlight Bay and

Who Were You With Last Night?. As usual Leo Connor's accompaniment was superb. Della's concert provided for us a real festive feeling for Christmas. How fortunate we have been in being presented with a wonderful night of this nature. Thank you very much, Della, for creating such happiness.

Earlier on in my notes I made mention of Sister of the Divine Shepherd, or Sister Theresa as she is now known. I mentioned that I located her in Edinburgh and in February 1997 I went with Filomena to pay her a short visit. After 41 years of not seeing one another it was with great happiness that we introduced ourselves once again. So much had happened in that time to both of us and we had great pleasure drawing on our memories of those years. Her Sisters in the convent were very welcoming and the visit to her was a fulfilment of a promise I made to see her, to thank her personally for all the prayers she had offered up for me. I promised her my prayers in exchange.

As you have gone through my story you will no doubt realise the impact that Our Lady and St. Joseph have had on us all. Sometimes one has even stood in for the other. Let me explain.

Dan Howard was one of our first patients. He was a supervisor of nursing homes for the local authority. He knew them all, but he also realised that there was no place for him.

Dan had been stricken with a nasty illness and was receiving treatment in Clatterbridge Hospital. We got to know about Dan's condition from one of his superiors and so Filomena and myself went to visit him in the hospital. He presented us with his dilemma and we knew that something had to be done quickly. We had just opened our Hospice in Thornton so we offered him a bed in our new Hospice dedicated to St. Joseph.

He had been praying a lot that a place would be found for him somewhere and he was full of apprehension at the thought. He was praying for a miracle basically. He was pleased that we had come to visit him and that we were trying to do something for him. He had been praying to Our Lady and had a small statue in his room in Clatterbridge Hospital. He knew we were from St. Joseph's Hospice and when he examined the statue he found it was not one of Our Lady but of St. Joseph and his joy and relief were boundless !! Poor Dan had a bedsore right down from his waist to the base of his spine and for this reason we used to give him his morphine half an hour before turning him and treating his pressure areas. To take his mind off his illness we also played his favourite Bing Crosby record which had an Hawaiian background. It was on one of these very difficult occasions that the O'Leary twins were called in by Filomena to dance for him and he thought he was in heaven. He was so enchanted by it all.

As I commit my memories to paper I realise how indebted I am to quite literally thousands of people, for their kindness and their expertise. For example, Brian Spanswick, whose wife Margaret is one of our senior nurses in Hettinga House, knows the ins and outs of new laws and regulations affecting nursing homes and I have relied heavily on that. The willingness of people to help in what has become a collaborative ministry–people who look after the flowers and the tidiness of our houses. I think of Maisie Johnson and her husband Arthur, Renee Lowe and Mary Wilson, who also leads our Legion of Mary Group so ably with Rita Horay, Jackie Culshaw and Anne Powell. Joan and Stan (in the Academy) and Chris and Joan (at Hettinga) can always be relied upon to provide a cup that cheers and a biscuit or two. Charles Evans and his marathons and Jack Moran who has done some notable walks to Lourdes.

Mentioning Jack Moran reminds me of a phone call I had when he had achieved his goal of walking from Crosby to Glenbuck. What is so special about Glenbuck you might say. Well, it was the birthplace of Bill Shankly, the former Liverpool manager who was greatly loved on Merseyside.

The village is no longer there, but Jack had planned to make a fuss about Shankly and intended to put up a plaque honouring his name.

He had received permission from Liverpool F.C. to bring to the attention of thousands of people his activities on our behalf, by walking round Anfield football pitch at half-time during the match between Manchester United and Liverpool. A needle match it was but unfortunately Liverpool got beaten. Jack was accompanied by a Scots piper and the television cameras were there to give it full publicity.

Well done, Jack, and congratulations to you and your team, particularly Gwen, Anne and Sandra who had a large part in making the preparations for this honoured walk. It was wonderful listening to Jack enthusing about his marathon and the way in which his team helped him to face 45,000 people at Liverpool F.C. But that was nothing compared with the spirit which must have inspired Jack to go so far.

It was amazing to realise that a couple of thousand people met him at the spot where the sponsored marathon ended. It was interesting also to hear how there is a football team called the Cherrypickers, which Shankly as a young lad used to play for, and that they received a challenge from a Liverpool team–the Shankly Reds. A wonderful experience for you, Jack, and something for us to be very proud of.

The telephone call I had was from a lady called Margaret Cloughley who lives at Burnsands, near Thornhill, in Dumfriesshire. She saw a notice about Jack's walk and saw St. Joseph's name mentioned. She thought how unlikely it would be, to be connected with the St. Joseph's she used to work for in Rawalpindi, Pakistan. How wrong she was ! Margaret told me that she goes back to the early days of our Hospice there and that she and her husband, who have now retired from Pakistan, spent many happy hours at the Hospice. She couldn't believe that in the wilds of Ayrshire where Glenbuck is, she would have the experience of reliving her first contacts with the Hospice in Rawalpindi.

It was an amazing experience really to be able to talk with her about old times.

Peter and Paul Derwent rode through the highways and byways from Hettinga House in Ormskirk to the shrine of St. James of Compostela at Santiago in North-West Spain. They started their marathon from Hettinga House and came back to record how they had ridden through the Pyrenees and eventually made their way to the shrine of St. James. That was a notable first for Hettinga House.

Two new rooms have been opened at Hettinga and one of them we have dedicated to the memory of Blessed John Finch who died for his Catholic Faith in the middle of the 16th Century. He lived in a house in Mawdesley, which is a village just outside Ormskirk, and so it is nice to have a local martyr to whom this room is dedicated and the patients who will use this room can invoke him for their protection.

I am thinking too of Jim and Sylvia Killen who have started a small group in Buntingford not far from Southend on Sea. Their example could be taken up by so many people who have time to think about us and who could be brought into our collaborative ministry in the care of the terminally sick.

I must mention Kitty, who as our chief receptionist, accepted thousands of telephone calls and put us in contact with so many important people. She was our ace communicator and was particularly adroit in protecting me from hundreds of people she knew I did not want to speak to ! Sadly Kitty died at the end of 1998 after many years of devoted service.

Another example of the joy and happiness which goes hand in hand with involvement in this type of work was when we had the great pleasure of joining in the celebration of two sturdy figures of St. Joseph's Hospice Association, John and Mary Carson. Their fortieth wedding anniversary is some time ago now, but the very fact that we all came together on that day to celebrate with Holy Mass and a nice meal is indicative of the fact that we can join our celebrations with the care of the sick who benefit by our enjoyment and festivities of that nature.

At this time one of the jewels in our crown shone brightly. Her name was Anne McQuaid. She made a recording for us which was absolutely stupendous. Not only has it given great pleasure to me personally but her recording of hymns and songs has been enjoyed by hundreds of our followers. She possesses a beautiful contralto voice, full of dark mysterious notes, and particularly she shone in Gershwin's Summertime, a beautiful piece full of sonority. Anne put a lot of hard work and money into this recording but it was so worthwhile. We thank her for the joy which she has given to her listeners.

When our first Hospice opened in Rawalpindi it gave great happiness to have in our compound the Franciscan Sisters. They had come under Mother Monica from East Pakistan (now Bangladesh). They were an enclosed order with strict silence. One of the joys of my day was when my school work and parish duties had finished, I used to go into the adjoining Church of the Sacred Heart, where there was Exposition of the Blessed Sacrament. The Sisters had Perpetual Exposition, and we all knew they were praying hard for us. One of them, Sister Bernard, who was a tiny person, four foot nothing, used to sing a Bengali lament at about midnight. I don't think she knew I was in the church but from behind the cloister this beautiful wailing, there is no other term for it, was sung and I used to listen with great attention to the wonderful melodies that came from behind that cloister. It was quite an eerie experience but a deeply spiritual one and most unusual. These Sisters are still in contact with us. Moka, whom I have mentioned previously, was sent by them to our Hospice in Thornton.

I have met up with Francis O'Leary on my return visits to Rawalpindi. I remember him coming from school with his exercise books in his hand and it was an unusual experience when he showed me his books, to read 'Francis O'Leary' on the front cover. He must be in his early thirties now and I hear he is doing well.

The mind makes its own flashbacks and the memory makes its own images. Let me recall one or two flashbacks and images from the past which gladden the heart.

Fr. John Ball wrote a play for the seminarians in Burn Hall, Co. Durham. I recall his being very chuffed when Fr. John McMahon came to him afterwards and congratulated him on his composition. He was also responsible for a very dramatic account of 'Murder in the Cathedral' at Mill Hill College, so very well performed during our Christmas holidays. I remember so much time and effort was put into the production.

Colonel Shales and his wife Molly were frequent visitors to our Hospice in Thornton. They were particularly interested in the work I was doing because they were married in the Cathedral in Rawalpindi so many years ago when he was in the Indian Army.

Fr. Piet Dirven was responsible for the whole of the 'O' Level class in Freshfield getting a distinction in Latin. I remember he was so delighted about it.

Thanks are due to Andy McDonald who for the past 15 years has called to see our patients every Wednesday with a bag of jelly babies. His visits always give us good cheer.

John Richardson and his wife organised the Car Scheme raffle in Southport for 28 years. It took a lot of organising and involved quite a bit of work. John eventually retired from that scheme because of his age–he is over 90 ! When the scheme started all those years ago the first prize was £500 which was the price of a Mini !

The Knights of St. Columba in the persons of Tom Holding and Ted Evans (friends of Jim Holland) have collected money for the Hospices. We are always thankful to the Knights for their endeavours of our behalf.

There are so many families to remember like the Tooheys from Seaforth and the Reaneys who have been such loyal followers for so many years.

I like to think, too, of Fr. Felix de Souza whom I met in Rawalpindi. Two or three times he came to visit our Hospice in Thornton and the Crucifix at the conclusion of our outdoor Stations of the Cross is dedicated to his memory.

Nigel Taylor and Nick O'Donovan, of Lonsdale and Marsh, have very dutifully done our accounts and we are grateful to them for their suggestions and help in the accountancy field.

Two of our regular visitors, who are very generous with their donations are Frances and Tricia, relatives of a former patient Sue Loughran. Sue and another patient, Frank McGrath, died within days of each other. It was wonderful to see our Faith exhibited by both their families and the expressions of Faith given to us by the patients themselves. Real gifts of God both people were.

And then there is Shirley Powell (Terry O'Leary's sister) who has been a constant source of strength to the O'Leary family and to us all. Their mother died in our Hospice a few years ago and so we feel very close to her.

I have also to make mention of more dogs: Geisha , Ricky and Sebastian who are our guard dogs in San Pedro Sula, Honduras, and Fran (obviously called after me !) in Guatemala. From the latest reports they are all doing extremely well and carrying out all the duties expected of them.

We have nine or ten videos which describe our work and thanks to Julie and Gerry Baden our activities are videoed regularly. We can supply nine or ten hours of really interesting viewing. So much time and effort have been put into the production of these and our thanks are due to both of them for this wonderful accomplishment. Julie and Gerry are two very valued members of our Management Committee.

I never cease to be surprised by the innovative ways in which people help us. Last year a lad called David Rushton came into my office with his friend Michael Matthews and gave me a cheque for £865, the result of collections he made while organising football matches. David had a daughter Denise who died while quite young and every year he has been organising a football tournament in her honour. A lot of people foregather for these matches and bring the crowds with them. The Memorial Cup which he instituted is a prized possession.

I suppose without exception we all go after prized possessions in our lives. It takes one form or another and can be of a material or a spiritual value. I reflect back on the time when the house and land we own in Thornton, and which became our headquarters, came into our possession. Not only did we experience a sense of relief but more a feeling of total happiness. This joy can be appreciated and experienced day after day. Every spring I look forward to the burgeoning of our camellia tree and the rhododendrons which surround our garden. They look particularly beautiful glistening in the sunshine. We are continually thanking God for the great beauty bestowed on us in these grounds.

I pointed out particularly the camellia tree to Fr. Bill Tollan when he came to visit me. I mentioned to him that I was writing my Memoirs and could he think of any funny stories from years gone by. He did recall one item which I thought was quite good. It concerned some students when we were in Mill Hill and the way in which we used to smuggle tobacco from Holland. One priest who later became a bishop, Fr. de Reeper, received in the post a big volume of Caesar's, De Bello Gallico. One of the students who was corrected for smuggling, Wim Bos, had noticed this huge volume on Fr. de Reeper's desk. He wondered what this tome was doing in Father's room. He opened it and found that most of the pages had been hollowed out and filled with cigars and so Johnny Fraughan did a wonderful cartoon of Fr. de Reeper sitting at his desk smoking a cigar while allegedly reading De Bello Gallico, smoke issuing forth from his nose and his ears. The case against the students after this episode was dropped and nothing more was heard about it.

I recall a drawing Johnny Fraughan did for me when I composed "The Call of the Prairie." We had one or two performances of this song with its rather corny harmonies. Johnny Fraughan's cover made it look respectable. We sang it at a smoking concert to honour Clemens van Pinxteren when he took his oath to our Society. I remember it received a big clap. Bill also reminded me of the suit I bought when I was at Glasgow University. Fr. Bill, Fr. Roger McGorty and Fr. Pat McDonald, who were also studying at that time with me, thought they would play a trick and succeeded admirably. A rather large priest, from a local parish, had recently died and one of his old suits had been passed into our house. I had gone as planned to Burtons and bought a black suit but didn't bother getting fitted out for it and brought it back home straight away. These aforementioned priests took my new suit and hid it and in its place substituted the suit of the priest who had died. Before I went out I thought I would dress in my best suit. When I opened the parcel and tried the jacket on it was at least three times too big !! I couldn't think what had happened and neither did I suspect my confreres until I saw them rolling on the floor with laughter.

I recalled to Bill the memory I had of Fr. van den Dries who was our rector in Roosendaal in the Netherlands. His nickname was 'Chefke'. He was an extremely nice man but at the end of every sentence he would repeat the last three or four words. One particular morning he was lecturing on Pedagogics and he said some sentence like "You can't wind up people like that, people like that, people like that, people like that or otherwise folk would say you were acting just like a gramophone, just like a gramophone, just like a gramophone." The study hall heaved with laughter and the poor priest didn't know why !

So many stories I could tell from college days that there would not be sufficient pages in this book to fit them all in, but space should be given to people like Patrick Deathe, a typical Irishman who regularly plants his potatoes on St. Patrick's Day and takes great pride in them, or Rose and Irene, two marvellous caterers. I must tell you about Bill McDermot who was with me when I was trying to organise the first meeting of our first Committee in this country.

He was on a business trip to Southport and I remember asking him to take me with him and leave me in the gardens there, to give me time and space to work out what I should do. After some time in thought I met up with him again in Southport, had an enjoyable meal and then I headed off to recruit my first members.

Most nights I do duty. Out of 50-odd patients there is always somebody who wants to see the priest. Before I leave, I usually pop into the chapel to say a prayer for all our patients abroad and here at home. I sometimes use the opportunity of telling the night staff that I got lost in prayer and saw a crowd of angels around me going mad blowing their trumpets. If it goes past 3 a.m. one of the night staff will say to me, "The angels won't be pleased tonight,

Father, because you're late." This has gone on now for many months and it gives me the opportunity of inventing certain expressions which the angels have said to me–something like "Tell the good looking nurse that we were asking for her" and each nurse protests that it is she to whom I am referring. There are so many variations on this theme that it becomes possible to invent the most outlandish statements which the angels have made.

One night I mentioned that the angels were very disappointed because they hadn't been included in my Memoirs. I protested in return that to get into the Memoirs you needed a photograph and it was impossible to take photographs of angels. The picture represented here was handed to me by one of the members of our Padre Pio group to whom I had told this story. Looking at this picture of angels with a sheet of music, one wag said to me, "They must be singing your Tango or the Call of the Prairie"!!!

One incident which gave me a lot of pleasure was being invested as a member of the El Camino group in San Pedro Sula, Honduras. Oscar, a great friend of ours, invited me to attend his prayer group meeting. Cath O'Leary knew where the meeting was being held and took me and her mother, Filomena, in the Hospice car. I remember hearing the strains of the singing before I went into the hall. They made a great fuss when I arrived and, to my surprise, they pinned on my lapel a small emblem to signify that I had been invested into their group. Their singing was magnificent. I often play the recording of this incident with great pleasure and wear my little badge with pride.

The beautiful grounds at our Hospice in San Pedro Sula, Honduras

One memory recalls Jane Hough. She was a young lady who came to us to work as an auxiliary nurse and having tasted medical life decided to go one step higher and become a doctor. She successfully passed her examinations and shortly after that got married to Chris McKeating. She requested me to perform the ceremony.

Chris' father Brian was in my class at SS. Peter and Paul's School. It made me feel so old when Jane told me she was to get married to Chris but I was delighted when she asked me to marry them. The wedding took place in Our Lady's Church in Formby. We attended a delightful reception in the Tree Tops Hotel afterwards.

I also recall a Mr. Philip Hawe F.R.C.S. I had the great privilege of meeting his son Dr. John Hawe in Guatemala. The Hawe family have been very good to our Association. I suppose it goes back to Mr. Philip Hawe's connection with my Sister Rita. He was an eminent surgeon and my Sister very often assisted him in his work at the Northern Hospital in Liverpool.

Dr. John has taken a great interest in our work and has visited our Hospices in Honduras and Guatemala. We thank him for all his kindnesses.

Another flashback concerns a delightful old lady called Senora Escalona. Filomena and myself had been travelling in South America and were desperately aiming to reach our Hospice in Honduras. It was the feast of St. Joseph and I was anxious to see our girls in that country on that day. But unfortunately the planes were difficult to come by there and the flights couldn't be arranged easily.

However, we were passing through Panama City and we decided to visit the cathedral. We felt quite lost at having no contact with friends and relations on this great feast day and felt rather stupid in having to fly, of all days, on the Feast Day of St. Joseph but something nice was to happen.

As I was wandering round the cathedral, an old lady came up the centre aisle and insisted on speaking with me and wanted to present me with a holy picture. It turned out to be one of St. Joseph. We were both delighted that he hadn't forgotten about us on that day.

I kept in correspondence with this lady for a long while but in the last couple of years there has been no reply to my communication with her, unfortunately. She obviously had no idea how much brighter she had made my day.

Another memory comes to mind which concerns Bill Glover. A few years ago Bill was a regular visitor to our Hospice in Thornton. He didn't impose himself in any way and even brought his own sandwiches. He made a great fuss of our patients and prayed with each one. He is a very simple man but deeply spiritual and the effect he had, not only on the patients but the staff as well, was wonderful. Sadly Bill hasn't been well and although it is some time since he last came to us, I know he prays for us.

Joe and Myra Lovelady came to our Aquinas Hall to celebrate their 40th wedding anniversary. They assembled with their family and friends. We had Holy Mass and put on a very pleasant reception. Both Joe and Myra have been solid friends and have raised considerable funds for us, for which we thank them. These people are the stuff on which Jospice is built.

Sometime ago I received a surprise visit from a gentleman rejoicing in the name of Dvorak. It turned out that he was a relation of the famous composer and he had a small group of people who were willing to put on a concert for us. A date in April 1997 was fixed. What a concert it was ! We had a wide variety of music with composers of different nationalities, German, Spanish, French, Italian, Welsh, Irish and English. They had a wonderful accompanist, Eva Warren, who was known to us from past concerts. So nice it was to hear her accompaniment through the various solo items which they presented. I suppose my favourites were the Song of the Flea by Mussorgsky and the Ave Maria by Schubert.

It was a great concert and all who came enjoyed the musical offering presented to us.

Hopefully we will repeat it very soon.

It is startling how varied and interesting one's day is. I received an excellent fax from Ecuador from Fr. Frank Smith who informed us about the visit to our Hospice there of Fr. Maurice McGill, the Superior General of the Mill Hill Fathers and how he was trying to cope with the huge number of people attending for care. That same day we were also thinking about Miriam Taaffe who went out to look at our Peruvian establishments. There was the funeral of Fr. Jukka, a de Montford Father who died with us. And, of course, there was the 40th wedding anniversary of the Loveladys mentioned above.

Other wedding anniversaries I attended were the 40th of Joe and Pat Mangan–Joe's mother died here 20 years ago–and the silver wedding of Dougie and Ann Wayne. Dougie had not been very well but he recovered sufficiently to celebrate his silver wedding.

There was a marvellous article in the Catholic Times by Norman Cresswell on the role of St. Joseph which did us all good and for your benefit I am reproducing it here since it is first class. St. Joseph has always held out a helping hand to us.

It's the hands–a craftsman's hands. Dry, strong, firm, decisive. No doubt scarred, too. Think of St. Joseph–as you surely must this week–and you can't ignore those hands. It was no accident that the carpenter was the one chosen to lead Jesus throughout his childhood. A good joiner is hard to find nowadays. And there's no reason to suppose that it was any different in Nazareth.

Joseph's position in the community would have been one of dignity. His skill ensured him a status among a people who have always prized dependability.

In fact, there are writers today who claim Joseph would have been a local businessman of some note, employing a small staff and perhaps advising upon the town's development.

Whatever his stature in Nazareth it was due to the endurance of his humility that he went largely unacknowledged until the Middle Ages and even then he was cast as the funny man in the mystery plays. It took Teresa of Avila to find him a serious role as the intermediary for a happy and holy death. And, very much later, those hands were recognised when he became ennobled as St. Joseph the Worker.

After his family's early journey to Jerusalem, Joseph's presence as foster father vanishes as the emphasis shifts to Jesus' Father in Heaven. Joseph the Worker is quietly redundant, his job done.

His anonymity is symbolic of those lost years of Jesus, covered so dismissively with the short comment that he grew in grace. But then, there are so many omissions in the New Testament which seem sent to tantalise us.

We know so much of the prophets–from boils to their fiery temperaments. Yet all we can know about the adolescent Jesus has to be deduced from our knowledge of the contemporary social conditions. But if the son is truly father to the man we can make some accurate guesses.

Particularly about Joseph. And the emerging picture has to be one that we in the pew can readily accept–that of a patient, caring craftsman whose hands are already sculpted to lead us gently through death with the minimum of fear in the gentleness of expectation. He is the layman's saint.

Great stuff, Norman !

Also I had the great pleasure of accepting an invitation by David Alton to be with him to celebrate the occasion of his retiring as an M.P. and his elevation to the House of Lords. David is high on our list of supporters and it was with great pleasure that Filomena, Terry and I accepted his invitation. He recently joined us on our sponsored walk along Crosby shore. He always makes a deep impact on our supporters and we have always felt secure in the fact that David is never slow to lend a helping hand. I proffered our congratulations to him on behalf of our Committee to let him know in what esteem he is held by all our members.

Congratulations, David. You are a great witness to the Catholic Church in our Houses of Parliament, particularly on the all-important questions of Life.

If only all politicians were as noble as you !

Someone mentioned the Football Echo to me and it brought to mind the great joy with which I used to receive a copy of it every week. My Dad without fail sent me a copy of the Football Echo every Saturday when I was in college and University and when he died my Mum kept up the custom and carried on sending it to me in Pakistan. It was impossible to buy nice chocolates in 'Pindi, so Mum used to put a bar of Cadbury's chocolate wrapped up in the Football Echo every week and it was wonderful to enjoy that weekly bar— even though it arrived suffering from the effects of the hot weather. It's only a small thing but it goes to show how much Mum and Dad since 1942 still cared for the welfare of their son and kept his affiliations with Liverpool Football Club and Merseyside !!!

A long-standing member of our Association, Eileen Phelan, died and Filomena and myself represented our Management Committee in St. Anne's Church, Rock Ferry, at her funeral. Eileen and her sister Nora always thought well of our Association. We as an organisation felt the same for them and during Eileen's last illness we prayed for both of these sisters because they represented something of which we are proud.

They were part of a marvellous family who gave great service to the Church and I know that they followed our activities very closely through reports about us in the Catholic Press. It was a great privilege to be there to represent our Association and to let their friends know how fondly we cared for them.

Quite regularly I receive reports from all our Hospices. The ones from Honduras submitted by Caroline Horsley were overwhelming. The amount of work which Caroline described in her report was very precise. The names of patients and their illnesses were documented so well that one could not but be impressed by the amount of hard slog which the nurses do.

Caroline's two helpers, Marie Cambray and Dawn Connor, both seemed to express great excitement in their work. When one reads reports of this nature one is not just taken by the detail but is affected by the attitude of those performing the work. To have on the one hand the expert administration of people like Caroline Horsley and to have on the other the joy and merriment portrayed by Marie and Dawn, one's heart rejoices.

Marie has been with us a few years and has in fact been to Honduras before, but Dawn, whose mother died with us some years ago, had spent many years at our Hospice in Thornton and had really looked forward to taking up a position with us in an overseas Hospice. She had seen many of the girls going abroad and had welcomed many who had come home.

The Honduras reports underline for me the importance of the origin of our work there and that those foundations which we laid 20-odd years ago were very solid. Anne Klapper and Rosemary Monaghan were responsible for these. We become more conscious of the efforts carried out by them so many years ago.

The reports from Guatemala are the same. This would not have been possible had not the hard work put into the project by Berta Mejia Medina, Bernadette Bradley, Maureen Keane and Toni and Mere Finnigan blossomed. Please God this work will continue. Today, Dr. Heino Hugel, Mary O'Sullivan, Sidonie Puech, Isabella Suarez, Manuela Friedli, Amaia Sarasti, Anne Bowers, Stella Kirkland and Anne-Marie Foster carry the flag for us.

By way of light relief I attended a beautiful wedding of Helen Bober, one of our nurses at Hettinga House, to David Marsh. Helen was one of our star nurses and we wish her and David every blessing.

As I was writing this part of my Memoirs the telephone rang to inform me that a great friend, Peter Brannan, one of our patients, was seriously ill. Kathie his wife, whose brother had died with us some years previously, was very attentive to Peter who fought his illness with great bravery. Sadly Peter died in the middle of 1998.

My Sister has just popped in with Ted Cleary and he was mentioning that Margaret his mistress was keeping well and hadn't seen me for some time. I assured Ted that I would go round to see her soon. (Ted is Dr. Marie Cleary's dog !)

I always keep a packet of biscuits in my office for Ted's arrival. He looks forward to the excitement of eating my biscuits and the first thing he does when he comes into my room is to sniff them out.

This recalled to my mind the fulfilment of one of my secret ambitions which was to mix some dog biscuits with ordinary biscuits when playing 'mein host' – and to get away with it. Each Friday after the Midnight Mass we forgather in the dining room to have a cup of tea and a piece of cake or a biscuit. I managed to mix some dog biscuits with ordinary biscuits and passed them around when my friends were enjoying a cup of tea. Ron Wharton put his hand out when the biscuits were offered to him and he chose a dog biscuit !! When we had finished eating Ron was still chewing but didn't like to admit that he had chosen the wrong biscuit. His reluctance to confess to this made us laugh even more and we were determined that he would finish it.

I was watching my favourite Bilko and I remembered the time when I used to go round to the house of Mrs. Quinn, whose son Tony and daughter Mary were students–one at the University with me and the other at Notre Dame teacher training college in Glasgow. Every Tuesday evening I used to sally forth along Dumbarton Road to the house where the Quinns lived. Mrs. Quinn used to expect me on Tuesdays at about half past eight. There was always something nice to eat and I became a good friend of their family.

That's when my interest in Bilko started and I suppose it was the excitement and the thrill which Tony, Mary and their mother would show when Bilko came on, which created my interest. My Mother used to come up during my summer holidays to stay with Mrs. Quinn and it was always a great joy to be with them.

The mind certainly makes its own reflections. One of these was recalled to me by our Chairman, John Carson. I don't know what prompted it exactly, but he reminded me of the time he kept a special brick for me. That brick was from the building my Father used to own in Bootle. On my return from Pakistan I often passed the site where this building had been situated.

It was being pulled down and they were constructing new houses on the site. I thought it would be a nice memento to take one of the bricks of the building as a keepsake. Not many people keep bricks !! They are a little burdensome to care for and so I asked John our Chairman if he would look after it until an appropriate time when it could be used. The time eventually came when we were building our small chapel in San Jose and I managed to secure a place for this brick near the altar. A small plaque was made and placed on the brick recalling the memory of my Mum and Dad.

Her Majesty the Queen awarded me the M.B.E. in the 1996 Birthday Honours List. I received it, of course, on behalf of the staff working for us here and abroad and who have done–and have always done–a marvellous job. The actual presentation took place 12 months later when the Lord Lieutenant of Merseyside, Mr. Alan Waterworth, came to the Hospice in Thornton. I feel extremely honoured at being selected for the M.B.E. but it does feel a bit strange that a person called O'Leary is a Member of the Most Excellent Order of The British Empire !

Incidentally, as I mentioned above, my cousin, Fr. Willie Russell, was awarded an M.B.E. many years ago for his work in Uganda and as an R.A.F. chaplain. So that makes two of us in the family to have received the same acknowledgement.

During the summer of 1997 the Metropolitan Choir visited us to sing some wonderful motets and our hearts were also thrilled when two of our helpers were admitted to the Secular Franciscan Order – Raymond McMullen and

Catherine Lavelle. We had a very enjoyable Mass for their reception. Theresa, Filomena, Lynda and the group received them with great joy.

Then we had the celebration of Jim and Maureen Hogan's Silver Wedding anniversary which was enjoyed by a whole host of their friends and relations.

Moira Billinge and John Cotter continually inspire us with their work for SPUC. They had a very successful sponsored walk in November which concluded at San Jose. Great people.

I received a great surprise when a young lady from London, Caroline Curtis, wrote to tell me she had adopted me and would pray for me. I was overawed by this act of kindness. So I say, "Thank you, Caroline, God bless you, keep praying!!!"

I have mentioned SS. Peter and Paul's Church quite frequently in my book, so it gave me great happiness to welcome the good people of that church to our Aquinas Hall for a retreat given by their parish priest, Mgr. John Furneval, the former secretary of Archbishop Derek Worlock. I have always been very proud to be a member of this parish.

Fr. Chris Cook, parish priest of Fakenham in Norfolk, rang me to pass on his good wishes. A memory I recall with Chris is sitting behind him in the study hall at Freshfield, with a very difficult arithmetic problem to solve. I passed it to him and within seconds he came back with the answer. I don't know how he got that sum solved, and it was difficult to explain my correct answer to our professor the next day !

What lies ahead for our Association ?

Looking back over these notes, I read once more the preface of our Chairman, John Carson. It was 1997 when he was asked to produce the preface and at the moment of writing we are well into 2000. A lot seems to have happened in the intervening years. At the end of 1997 we had our Christmas Pageant as usual with Midnight Mass but the weather made it impossible for us to have our normal Pageant. Winds roared, branches snapped, trees were uprooted and the grounds were in quite a sorry state.

However, Jenny our treasured donkey came over to carry Our Lady and our Christmas celebration was held in the Aquinas Hall. Rachel Birch, who worked for us in Honduras, and her husband, Dr. John McKay, took the parts of Our Lady and St. Joseph and their young child played the role of Jesus in the manger.

Early in January 1998, Mgr. Hector Flavio, secretary to the Colombian Bishops' Conference, visited us with Fr. John Mahoney, who had been working in the diocese of Cartagena in Colombia. Fr. John had taken up a position with the hierarchy in caring for the rejects of society, particularly in Bogota. Both of them earnestly requested us to put our minds to the establishment of a Hospice in Bogota for these poor unfortunates. We are working on this project at the moment and hopefully will conclude our plans shortly.

It will be difficult because we also have to apply our minds to our new Hospice in Mexico. Mary O'Sullivan called in to see us from Guatemala to remind us (if that were necessary) about our new building there. The President of Guatemala has assigned a plot of land for us on which to construct a purpose-built Hospice. Mary explained the ways in which this new building could be set up. We were grateful to her for her comprehensive report on our Guatemalan work and praised God for the graces which He has given to us in that country.

Our Guatemalan Hospice

Whilst we were dealing with all these problems, we had to set some time aside for a Gala Concert on March 21st. We wanted to make this Gala Concert (our third) a great success. As usual it was great fun entering into all the ordinary arrangements which are necessary to stage a successful concert. We had the Royal Liverpool Philharmonic Choir and their conductor Ian Tracey to help us in our planning. Fortunately I was able to obtain the services of Eirian Davies (soprano), Della Jones (mezzo-soprano), Jeffrey Stewart (tenor) and Michael George (bass-baritone).

We had a wonderful programme arranged but on the morning of the concert at ten minutes past ten, Michael George rang to tell me that he could not come because he had lost his singing voice ! It was impossible for me to arrange a substitute at such short notice and I asked him had he anybody in mind. He said he would do his best, so once more I asked Our Lady and St. Joseph to sort out a suitable substitute bass since they were in charge of our concert. Ten minutes later the phone rang again and it was Michael George telling me that he had found a replacement in the person of Simon Birchall who was a chorister in the choir of Westminster Abbey. Simon in turn had to find a substitute for himself before he could travel from Wimbledon for our concert. Thankfully Simon arrived at the Royal Philharmonic Hall in time for a rehearsal and our fears were laid to rest.

The first part of the concert, as before, was entitled Missa Mosaica. We began with the Kyrie from Mozart's Requiem, which was followed by the Gloria from Mozart's Missa di Credo. Then an Offertorium Gloria et Honore from the Missa Sancta by Weber was sung. This was followed with the Sanctus from the Messe Solennelle by Gounod. We also took the Benedictus from that same Mass and the Missa Mosaica was concluded by my Dad's Agnus Dei from his Mass of the Sacred Heart. A beautiful rendition of Soul of My Saviour and a magnificent performance of the Inflammatus from Rossini's Stabat Mater formed part of our recessional. The first part of the concert concluded with the Dies Irae from Mozart's Requiem.

Lord Alton, our master of ceremonies, who had already greeted the soloists, choir, orchestra and conductor at the beginning of the concert introduced us to the second part of the Gala Concert. It opened with the famous overture Poet and Peasant by Suppé and Simon Birchall gave us a very telling performance of an aria from Tannhauser by Wagner. Della Jones then came into her own with a scintillating performance of Una Voce Poco Fa from the Barber of Seville by Rossini and followed this by La Vergine Degli Angeli from The Force of Destiny by Verdi.

As you can see we had a nice selection of composers whose music everyone enjoyed. We were all in the mood now for a change and enjoyed a performance of my Tango. Mgr. Hughes followed this by giving us his Blessing and saying the Jospice Prayer and encouraged us all to take part in singing the Jospice Hymn. The second part of the concert was concluded by a wonderful performance of In Sempiterna Saecula Amen from Rossini's Stabat Mater. This is a spectacular piece and formed a fitting conclusion to our Gala Concert.

Many of us retired to the Rodewald Restaurant in the Philharmonic to take part in an enjoyable meal. All in all, a wonderful night !

We look forward to our next conference in the Academy. It is entitled "The Missionary Image of the Church." The concept we want to enlarge, is how did the present day situation in the Church arise from those first missionary journeys of St. Paul and the other Apostles. We have to plan our day along those lines. We hope to have good speakers and from our talks, I know we will have our own inspiration renewed.

On October 22nd, 1999 a very important occasion took place and has pride of place in our annals. It was the comemmoration of the Silver Jubilee of the establishment of our first Hospice in England at Thornton. It was an opportunity to celebrate in grand style and we invited Cherie Blair, the wife of Prime Minister Tony Blair, to be guest of honour. It was very fitting that we chose Cherie, because she had many friends in this region and had at one time attended Seafield Convent, one of the principal schools in the Crosby area. The festivities were centred in the Formby Hall Golf Club restaurant and 270 people attended the Silver Jubilee dinner. Cherie stayed overnight with us and on Saturday October 23rd, visited both our Hospices here in Thornton and spoke to every patient. We thank Cherie for spending so much time with us despite the heavy schedule of events in which she is occupied as the Prime Minister's wife and we all felt so pleased that Cherie graced this occasion by her presence. Thanks to Pat Murphy our fundraiser for organising this event.

As I have said before, as one comes towards the end of the Memoirs, it is hard to encapsulate all the events which continued to take place as the weeks went by. However, there is one happening which I strongly feel should be recorded.

On Sunday November 21st, the B.B.C. and Thames Television celebrated the thousanth presentation of the "This is Your Life" Book and called together all those who had taken part in the "This is Your Life" Programme to celebrate this event at the B.B.C. Television Centre. I accepted the invitation with pleasure and travelled down to London with Terry O'Leary.

Michael Aspel hosted the evening entertainment which included many well known artists. The show was enjoyable and afterwards I found myself having dinner with Sir Harry Secombe, Dame Vera Lynn and a host of other celebrities. It was an odd experience to meet up once again with Jack Crawshaw who produced my "This is Your Life" programme in 1973. After we had shaken hands he immediately recalled a phrase that had been used in my programme, "He stood on the threshold of a dream", which I thought was particularly brilliant. How he remembered that phrase, after such a long time, left me astonished.

My day was further enlivened by receiving a visit from Caroline Curtis and her mother who live in the London area. I have mentioned Caroline before as one of the special people who pray for me and so I was honoured by her visit.

I value her prayers very highly and I feel that her intercessions on our behalf has contributed to the success of our work.

I was very anxious about celebrating the Millennium in a special way when lo and behold two big problems confronted us.

The first was in Honduras. Unfortunately, our staff in the Hospice there were savagely attacked and the project almost came to a full stop. However we were baled out by the good offices of Filomena, who volunteered her services immediately she heard of the tragedy and went out to that country to see what she could salvage. She was followed by her daughter, Catherine and between the two of them came up with possible solutions, one of which they chose and is now in position today.

We hardly got over the shock of that problem when a huge 80 ft. tree in our grounds in Thornton, crashed against our new Academy. The winds that night were very severe and the tree came tumbling down on the roof.

The damage was quite horrendous. Fortunately, no one was killed and all our patients were safe but we had to evacuate them all to our other Hospice in Ormskirk. You can imagine the mess which ensued when the tree went right through the roof. Fortunately the insurance covered us and hopefully everything will be back in order soon.

On April 23rd Filomena rejoiced in the company of her husband and family on the occassion of her 70th Birthday. A special Mass was said in the Academy.

I feel a little sad and overawed that I am coming to the end of my Memoirs. In 1997 I read a booklet containing the life story of Bishop de Wit, a former Superior General of the Mill Hill Fathers whose great capacity for smoothing troubled waters had been of immense help to us. I found it fascinating and thought that if he can commit his memories to paper then I am glad I have done the same. Not everyone will see my point of view and I am conscious that my classmates and colleagues will be saying to themselves, "Why the hell has O'Leary written his Memoirs ?"

The answer to that question is, quite honestly, I don't know. I suppose it is to commit to record some of the nice things which have happened to me during my life as a priest. Maybe a reason for writing these down, is to thank God for all His graces and blessings bestowed on me and to thank Our Lady and St. Joseph for protecting my family, friends and members of my Management Committee and for guiding my steps in the way they have.

I hope these Memoirs are a source of inspiration to some. I haven't written them with that in mind because the more I think of it, the more audacious an act it appears to be, to commit these events to paper. Anyway I've done so, for what they are worth.

I have said these Memoirs are coming to an end, but, really this is not the end, because every day brings new surprises and one finds that God is working mysteriously within one for reasons He knows best. And so it goes on . . .

In summary, these memories and vagaries are a humble attempt to record events and happenings of the past 50-odd years. Personal feelings and reactions have not been included in any detail but the day-to-day and year-to-year events have brought their moments of fear, sickness, anxiety, frustration and at times a natural feeling of helplessness. Still the urge to go on persisted. These have been completely overshadowed by joys and blessings untold, giving one a sense of achievement which has not been acquired by me alone, but by those who have been involved to a greater or lesser degree by their unflagging footsteps, dauntless faith, unfailing loyalty and, above all, their commitment. Not my way but God's way. I honour and salute them.

Deo Gratias !!

Terry and Filomena O'Leary and their family in the late sixties
(left to right): John, Anne-Marie and Paul are at the back.
Catherine and Ruth are in the middle with twins Bernadette and Claire in front of them.
Inset: Elizabeth and Patricia.

The family are not related to me but are good friends and wonderful helpers.

Envoi

Like so much of life, what is written here is a shadow, a poor imitation of the truth, inexpressible. Each of us is a part of that truth, of which only God is the entirety.

Many people in their everyday lives, humdrum as they may be, achieve heroic heights. Despite themselves and their misgivings, a divine spark keeps them enhancing the ordinariness of their existence to their own and others' surprise. Some people like Fr. O'Leary do it brilliantly.

Each of us armchair experts could have written this book much better, more wittily, more dynamically, changed ourselves and the world around us, written a best seller, made a film 'a life in the day of' – we may still do it.

The fact is we didn't. Fr. Francis O'Leary did it, in between worries and the thousand and one arrows of outragement and good fortune that beset his life.

He is a 'can do man' in a 'can't do world'. He makes things happen. He never takes no for an answer.

Already, many millions of people witness to the experience of an encounter with him, each one unforgettable.

In the future, perhaps, many people will tell his story.

The important thing is, he is a living example to all. You may not have enjoyed the book.

You might have written it better. It will certainly make you think. Be certain that you or I have not done it–he has–and that is the essence of this man of God. If it's worth doing wholeheartedly, even badly, God supplies the magic dynamic for a man who is a Morning Star for all of us. For many people he is a light at the end of a very dark tunnel. Long may he shine !!

Filomena O'Leary, R.G.N.
Nursing Superintendent, and Hon. Secretary,
St. Joseph's Hospice Association.
Thornton, Liverpool.

The St. Joseph's Hospice Association Prayer

O Divine Child whose wish is that we all love one another and show this love daily in our lives, grant us a true understanding of the needs of poor people everywhere and the courage to make sacrifices so that we may help those who are sick or destitute.

Our Lady, Mother of Sorrows and our Mother, please comfort all who are afflicted by sickness or destitution.

We beseech thee, O Lord, to help us through the merits of the spouse of thy most holy Mother, and what our own efforts cannot obtain, do thou grant us through his intercession.

St. Elizabeth, Patroness of Nurses, pray for us.

Bless, O Lord, St. Joseph's Hospice Association and its members. Shower down your graces on all those poor people who are in need of help and consolation. Amen.

We thank God and our Patron Saints for the Graces and Blessings bestowed on St. Joseph's Hospice Association over these past years.

St. Joseph's Hospice Association Hymn   *H. F. Hemy (1818 - 1888)*
(Words by The Management Committee of St. Joseph's Hospice)

When St. Joseph loving Patron,
   Jospice sends its prayers through thee.
Asking for some special favour,
   Listen then and grant our plea.
Now St. Joseph let us thank you,
   For the gifts of earlier days.
We who call you friend and leader,
   With our voices sing your praise.
From the plains of Rawalpindi,
   To the mountains of Kashmir,
On the Caribbean Coastline,
   Jospice helps the sick we hold dear.
from the heights of Machu Picchu,
   Down to Lima's desert shore.
Also here at Jospice, England.
   Joseph helps and guides us all.

Appendix

The Jospice Imprint by Dr. Phil Callahan
The Physics of Sacred Images
Liverpool

In the discovery of photoelectrets it was found that the thermoelectret state can be produced under conditions analogous to those used to form photoelectrets.

(Photoelectrets and the Electrophotographic Process – V.M. Fridkin and I.S. Zheludev)

About the middle of June 1995 my phone rang and a pleasant female voice asked if I were Dr. Callahan. After affirming my identity she asked me to hold for Fr. O'Leary.

Fr. O'Leary told me he had heard about my work on the miraculous image of the Virgin of Guadalupe from a priest he met in Knock, Ireland. He tracked me down through the University of Florida. "Where are you located, Father?" I asked. "Liverpool, England," he replied.

I was quite sure he was calling from somewhere in Florida. It is not uncommon for connections from England to be clearer than those from Daytona Beach or Jacksonville. This brings to mind that such a message is travelling on radio energy from satellites of about 10-12 watts.

Lightning at the Earth's surface can generate up to 10,000 volts per metre of air space and thousands of watts of energy. Despite that simple and undeniable fact modern materialists are so enamoured with their self-satisfied intellectuals' abilities that they believe they can talk over thousands of miles on 10-12 watts [one million millionth of a watt], but that God, who designed the entire system, cannot paint a picture with 103 watts (1000 watts).

A newspaper survey showed that 92% of Americans are ignorant of any real scientific understanding. It is incredible that most biologists are just as ignorant of basic physical principles.

In 1922 a Japanese scientist, Mr. M Eguchi discovered in plant waxes a phenomenon he termed the ELECTRET effect. Electrets are formed in wax by the combination of heat, electricity and light. This is not a treatise on physics but in simple terms wax formed by light, with heat and electricity, into an electret is in essence an "electrical field" magnet, that has a plus field (+) on one surface and a minus (-) on the opposite. Plant leaves are weak electrets because they are coated with wax. The charges, as in a magnet, are permanent. Most modern microphones are made with teflon (not wax) electrets – thus joggers have a permanent magnet in their ears – not a good idea when one considers that blood is doped with iron (Fe).

Electrets, as in the case of magnets, are highly attractive to iron molecules. Both the Shroud of Turin and the Tilma of the Virgin of Guadalupe are doped, that is, have scattered on the fibre particles of iron oxide (Fe_2O_3).

Hematite (iron mineral) is one of the main components of the basalt volcanic rock which surrounds the Sea of Galilee and of which Tepeyac Hill in Mexico is formed. The Virgin Mary appeared to Juan Diego on Tepeyac Hill.

All Mary apparition sites are highly paramagnetic – contain weak magnetic forces. Such places are conductive to high radio and electrical energies. I have been measuring air voltages and ELF waves for many years. See my book My Search for Traces of God.

Since electrets are such an important part of my theory and experimentations on Sacred Images I was excited and intrigued when Fr. O'Leary informed me he was the director of a Liverpool Hospice for the dying and that one of his cancer patients, a very devout young man named Les, had died (in March 1981) leaving a Shroud-like image of his hand on the mattress cover.

The mattress cover is made of polyurethane coated with rosin – a material on which, with even an extremely weak current, one can form an "electret" image. I refer the reader to the English translation of the Russian work Photoelectrets and the Electrophotographic Process by V.M. Fridkin and I.S. Zheludev (Consultant Bureau, N.Y.). In that book the authors show a picture of a beautiful sunflower made with polycrystalline yellow sulphur and asphalt.

This is a process where the yellow sulphur and the black asphalt molecules migrate (move) to different charged areas on the electret surface. Those areas are made by projecting with visible light the image of a sunflower. Yellow molecules move to the petals and black molecules to the stem and leaf – an ELECTRET PHOTOGRAPH.

Fr. O'Leary was setting up a conference on the Shroud of Turin and Hospice and graciously included me. I was to speak on my infrared work on the Virgin of Guadalupe. He also promised a real piece of the mattress cover to take home with me to my Gainesville lab for study. My own "Shroud of Liverpool" to work on.

On arriving home the first thing I did with my 6 x 9 inch piece of the mattress cover, that Les died on, was to measure its electrical properties. I already knew, due to the high electric charges (500 to 600 mv per cm of air space in the death room) that the mattress would have a fixed electrical charge on it – plus on the rosin side, minus on the polyurethane side. There was in fact a

12.4 millivolt difference between the rosin side and the polyurethane side (42.9 mv - 30.5 mv).

I was also aware the Hospice building was in essence paramagnetic cave since it was constructed of highly paramagnetic brick. Paramagnetism is a weak alternating magnetic force (1/1,000,000 gauss). It is important to plant growth. See my book - Paramagnetism Rediscovering Nature's Secret Force of Growth.

The human body has approximately a 200 volt potential between head and toe. Lying down the potential would measure in the range of 1/4 metre of air space, eg. 50 volts. The body air interface would be air, 500mv (=1/2 volt) to the 50 volts of the body. The temperature of such a sick person, 102 to 105 F, is quite enough for the electret phenomenon to occur. For the image to form by the electret process, light must "develop" the image. Photoelectrets are sensitised in darkness by charging the photoconducting layer surface, eg. under the sheet in the dark Hospice (room electricity). The image would not appear until the bed was stripped in daylight.

The Experiment

In an experiment such as my sacred image experiment one is dealing with a rather modern form of maths called complexity. It derives from chaos mathematics. The best analogy is the test for colour-blindness. It consists of a field of different coloured dots. A colour-blind person sees only chaos (no figure). A person with normal colour vision sees a 6 or 7, or some letter or other number.

The non colour-blind person has gone from chaos mathematics to complexity. They see not chaos but a complex figure (message).

In these image experiments I have gone through a whole series of life experiences, physical phenomenon, religious beliefs (e.g. Catholicism) etc. etc. A list would include a knowledge of art, pigments, soil, rocks, plants, cloth, biophysics, biochemistry, biology, electronics, meteorology, special relativity etc. etc. They all come together in this one simple experiment. It is the type of experiment in which the physicist, who does not accept my work, will say, "That is too simple and we knew that all along" - the excuse of a reductionist scientist. A natural philosopher of complexity is an observer of what God does with nature.

Obviously a dying man is sweaty and such sweat contains numerous chemicals. One cannot know for certain what chemical was involved in the Hospice image.

Since sweat contains iron oxide from blood, ($Fe+2O-3$) it is the most likely candidate.

Iron oxide is easily obtained from a rusty paper clip (one soaked in sweat). Sea water is close to the same composition as sweat, so I soaked a paper clip in sea water and put 500 mv of electrical current across the damp soaked mattress cover and paper clip. The voltage was generated at 60 Hz (hertz) with a function generator. The electrical charge in the Hospice room would be 50 Hz (English).

Within one hour at 500mv (1/2 V) a paper clip image (negative print) was deposited on the mattress cover cloth.

The Hospice print, unlike the Shroud of Turin, is positive because the sweat (sea water) flowed down the body wall and deposited around the body. Iron (Fe) is magnetic, but iron oxide (oxidised blood) is paramagnetic (CGS of 7200 for the physicist). The negative iron oxide ions were attracted to the positive (top) side of the electret due to opposite charges. The oxide fixed itself permanently on the electret mattress cover.

The iron oxide outlined the still alive body (shadowed it) leaving a "Shroud-like" image of a very holy man. His devotion to God was vouched for by Fr. O'Leary. The sweat on the body itself left various shades of grey depending on its amount of sweat, e.g. more in the palm creases where it collected than elsewhere. It should be noted that the stain is most in evidence at the tips (curved surfaces) of both the fingers and of the paper clip. Charges are always set highest at the sharpest points.

The paper clip experiment imprint is, of course, a negative not a positive image as the paper clip is light coloured (silver). The iron oxide also moved to the crease (stitch holes) along the edge as it did on the palm creases.

In other words the iron oxide image of the paper clip is very close to the image of the Shroud of Turin.

At this point we enter a raging controversy between a group of highly competent and totally honest scientists. They are caught up in the reductionist practice of science, which in truth never works for pure science (new discoveries) but works very well for technology.

To make a long story short the pro-Shroud group say iron oxide, (FeO, rust) could not be involved, and a very competent expert (on ink and pigments), Walter McCrone says it is – reductionist (either or science).

The real truth is again hidden by the complexity of life.

Both are correct as the negative paper clip image and negative Shroud image were with certainty formed from the very few iron oxide (rust, FeO) molecules moving to the portions of the cloth that touched Christ's cold dead body, or a cold paperclip touching a mattress cover (negative photo). The Liverpool image formed on the mattress cover with sweat around a warm dying body (positive image). The molecules were from the dripping sweat of a warm body. That of the Shroud and the paperclip formed on the cold body of Christ and cold wire touching the Shroud cloth or mattress cover (negative image).The iron oxide moved to the touching high points.

St. Matthew writes (28, 1 to 6): The Resurrection of Jesus.

After the sabbath, as the first day of the week was dawning,

Mary Magdalene and the other Mary came to see the tomb.

And behold, there was a great earthquake; for an angel of
the Lord descended from Heaven, approached, rolled back
the stone, and sat upon it. His appearance was like lightning
and his clothing was as white as snow. The guards were
shaken with fear of him and became like dead men. Then the
angel said to the woman in reply, "Do not be afraid ! I know
that you are seeking Jesus the crucified."

Earthquakes generate considerable atmospheric light and electricity as does of
course lightning. Research on lightning demonstrates air voltages of up to
1,000V per cubic metre of airspace. Earthquake light is of a similar degree.
Temperatures are excessive. Electrets of teflon are easily formed in my
laboratory with 2,000V. Wax-resin electrets are slightly heated and form as
they are allowed to cool – exactly the same as would happen to a waxed
coated (flax) cloth (unbleached) heated by earthquake and lightning then
cooling on a cold and dead body – proof of Christ's DEATH. The electret
charge on Christ's nose would be higher than lower spots so iron oxide would
move (as in an electrophotographic process) and stain the touching cloth. At
10,000V and 1,000 watts the image formation would not take one hour (as at
500 mv) but would occur instantaneously.

Lastly to maintain that a shroud placed over a body with iron nails in the hand
and feet, and scourged all over the body with iron (probably rusty) dumb-bell
tips, and also laying on dust from basalt rock (hematite, FeO) would not have
enough iron oxide on it to concentrate at electret charges and form a very dim
image borders on ludicrous. If I can do it with a paper clip at 500mv over a
one hour period then surely God could do it for Les over a six hour sweaty
period and also do it to His own body with an earthquake focused into a
resonant cavity (tomb) over a microsecond period. The apostles would not see
the image immediately (in the dark) because light "develops" such images
and it would slowly become visible as it came into sunlight.

I have a very difficult time believing that ancient Indians or Hebrews had a
modern control of complex electrophotographic processes, or alternating
current at their disposal (year 33 and year 1531). I have no difficulty in
believing that God has known about the entire process for ever (before and
after) and that I have known about it since 1962 when I first investigated
electret phenomena with the help of the Russian book on the subject.

In my next article I shall demonstrate how iron oxide and copper oxide from
soil, through the photoelectret process, can draw a beautiful image on
unbleached cloth and how it "codes" up in electret spots to fill and "cake" the

spaces between cloth fibres. In short I shall produce a crude electret photograph with the two minerals which I predicted in 1979 formed the Virgin of Guadalupe from the flower root soil on Tepeyac Hill.

MAN COULD NOT IN 1531 PRODUCE SUCH AN IMAGE.
GOD THE ULTIMATE PHYSICIST-ARTIST COULD.

I have to thank Dr. Callahan for all the hard work he has done in comparing the Imprints

F.O'L.